FIZZY DAYS AND PLASTIC MONKEYS

from Crewe to Malibu

FIZZY DAYS AND PLASTIC MONKEYS

from Crewe to Malibu

written by

Mark Millicent

First Published in 2022 by Fantastic Books Publishing
Cover art by Mark Millicent

ISBN (ebook): 978-1-914060-34-2
ISBN (paperback): 978-1-914060-33-5

For my Nan, Ellen
who loaned me the money
to buy my first proper road going motorbike.

ACKNOWLEDGEMENTS

To Luisa – for entertaining all this nonsense.

CHAPTER 1

The start of it

Dear Writer,

We are not currently accepting any scripts. But I thank you for reaching out and I wish you all the best success. Please do not contact us again unless you have an agent submit.

Sincerely …

Dear Writer,

Keeping in line with our policy not to accept unsolicited submissions, I have deleted your email regarding your project. I wish you all the best in your future endeavors.

Sincerely …

Dear Writer,

In keeping with our rule on unsolicited submissions we have deleted/destroyed your submission. Once you have an 'A' list cast, crew and finances in place, and a sales deal, please re-submit.

Best …

Dear Writer,
Thank you for getting in touch. I don't think it's a project for us as we are unable to look at it at this time, but best of luck setting it up – it looks like fun. If you approach us again, we will use the law to its fullest extent against you. If you own a pet, we will find it.

Best wishes …

Dear Writer,
Stop sending us your fucking scripts! We will NOT read them!!!

Best …

Dear Writer
Fuck off!!
Sincerely
FUCK OFF!

Somewhere between 30,000 and 50,000 screenplays are registered with the Writers' Guild of America each year. Would people embark on this thankless, clichéd crazy writing endeavour if they gave those figures some thought? The wannabe scripters of movies that no-one is ever going to see because they don't stand a hope of being picked up and produced. Would they continue the quest if they actually knew how fuckin' hard it really is?

One speculative screenplay is sold for every 5,000 tossed into circulation. Undaunted, there are thousands of 'don't stand a chance' screenwriters out there, and I was one of them. The odds are fairly great that fate will be against you, though not as great as, say, dating a supermodel, trying to win the lottery or marrying a millionaire.

But 5,000 to 1 odds? Let's put that figure into perspective.

Odds of getting a hole in one: 5,000 to 1
Odds of being murdered: 18,000 to 1
Odds of being the victim of serious crime in your lifetime: 20 to 1
Odds of fatally slipping in the bath or shower: 2,232 to 1
Odds of being considered possessed by Satan: 7,000 to 1
Odds of dying on a bicycle: 4,472 to 1
Odds of dying in a car accident: 18,585 to 1
Odds of winning the California lottery: 13,000,000 to 1

'Never give in, never surrender!'
Enrico Colantoni, aka Mathesar,
leader of the Thermians, *Galaxy Quest.*
Dreamworks Pictures 1999

So maybe today will be different? Because today is the start of it. This was going to be a different day, a 'red letter' day when everything finally comes together, when all the hard graft will turn out to have been worth it. The doubt, that nagging feeling that you were wasting your time, your life, on something that would never see the light of day, is gone. So maybe they were right after all, those placating folk philosophers: that if you work at something hard enough, 'It's bound to pay off in the end'.

How many times had I questioned that well-worn mantra? But I can now say it's true! I'm holding the proof in my sweaty little hands. Because today my contract arrived.

A contract for what, you might ask. A contract for my film. Hollywood here I come! I say that as if I'm on another planet, which for the movers and shakers in this industry is probably true. But geographically speaking, I'm actually not that far away. On a clear day you can see the white letters of the Hollywood sign from the top of the sand dune at the bottom of our street. It's a few miles north, off the 405 freeway, turn right along Sunset Boulevard and head east for a few more miles, as it winds its way towards Highland Boulevard. You run straight into the glitz, I can almost smell it – the bright lights, fame, fortune, stardom, the smell of success. It sounds pretty glamorous, doesn't it? Can you believe it? Finally, after all these years I'm making a film. I'm making my film.

So let me tell you, up until this point I had felt like the lowly dung beetle (*Scarabaeinae shittyicus*) perpetually pushing my little ball of shit in front of me. Then suddenly, like a giant switch had been flipped, I felt vindicated, like a tiger, or at least like a dung beetle on steroids. I was through with constantly pushing my little ball of rolled dung up hills that kept getting steeper. But not anymore, no sir. That daunting incline now looked almost like a downhill slope, my ball of shit now practically a fart! I was on my way. I was a happy beetle. In fact, the day was such a milestone that I decided to write about it. January 7th, 2007, the day my movie contract arrived after five long years of hustle and hassle and getting nowhere. A very sunny day indeed.

In fact, let's back up a little. I had always wanted to work in the movies. A long time ago, far away from planet cuckoo USA, I once worked in a cinema. I grew up in the north midlands of the UK, and one of my first jobs from school in the post-punk ashes of the late seventies was as a tyre fitter. Your car needed new tyres? I was the man, or at least the youth, to see. One of these businesses was based in a former cinema. As a teen, I had worked part-time at weekends in various retail tyre outlets, so I knew a little about replacing rubber. It seemed a logical move that my first proper full-time job should be as a full-time tyre fitter. With the optimism of youth, I think I probably figured I would move on to greater things as life dealt me the cards to do so.

The old cinema that had been my place of employment was The Grand on West Street near the town centre of the not too glitzy or glamorous Crewe. Bill Bryson described Crewe as the armpit of Cheshire in his book Notes from a Small Island, a little harsh, I think – armpit. More of an elbow? Fresno might be a US equivalent, if you were looking for a transatlantic comparison. If you were looking? So, Crewe was where I got my first full-time job after finishing at Stoke Art College. I was hoping that tyre fitting would be just a fill-in, as my qualifications leaned to the more creative. But I had not been able to land a position anywhere in the art world, and out of necessity and desperation I took anything that would pay me any fuckin money! So, tyre fitting it was, 'for now'.

Crewe is a working-class industrial town in the North-West of England. It is somewhat famous as the home of Rolls Royce. It is also home to one of the largest railway hubs in the UK, so they make a lot of trains there too. Anyone traveling on a train going north or coming south in the UK will have been through it, but not so many will have alighted. I have a tenuous connection with the rail station, as my uncle Jack was the platform announcer for many years before retiring to a modern grey high-rise tenement building overlooking the station with my auntie Mary and her colourful glass animal collection. I don't remember much about him other than the serious injury he'd suffered as a young man in a motorcycle accident. As an adult he walked with a stick and wore one of those big, black, built-up orthopaedic boots. My mother always reminded me darkly about Uncle Jack's big black boot whenever I showed any hankering for motorized two-wheeled transport. 'You'll end up with a boot like your uncle Jack!' she would say between peeling the potatoes.

But my yearning was obvious from the gallery of magazine pages depicting motorbike heroes of the day – Barry Sheene, Mike Hailwood, Ivan Mauger, Barry Briggs and Kenny Roberts – with which I plastered my bedroom walls. These images shared wall space with my plastic model kits of motorbikes, monsters and planes, pinned alongside the odd picture of Lyndsey de Paul torn from a pop magazine.

Crewe Kings were the local speedway team. Some special Saturday nights my father would take me and my younger brothers Paul, and Nick to support them.

At the Earl Street stadium, we were swathed in the unforgettable smell of Castrol R as our ears were assaulted by the unbaffled roar of the 500cc single-cylinder Jawa engines. The likes of Phil Crump and Dave Morton did battle, screaming at full throttle round a quarter-mile oval of brown shale track. Between heats, the PA system blasting out the latest seven-inch singles; the glam of Slade, Mud, Sweet and Glitter. Earl Street Stadium has since gone the same way as the Grand. It's now a retail park and home to a B&Q big-box hardware store.

Even squinting through rose-tinted spectacles, Crewe is a bit of a grey town. My father Brian still fervently supports its football team, Crewe Alexandra, and has a season ticket to go and cheer them on every Saturday. He must have been more than a little disappointed in the sporting prowess of his eldest son, having himself played for Stoke City's A team and try-outs for Wolverhampton Wanderers as a youth. I guess it just skips a generation sometimes. Sport was never really my bag. I got all my exercise being chased by bored policemen and angry store detectives or irritated night-watchman. I'm glad to say his grandson is a lot more soccer inclined than I ever was.

As a nipper I did enjoy the thrill of petty thievery. It was my sport, my exercise. Filling my pockets with unpaid-for Mars bars and cans of Tizer or the odd crate of Brown Ale from the back of the workies' club was as dangerous and as big time as it got. Hardly a 'Ronnie Biggs'; and how many people would remember that name today and what he was famous for? The drinking man's footballer, George Best, is probably the most prominent sporting name I can recall from the time, so that's some indication of both my age and the extent of my sporting knowledge.

As a twelve-year-old boy and bona fide Artful Dodger, I remember one Saturday morning session after the swimming baths with a pal. An overly observant store detective caught us busily shoplifting our way around Woolworths and gave hot pursuit through the town. I don't think we'd ever run so fast and so hard and for so long! The skinny guy with glasses and an anorak didn't look like a runner, but then he didn't look like a store detective, when in fact he was both!

'Just a minute, you two!' were the only words we needed to hear as we left the store, sniggering with the goods stashed in our damp towel bags. Fight or flight kicked in and we were off. With wet hair and the heady smell of chlorine in our nostrils, we did a whole circuit of the town square. The extremely fit store detective kept up an alarmingly close pursuit, but luckily not close enough. We lost him through the buzzing crowds of passengers and feral pigeons at the bus station. Nicking fishing tackle and handfuls of Pic'n'Mix along with plastic kits from the local Woolworths, crates of ale from the local social clubs, and setting the odd fire … Ah, fizzy days indeed! The Woolworths is long gone, as well as the swimming baths, like the many obsolete cinemas and speedway stadiums and small sugar mouse selling corner shops across the changing face of today's Britain.

The town itself was grey so we probably needed to do stuff that was a bit colourful just to brighten it up, and for me petty thievery seemed to fit the bill. I don't think I was a particularly wayward or dishonest, but when you don't have much – and much, relatively speaking, becomes available for no more than a little creative thinking or minor risk taking – then it's all too easy to succumb to opportunity. Creativity fuelled bouts of mischievous invention to aid me in my larceny; I devised contraptions to stop purloined tools falling from my sleeves or trouser legs on shoplifting escapades to Halfords and other hardware stores. Of course, I was caught and questioned on a few occasions about things that went missing, disappeared or burnt down, but it was never me, so I managed to avoid any serious repercussions.

After dark, rather than do homework, I sometimes spent

school evenings wandering round the local meat-pie factory or social clubs or nearby derelict buildings. Roofs were always good. I gained access to places through the small lavatory windows of local retail establishments, thinking I was James Bond. I managed to get into the local sewer works, railway signal boxes, bus depot, engineering shops and any used or disused premises that looked like fun. Just like James Bond.

At night we had the run of these places once we had squeezed in through an open toilet window or vent. Being all of nine stone at the time, I was able to squeeze into a lot of buildings. In fact, Paul McCartney may have written, 'She came in through the bathroom window,' from the Abbey Road album because it was always easier to get in that way; no one expected you to! A bog window, inadvertently left ajar, might as well have been an open front door. It was the same with local clubs and licensed premises, schools and factories. Everything seemed fair game as long as there was gain to be had and our adrenalin was driven faster by doing it. Consequences were never considered. It was just a phase. But at the time, I was no different from any other kid I knew. Of course, I hope mine don't go through the same phase, but all in all I loved my early teenage years. They were bloody good fun.

Most of the time I kept within the rules; nothing bad, never stole a car, not a whole one, though I must admit to quite a few radios and wheels, dashboards etc. I was a piecemeal car thief. Or annoying little twat, take your pick. Never burgled a house, no joyriding. Did take a bulldozer for a spin once at the local sandpits and excavated for a while until the police turned up. Again, we were chased, albeit slowly, lights flashing. I remember a lot of 'We've got your mate,' being shouted. People always seemed to shout that when they're chasing you. The old sand quarry is now covered in little red Barrett homes, a sprawling suburban estate, not a tree in sight. I had my crappy field bikes by then; different engines, different frames, my Tiger Cubs or old Villiers or BSA Bantams, worn out Lambretta or Vespa scooters. So, I never saw the need to take other people's cars and bikes – and whole cars, well, they were a bit more serious.

I'd made a pact with my mother and father that if they let me have motorbikes for the field then when I became old enough for road-going equipment I would be happy to move on to a much safer mode of transport – a car, maybe a Vauxhall Viva or Ford Escort. The only occasion I ended up in court as a nipper was at Crewe Magistrates, where I was fined ten pounds and received a stern warning on being conditionally discharged for a period of one year. The charge was avoiding arrest and disturbing the peace whilst being pursued on an old James Captain 250cc field bike. The bizzies had chased me all over the place like Steve McQueen in the great escape and if I hadn't run out of gas, they never would have caught me. That was a memorably fun day.

So, at fourteen years old, I got a criminal record for pissing about on my crappy old motorbikes and taking up valuable court time. Lionel, a ginger-haired miscreant youth from the next village, was up before the same judge that day. We waited outside the courtroom in the corridor together. A big lad for his age, his case was for GBH and assault. I knew Lionel from a previous school, in the nearby Staffordshire village of Audley. He was a bad egg, a fighter who liked fighting and was good at it. I was to see his face again when I read about him several years later in a national newspaper. He played a role in the Heysel Stadium football riots that killed so many people. There are degrees of bad, and I think I wasn't that bad as a nipper, and maybe pretty good on the whole. Certainly not a Lionel.

However, I did find out a few years ago that a rather notorious, if tenuous, line of criminality runs in the family. I am distantly related to the Kray Twins, the iconic 60s London gangsters. Really. My mother's eldest brother, my Uncle John, had a step-wife Margaret; her youngest daughter Roberta married Reggie Kray while he was in prison and remained his wife until he died in 2000. So … maybe I am something of a badass!

And as for the motorbikes, well this is really where my story begins or rather has its roots. At sixteen, too young to own a car and with a love of motorcycles. Like many others I got a Fizzy. A Yamaha FS1E. A small Japanese 'popsicle-purple' 50cc moped. Purple was the most sought-after paintjob. A legend of a little bike that so many UK youths of the 1970s remember as their object of desire. Their first proper road-going motorbike … with pedals.

1970s bikers – author 2nd from the right

The Fizzy was more than a bike, it was the transition from boyhood to manhood. It was the autonomy of the open road and of course the independence that came along with that. It was exciting, it was girls, it was music, it was glam – and it would do nearly fifty miles per hour, lying down on the tank with the wind behind you, its exhaust note screaming like a rabid bee. But a main driving factor was that everyone knows if you've got the right ride; you can pull the birds!

Dear Writer,
What is the matter with you? Stop! No one cares … that said, we enjoyed your project and wish you every success – just not with ourselves.

Sincerely …

CHAPTER 2

In the Grand

I was twenty-one. I now worked somewhat happily as a tyre fitter in a building that had once been a cinema. The Grand on West Street, Crewe.

My work colleague and fellow tyre fitting buddy was a Welsh lad called Aled Jones. Not *that* Aled Jones, the Welsh former choirboy now radio presenter, who sang The Snowman theme. My Aled was a few years older than me. My Aled Jones was short, a stockily built lad with a dirty blonde pudding bowl haircut. He must have been a bit of a trendy geezer at one time as he wore a pair of red crepe-soled Teddy-boy boots to work. Looked totally wrong with his blue oil-stained overalls but life at that point wasn't really a fashion show; nobody gave a fuck, least of all me. Originally from Cardiff, his family had moved to Crewe in search of better things. Some people choose resort towns in Spain or Australia, but Aled's kinfolk had chosen Crewe. He lived with his wife and their three kids in a small brick terrace, several streets away from the Grand, where we worked. He still retained a thick

Cardiff accent and now and again the occasional 'Boyo' would leap from his lightly moustachioed lips.

'I'll do the Cortina, Boyo, you do the Maxi.'

To my undiscerning eyes, Aled seemed really old, him being a few months the far side of twenty-five and me just into my early twenties. He carried himself with a knowing air of maturity in those red suede brothel-creeper boots. He'd told me one day over a mug of tea that he'd fathered the first of his brood with his wife Sandy at the age of fifteen. He seemed to be very proud of this, and to be honest I remember being pretty impressed; Sandy, his wife, being only fourteen at the time of conception and both of them still at school. The social workers had got involved and it was all a big to-do, but they'd remained together and had carried on from there. Every day, sometime during the morning, Sandy would pop in with Aled's lunch, baby in the pushchair and a young 'un either side. She would have been in her early twenties but still looked like a girl, a tired, pale-skinned girl with lank hair and large breasts but a pleasant enough smile. She looked to me like the fourteen-year-old he'd described from his amorous prenuptials, not the mother of three snotty-nosed kids. She never wore any makeup, but there was always that pretty smile for Aled as she handed him his foil-wrapped package, usually 'sandwich spread' sandwiches, a bruised banana and a packet of crisps.

'I've put something extra in for ya,' she might say in a broad Potteries accent. I always took that to mean a Penguin or Club biscuit. Or if his luck was in, a chocolate-covered Wagon Wheel, though the grin suggested more was in the offing once the kids had been tucked up in bed for the night.

1981; it was a hot summer that year. I still remember it fondly. I remember the smell of new rubber, vulcanizing cement, and Swarfega hand cleanser, with the constant whizz of the pneumatic air wrench as the lug nuts were pried from the wheels of cars needing new tyres. Paul McCartney's *Waterfalls*, the Human League's *Don't you want me baby?* and Madness's cover of Labi Siffre's *It must be love*, were all played in rotation on Radio One by Steve Wright and his afternoon boys, all belting out loudly between the industrial racks of new tyres. The real future was uncluttered and bright. Mortgages and pension plans, life insurance and annuities were so far off as to seem like words from another solar system. I'd settled into the job and I was looking forward to summer day-trips out to Conwy and Llandudno and other exotic extravagances as I was on decent wages now. All the spending power that went with fifty-two quid a week and as many used tyres as you could pilfer and sell without Ken the boss noticing. My proper future would be along shortly, I figured, with the naive optimism of youth.

Most towns and cities across the UK had their Gaumonts, their Odeons, their Ritzes or their Grands. At one time, Crewe could boast of half-a-dozen movie houses, but by the early 1980s multi-screens and Cineplexes had left just one of them standing. The Grand was a casualty of the same process – no longer grand, it was now just old, sad and smelling of used engine oil, hand cleaner, various industrial lubricants and just a hint of cat piss. Where once had been the romantic whirr of the massive Cinemeccanica projectors, the walls of the building now hummed to the sound of industrial compressors filling their tanks with air; the day-to-day routine noises and smells of a retail tyre-fitting business.

It was a long time since the Grand had closed its doors to a cinema-going audience. The kids who had queued excitedly on a Saturday morning outside those doors, waiting to be let in by the uniformed usher, had then raced down to the front to watch Buster Crabbe as Flash Gordon do battle with Ming the Merciless, or the black-and-white antics of Korky the Kat or Laurel and Hardy, Abbott and Costello. It was a time when people didn't stare transfixed at phones, a time before Xboxes, PlayStations, iPods and iPads, when 'face' and 'book' were still separate words and 'twitter' was something the birds did. Before the world and his wife donned matching soccer tops to shop in the likes of Asda and Tesco and Aldi superstores. All of that seems as far off now as when Churchill proclaimed ... 'We will defend our island ...' When Britain was great and upper crust Pathe-News-voiced announcers told us how things were. We had a thriving homegrown movie industry along with a car and motorcycle industry, steelworks and coal mines. A little bit of pink empire still remained on every schoolroom map.

All a long time ago, and getting further by the minute, although Chariots of Fire was a cinematic bright spot back in 1981; the academy award-winning drama about two British track athletes set in 1924. But that last gasp of a renaissance petered out, like the diminishing identity of our solid Britishness that it represented. All that remains is Vangelis's hope-inspiring soundtrack fading into the distance, with maybe Terry Thomas admonishing us through his cheeky-chappy gap-toothed smile, 'You're a shower, an absolute shower.' I think he may have been right to a certain extent. Today, we probably all are an absolute multicultural shower!

As kids my brother and I were dropped off at the Odeon while Mum and Dad did the weekend shopping in Crewe town centre. We would watch the Saturday morning matinee in the former Odeon; it's a McDonald's now. A few years later, it was Saturday morning TV that we watched transfixed. Heavily dubbed European imports, with great theme tunes, Robinson Crusoe, The Flashing Blade, Belle and Sebastian, The White Horses and so many more – magazine shows like Swap-Shop and the mad flan-custard world of TisWas came later.

Assorted Gerry Anderson puppet shows played such as Thunderbirds, Joe 90 and Captain Scarlet – or Fireball XL5 with Steve Zodiac and his hot-stringed sidekick Dr Venus along with the rest of his puppet rocket crew. That was my fondly cherished boyhood. Of course, I had indoctrinated my own two young offspring many years later with my pop culture obsessions. I have a fond memory of Zack my young son announcing he was naming his maimed monarch butterfly, 'International Rescue,' while dressed in a baggy batman suit in our LA backyard standing all of three-foot high at the time – he now stands over six. International rescue flew off years ago as he was in kindergarten at the time.

Those TV shows would compete for our Saturday morning viewing, vying with the polish of the syndicated American shows. We had some US shows, Kermit and Sesame Street, of course, but it was Hollywood that produced the syndicated biggies: Adam West's Batman, Gilligan's Isle, Voyage to the Bottom of the Sea, The Beverly Hillbillies, Man from Uncle, The Munsters, The Monkees, Bewitched and the whacky antics of the The Banana Splits. Cue the theme song!

The mid 60s produced a slew of great TV, still revered and in syndication today. The little Grundig gogglebox was as much an object of trancelike devotion for my generation as an iPhone screen is for kids today. Of course, while the phones have got smaller, the TVs have got bigger; but back then, to have a new 26-inch screen was something of a status symbol, which only people who took foreign holidays could afford. We had a 17-inch black and white, so it was a big day in the Millicent household of 1970 when the colour TV arrived.

Back to me working “in the movies”. The Grand hadn’t really been converted; it had just had a sizeable portion of wall removed to make an entrance. A roll-down metal door was fitted and the original rows of velveteen-covered seats torn out. The floor space freed up was enough to accommodate several cars at a time. It looked like the whole transformation had taken place over a short weekend. It breathed the air of a condemned building – cold, and clinging to a glorious past. Michelin, Goodyear and Firestone had replaced Bogart, Hepburn and Tracy. The bones of the old building, the musty cinema, were still visible – moulded, fluted columns running to the high-roofed ceiling, ornate cornicing and the odd dusty exit sign – the recognizable fabric of its glory days. As people waited for their tyres to be changed, you could catch them looking around, occasionally remarking, ‘Didn’t this used to be an old cinema?’ Or if they were local, smiling and pointing: ‘I used to come here with our lass before we were married. We did some courting here, sat up there.’

“Up there” was the balcony, where countless courting couples had held hands and embraced in the darkness. But the rich Venetian reds and warm golds with which it had been painted had been replaced by a pale-bluish, whitewashed colour, the bland pallor of death. The balcony was now home to industrial metal racks of new tyres, boxes of valve stems and inner tubes, worn tyres that you could sometimes sell for a few quid, and gallon tubs of Swarfega. The once-posh seating above the circle stalls, dusty cramped storage space now, slanted on an incline for seats that were no longer there. From the balcony you could look out over the day-to-day business of tyre-fitting at what would once have been the screen, where a huge Avon Tyres banner now stared back. Imagine that today: a cinema with just one screen!

At the rear of the balcony on the back wall was the sad sight of the engine deck, the former projectionist's box. It had once housed two big old arc-light 35mm projectors, now long gone, with just the bolt holes on the linoleum floor where they had rested. Four small square openings in the wall were still there. They had let the movie project on to the screen opposite. The former projectionist's sanctuary was now Motorways' ad-hoc brew room and kitchen. Beside PG tips and Hobnobs biscuits it was here that certain other goodies could be found.

A projectionist room is now a relic of the past, unseen in today's modern movie houses. It's all automated and digital. Back then the projectionist was like the captain of the ship, guiding his audience. The projection room still had all the brown Bakelite controls and switches for lifting the curtain, adjusting the screen size, and controlling the lights and sound as well as the music, all still legibly labelled. From this room, the projectionist's main job had been to load and keep the film in focus. Changing reels and watching the movie until the circular flash appeared in the top right-hand corner of the screen. This was the signal to start projector number two. When the second flash appeared, projector one was turned off and projector two took on the leading role. The next reel would then be readied on projector one and the process repeated every 15 or 20 minutes. No wonder it's automated today. What a palaver!

The wrecked projectionist's room was manky and had a distinct stink of cat piss, but not enough to put you off your lunch. In a quiet moment, if you closed your eyes, you could almost hear the whirr and click of the projector as the film wound its way over the turning cogged spools. When we had locked up for the day, the walls still softly echoed with the sound of people in hats, laughing at British cinematic royalty – Will Hay and George Formby or Norman Wisdom, and maybe later the odd Carry-On film – laughing in black and white then later in colour at the movie stars of decades past. Some rainy days the ghost of the old projectionist could be felt as if he still worked here, sipping his mug of tea, puffing on a Capstan unfiltered between reels.

It was less than hygienic but interesting, as the treasures in the brew room were mainly lobby posters strewn around the floor in pieces, crumpled and yellowing. One-sheet posters advertising old B-rated stuff, Saturday matinee comedies from Ealing, Pinewood and Elstree. All were damp and disintegrating, way beyond saving. We would sometimes try and piece them together, like jigsaws of the past, to see what was showing on a given matinee in the mid-sixties and seventies. Aside from this detritus from the golden age of cinema, there was the usual stuff you would see in any brew room of the time: an old sofa, an electric kettle, a couple of mugs and plates, last week's fish-and-chip papers and milk bottles. The obligatory reading material of a couple of well-thumbed nudie mags – Parade, Penthouse and Playboy. A smiling, topless Samantha Fox or Linda Lusardi torn from the centrefold and now pouting breathlessly from the damp walls.

There were also dozens of dented film cans, which at one time had held 2000 feet of Kodak film stock. Rolls of paper admission tickets in different pastel shades in pre-decimal currency – 1/6d for circle and 2/3d for the balcony – green for balcony, pink for stalls. All of it left lying there like there might be another Saturday matinee scheduled for the coming weekend. A gold mine of rotting rubbish that would probably be worth a small fortune on eBay today.

But to me, the most interesting bits were the pieces of shiny celluloid film frames – mouldy offcuts dotting the floor, sometimes several uncut frames together, intact, that you could run through your fingers. I learned later on that the cat-piss smell was very likely the vinegary odour given off by nitrate-based film stock as it breaks down over time. Sometimes scenes were discernible; images revealed themselves more clearly when I opened the door leading to the roof, at the back of the projectionist's room. From the rooftop was a panoramic vista, between the chimneys and TV aerials out over the surrounding buildings, an industrial North-West urban landscape: Crewe spreading out in all its grey glory.

A couple of old car seats and an upturned milk crate served as furniture at our improvised roof top café. A coffee table constructed from a few stacked tyres under a piece of chipboard; al fresco luxury for when the sun shone. Holding the little fragments of film up to the light of a sunny day I tried to imagine what film the frames were from. From Here to Eternity, Saturday Night, Sunday Morning, Richard Attenborough in Brighton Rock ... or even Orson Welles in Citizen Kane. Well, perhaps for Crewe, make that Trevor Howard and Celia Johnson in Noel Coward's *Brief Encounter*.

The rooftop café was a peaceful and tranquil retreat to get away from customers wanting radials or cross-plies. At lunchtime or anytime when it was quiet, I would take my sandwiches or locally-made Wright's pie and chips and gather up a mag and a handful of film cuts from the floor to see what I could see. Sometimes, if business was slow, Aled would join me and, for a few moments, we'd both escape the world of vulcanized rubber by squinting skyward at the bits of ancient celluloid. We'd discuss our plans for life and the future, although it has to be said that Aled's future seemed pretty much mapped out by then.

If we were really lucky, on the odd sunny afternoon we'd be treated to the sight of a bikini-clad, chubby red-headed mother and daughter team sunbathing in the back yard of the council flats below. I'm not sure if it was genuine lustful voyeurism or just plain curiosity at what happens when that amount of wobbly, ivory English skin is slathered in coconut oil then bathed in sunshine. Whatever it might be, they had our attention, even though these two would have been a very rough two-thirds of Charlie's Angels. It was dead glamorous for Crewe, and we waited expectantly for bosom or buttock to pop from the strained Marks & Spencer's bikinis that were holding everything in place. Peeping over the lip of the walled roof like two immature schoolkids. Would they or wouldn't they go topless? Of course, they never did. After all, this was Crewe and real life and not Saint-Tropez.

CHAPTER 3

BeefyMeat

The part I remember not being keen on during my cinematic tyre-fitting days were the Saturday trips to BeefyMeat, the pet-food processing plant on the outskirts of the town. BeefyMeat was a different story. The eviscerated animal stomachs, spilled acids and bovine juices played hell with the tractor tyres, degrading them to such an extent that the fragmented shards of bone would puncture the softened rubber. Unfortunately for me, Motorways had a contract to service those vehicles.

BeefyMeat was an isolated collection of old farm buildings at the bottom of a field laid out around a central cobbled courtyard. You could smell it over a mile away if the wind was blowing in the wrong direction. Normally, you stand anywhere near a Cheshire field and the wholesome country smell of 'cow shit' assails your nostrils, dairy farming being a main staple of the county. It's funny that cow poo or cow manure or cow shit is never referred to as faeces, a word that has a whole different connotation. But cow 'poo' was good; cow poo was something you rolled into a ball with your bare hands and threw laughing at your mates as a kid, a sort of brown, chewed-grass snowball … that smelled.

But BeefyMeat had the smell that the word faeces evokes, a poisonous, acrid, dead-skunk type of smell causing a physical reaction that was drawn from your gut on arrival. The BeefyMeat smell was barbed with talons that stuck in your throat. BeefyMeat produced pet food for dogs and cats made from anything that died on the local farms and of course anything that was killed in the building with the big blue doors at the bottom of the field. This was before EU rules and regulations kicked in, so pretty much anything dead went into pet food at that time. The tyres on the vehicles used to pull the carcasses around were all well beyond their usable service life. The owners of BeefyMeat saw no reason to replace them if they could be repaired … again and again. The whole establishment had something of a surreal quality to it, from the skinhead slaughterers to the strange displays of animal parts they would assemble in macabre sculptures around the farm. I never liked going there.

On my very first excursion to BeefyMeat, I was literally given a taste of what life as a 'slaughterhouse monkey' could be like. I drove the half mile down the wet unpaved single-track lane that was the only approach to the farm. The lane was shrouded by hawthorn hedges and ash trees that lent a tunnel-like effect to the journey, as if you were entering a nightmare Narnia, and believe me you were. At the end of the tunnel, I was greeted by two mangy collie dogs chained to a piece of rusting agricultural machinery. They were so friendly that I always felt sorry for them. I certainly never saw any reason for the chains, and on later visits I would bring biscuits for them, Hobnobs or Bourbon Creams, from Motorways' brew room.

The grey day of my first visit to Beefymeat was a memorable one. It was late summer. I parked my flatbed pickup with its compressor and tools next to a rusty old Massey Ferguson tractor; obviously, the reason for my visit. It looked to be in need of my services as it rested lopsidedly on a rear tyre that was as flat as a witch's tit. Looking around, sniffing the noxious air, I left the sanctuary of my cab. No birds sang at BeefyMeat, even the quietness seemed to have a foul nauseous odour. A pair of silent crows perched on a barn's heavy slate roof stared at me. I scanned the vicinity for zombies. A dilapidated, two-tone single-axle caravan bore the sign 'Office.' Through the open door I could see its walls were plastered with the most explicit pornography available in the Western Hemisphere at the time.

No-one was about; the odd 'pop-pop' noise came from one of the corrugated roofed sheds across the courtyard; a bit eerie. Making it more so, lying on the cobbles was the huge, dead carcass of a fly-covered unicorn. It was still attached to the tractor by a chain around one of its legs. Well, perhaps there wasn't a horn, so more than likely it was a dead horse. A huge dead horse in the sense that it was swollen up like a balloon. Each leg sticking out stiffly from its body. Bloated by the decomposition process. It looked almost as if it might stand up if you could get it upright – like a fly-covered, life-size plastic toy.

After a moment, the popping stopped and a rough-looking, tattooed skinhead appeared frowning from behind a blue door. He looked to be a few years older than me, his leather apron covered in blood that dripped down to soak his jeans and wellies. Every inch of skin on his sinewy arms and neck were decorated with badly drawn tattoos. He acknowledged my presence with an unsmiling nod, flicking a worn but sharp-looking paring knife between his fingers before slipping it back into a bloody sheath. Taking half a ciggy from his lip, he pinched the butt between thumb and forefinger, and flicked it at the dead horse. He then fixed his gaze on me, frowning, as if I might have interrupted a particularly satisfying shag, which given our surroundings didn't bear thinking about.

'You the new tyre bloke, eh?' he asked grudgingly, now staring at the horse.

'Er, yes, I am,' I mumbled, as I tried to look hard and tough too.

'That's it.' He pointed his knife at the tractor's huge, flat tyre, which was covered in animal guts. Maybe I just looked stupid rather than tough. It's probably something I should have practised more on my way in.

'Just patch it, you don't need no new tube or owt like that, so don't go saying it does cuz it doesn't. Just a patch, right!'

I nodded. I understood. 'I'll just patch it.'

It wasn't the friendliest work order I'd ever had, and this guy looked like he could chew nails, so smile and comply seemed like the best path to take. He didn't strike me as a talker.

'Right, er, you keeping the horse … on?' I asked.

'Well, it ain't fuckin going nowhere, is it?' He spat, smiling contemptuously, baring one or two gapped yellowed teeth.

'Right.'

I'm not sure if it was for my benefit or just this sicko's amusement, but with an evil grin he unsheathed his knife then bent over the carcass.

I stared wide-eyed as he pushed the blade into the bloated belly. Like a macabre party balloon, it popped! The putrid gasses blew open the flappy little slit he had made. The horse deflated. A black shadow of bluebottle flies, *Calliphora vomitoria*, lifted off the carcass, then instantly resettled.

The stink was indescribable. I tried not to react but couldn't hold back an involuntary 'girly' gagging sound.

He looked at me, made some sort of judgement, smiled as he re-sheathed the knife.

Mistaking this for a friendly gesture, I smiled back as best I could – hard men together, or so I imagined. He said no more, retraced his steps through the big blue door and was gone. Crikey!

It started to rain as I slithered underneath the tractor to place the jack. I cranked away lifting the rear axle, ever mindful of Mr Ed still chained to the towbar. The wheel and tyre came off a lot more easily than I'd expected, everything being slippy, soft, stinky and gooey. I was covered in the stuff, but 'hard graft maketh the man'.

I took a break for a moment and wandered up to the open doors. The sight that met me brought me up short. Wall to wall was death and dismemberment. I stood shocked but tried to make out it didn't bother me; I was a hard case, too. To reinforce my studied nonchalance, I made the mistake of asking the guy who'd deflated the horse, 'Hey, mate, how do you put up with the stink?'

The slaughter barn fell silent.

He froze mid-slice and spat another half-smoked ciggy on to the velvety blood-covered floor, turning – eyes blazing like an enraged cast member of "Zombie Apocalypse".

'You what?!'

'The … er … smell?' I mumbled.

'What fuckin' smell?'

'Got used to it then?' I foolishly pressed.

He put down the still-twitching animal part he'd been holding and got a bit in my face.

'Whatcha' sayin?'

'Nothing,' I whimpered, glancing at his knife, still dripping with blood.

'Used to what?' His two eyebrows met and formed a distinct V.

'The er …' I tried for another smile and scuttled back outside to carry on with the job. He was a big bastard, covered in badly spelled tattoos that were obviously his own work, and, as far as I could tell, not a conversationalist who needed a new buddy.

Twenty minutes later I was nearly done, lying on my back beneath the tractor, twisting away at the handle of a rusty bottle jack to lower the huge rear axle and the newly repaired tyre. I was just about stifling an urge to vomit at all the body parts and fluids I was lying in when, without warning, the contents of a fifty-gallon plastic drum rained down upon me.

Pound after moist pound of warm, wet, slithering animal guts engulfed me. I was drowning in the warm fresh vat of offal from several animals. As it splashed over me, the slaughtering Neanderthals were beside themselves. I thought of a gaggle of frenzied bonobo chimps surrounding a victim. Covered in blood and guts themselves, their pale skin almost black with their badly spelled tattoos, they whooped and hollered in the rain.

I scrambled from beneath the tractor and spat something warm, soft and unidentifiable from my mouth.

The horse-stabber shouted, 'Hey, I can smell that fuckin smell now!'

'You bastards!' I managed, but still tried to smile, while hauling a few yards of small intestine from inside my overalls, wiping the foul-tasting, viscous animal fluids from my eyes, mouth and ears.

They laughed as hard as they could, then at some unseen signal, they stopped. Their eyes glazed over, like they had all heard a siren, inaudible to any human ear, but clear as a bell to a primitive slaughter monkey. A siren signaling they should cease all merriment. This they did and immediately went back to the business of killing things and cutting them up. That was my baptism of fire at BeefyMeat. I staggered away, shocked, shaken and stinking.

Aside from BeefyMeat, fitting tyres over the summer at Motorways in the old Grand wasn't too bad a place to work. I enjoyed my time as a tyre fitter; a cinematic voyeuristic tyre fitter. I may be romanticizing it, but when I look back at working in the old movie house, it sort of reminds me of the film *Cinema Paradiso*. A haunting score by Ennio Morricone – an off-key piano refrain – and the smell of Crewe Works and Wrights Pies and cat piss mixed in with an eclectic soundtrack of early eighties anthemic pop songs by the Human League, Madness, The Jam and The Cure. The secret retreat on the roof of the old Grand. Dashing for cover from a summer shower, cursing the fact that nobody down below had got their tits out and with just a hint of a taste of something indescribable in my mouth. It's almost poetically romantic, in a fragrant offbeat kind of way. At least, I think that's what it was like. If I didn't do something about it, just like Aled, this would be my world. I needed to move on.

Dear Writer
Thank you for your interest in our company. Your project submission has I'm afraid been tied to a post and shot in the head early this morning. Do not try and retrieve the remains as this will only lead to more bloodshed. You choose to ignore our submission criteria: you pay the price. We know where your children attend school and where your wife shops, so further correspondence with ourselves will have dire consequences. Do we make ourselves clear?

We wish you every success in your further creative endeavours:

Now, F U C K off!!

CHAPTER 4

Further afield

I thought I was going to be something in the art world. But I wasn't, I was a tyre-fitter. It was starting to grate as the weeks turned into months. The urge to get out and move on grew stronger like the lingering smell of Beefymeat on my overalls. The realization dawned on me that I was not going to make the big-time fitting tyres in Crewe. I had finished my education with a bag of memories but, more usefully, a college degree in illustration; I should use it.

Prior to the tyre fitting, I'd had various positions of temporary employment, part-time or full. I'd been a bartender; I'd worked on farms. A scaffolder for a short time on new Barrett housing constructions beautifying the countryside with little square brick boxes. I had been an early-rising 'crumb-brusher' in a bakery, my job being to keep the production lines of the ready-sliced bread clear of crumbs. The slicing process could stop a conveyor belt in the blink of an eye. It needed constant attention; a position of great responsibility. I'd been a gardener at an ROF munitions factory and then a septic-tank serviceman. I was a "hole driller" for a while, drilling small holes in things I can't remember at a company whose name I've now forgotten. A scruffy little engineering firm in Stoke, beneath a bridge on the orange-coloured Trent and Mersey Canal. I do remember Earth Wind and Fires, Boogie Wonderland playing on the brew room radio a lot. When I hear it today it takes me back to sitting by that canal side at lunch times eating my own sandwich-spread sandwiches. I'd pumped gas, and I'd bartended at a Butlin's holiday camp.

Butlin's was a bit of an eye opener. On the first day on the job in Skegness, the orientation focused more on avoiding STDs than the actual job in hand. 'Skeggy' was the oldest of Billy Butlin's chain, and the women, both guests and staff, were very friendly for the most part. They thought I sounded posh with my Cheshire accent, something that served me well, making company easy to find after an evening behind the bar. In fact, I had started off bartending but after a few weeks I was demoted to glass collector due to discrepancies on the cash tills. I was then a warehouseman and busboy. I was a shelf-filler and Saturday lad in a local supermarket. Then, as I got better at shelf-filling and honed my skills, I became more talented – yes, talented – at handling a price-ticket gun. I could price up an opened 24-tin box of Heinz Alphabetti Spaghetti or Bird's Custard in 5.7 seconds. Talent like that doesn't go unrewarded, and I was soon promoted to a job with Asda. I was a shelf-filler at the top of his game. Life was on the up.

As a younger kid, the summers saw me potato-picking or hay-bailing on local farms.

While I was at college, the position of arts & crafts

counsellor came up with the Camp America summer-camp programme. That beat everything else hands down. In this role of teaching art to the offspring of wealthy Americans in both Wisconsin and New York, I got to know America a little better each year. It became somewhere I imagined I'd be quite comfortable moving to.

At the end of my summer term of employment, for three years in a row, me and a carload of other travel-hungry counsellors – usually from Britain and as eager as I was to rough it and see the world – would traverse the USA, driving across the States delivering cars to people who had moved house and needed their vehicles delivered to them at their new homes around the country.

We used the cars as a way to see the country, zigzagging en route to as many of the most scenic wonders as we could. They were also where we slept, parked in a truck stop or hotel car park. I pretty much got to see every state in the Union courtesy of these car drive-away companies. I hate to think what the owners would have said if they had seen what their cars went through to reach them. I remember one little yellow Volkswagen Rabbit being pushed to its very limit along the painted centreline of the Bonneville Salt Flats in Utah, following in the footsteps of Malcolm Campbell, but no land speed record was broken that day.

When camp was over on the last of my years of counselling, we left the beauty of Upstate NY and the Adirondack Mountains and Camp Idlewild, took Interstate 87, and headed for New York City. But having crossed the Henry Hudson Parkway, we found that none of the drive-away agencies in the city had a vehicle of any description going anywhere. What were we gonna do? Four young men looking for travel and adventure in Uncle Sam's USA.

The troupe I'd joined forces with as a travelling gang that year were; Smithy, my long-time good friend from the UK, a committed agnostic; Rob, a wandering Hasidic Jew; Steve, a practising Mormon; and me, an ardent Slade fan. I mention the religions only because Slade are a seventies and eighties British rock'n'roll institution – a much-underrated four-piece rock band from Wolverhampton who, like the Jedi, ought to be a viable religious option.

As an alternative to being marooned at the Travelodge on 42nd Street in New York City, we had been told that cars were cheap in Queens, a suburb across the Hudson River. So, hot and sweaty, we backpacked our way aboard a graffiti-covered subway train to Queens. Sitting forlornly behind a chain fence on a seedy, used-car lot we found our transport: a gold 1970 Oldsmobile station wagon on whose dirt-encrusted windshield someone had written $400 with their finger. After some haggling, the price paid was $250 and we had us a deal. Or so we thought.

We drove it off the lot, no papers, no insurance and as it turned out no brakes, but we owned it. As we cruised up to the first set of lights and attempted to stop, we instantly became the centre of attention. The car tried to grind itself to a halt by juddering uncontrollably, but only stopped if the driver slammed both feet on the brake pedal and pulled with everything he had on the steering wheel. Once stopped, the car stalled and refused to restart, stranding us in the middle of a bloody busy thoroughfare in a pretty downmarket area of Queens.

A cacophony of car horns burst out. 'Get that piece of shit off outta here!' They don't like stranded vehicles in Queens.

All of us got out and started to push our new purchase back to Honest Jamal's Autos for a full and instant refund. He had seemed like an understanding and fair Rastafarian proprietor in our recent negotiations.

'What the fuck yo talking about, man? Wha'dya expect for 250 dollars, man? You can't even get no TV set for that price! Yo mother couldn't buy no tricycle for no 250 dollars! Get the fuck outta here, and take that piece of junk shit with you before we kick yo sorry Limey asses. Go on, get the fuck out of here. You didn't even get it from me. I ain't never seen you guys before now. Just take your motherfuckin' car and fuck off out of my motherfuckin' shop, man. You Limey motherfuckers expecting some Cadillac Rolls Royce shit for yo 250 dollars, now get the fuck out of here!'

'So, you won't fix it?'

Ultimately, they agreed to help us 'motherfuckers' get it running if we paid them more motherfuckin' money. They fitted a new starter and battery, and eased the brakes enough for us to put new pads on and drive it away, all the time cursing us 'motherfuckin' Limey English fag boys'.

So began a month of driving from state to state. Pittsburgh was the first unplanned stop, owing to a monumental failure of the repaired but fragile braking system on an early steep downhill part of the journey.

The first we knew was when Smithy, white knuckled and frantic at the wheel, screamed, 'The brakes have gone!'

Joining the panic, I pushed my door open. Rob did likewise as we searched desperately for a suitable place to jump, screaming at the others to do the same. The ground rushed beneath us. Jumping would have been suicide.

Smithy fought the wheel, his face frozen in concentrated terror.

By some miracle he maintained control. Our runaway transportation picked up speed as we careered through a God-given gap in the traffic at the bottom of the hill. Screaming horns and squealing tyres never quite became the clash of metal on metal. We got away with it, but were a hair's breadth from being involved in a major newsworthy tragedy. No one said a word for a moment as we decreased momentum and slowly ground to a juddering halt on the hard shoulder.

'Fuck.'

We knew we had to get the car fixed if we were to remain alive. Still shaking, we stopped for repairs in Harrisburg, Pennsylvania, sleeping three days in the car behind the repair shop as we waited for parts to arrive. From there it was up to Niagara Falls and on into Canada, back down into Michigan and Wisconsin, then Chicago before heading west. We did Route 66 and every other detour that looked interesting. We slept in laybys and truck stops, and washed in lakes and rivers. We drove through Minnesota and the rolling plains of South Dakota's Badlands along to Mount Rushmore.

Every state we reached, something would seize up or fall off. The car was using as much oil as gas and every time we stopped, we added a gallon or so from the five-gallon drums of used dirty drained sump oil that the garages would give us for free as we got our repairs along the way.

In Wyoming we started to dribble more oil than usual from the cracked sump and rocker cover. Then we blew a radiator hose in Yellowstone and threw a valve in Rapid City. Each unavoidable repair stop came with a bonus; we could stay a little longer than we might otherwise have done in places we'd never seen before. We spent a few enforced days on the northern rim of the Grand Canyon courtesy of a sheared universal joint on the drive shaft. In Vegas, the muffler left the building or rather the vehicle. In California, the fan belt shredded, but we made it to LA and down into San Diego for an Elvis Costello concert and then over the border on into Mexico. At Rosarito Beach the car stopped inexplicably for a couple of hours, before – with nothing more than the power of prayer – we were able to get it started again. Back into the USA and up to city on the bay, San Francisco. We halted here.

Rob had said we could all stay with relatives he had living there. The remaining three of us spent a week in San Francisco international airport before Rob returned and delivered the disappointing news that he couldn't square it with his relatives.

At this point Steve had had enough and boarded a flight back to the UK. Rob made his apologies and disappeared into thin San Francisco air ... Leaving Smithy and me to decide on a course of action.

We headed for the YMCA. Outside which, we sold the car to a Rastafarian musician who needed it to transport his colourful collection of West Indian steel drums. It's what Honest Jamal's Autos would have wanted. There we also made a decision.

As luck would have it Smithy, my best buddy, and still someone I share a drink with on a regular basis, had been injured in a car crash prior to our American escapade. Not badly, but badly enough to be the recipient of an insurance settlement amounting to a credit card and a couple of grand in his bank account. We agreed, or rather he agreed, to spend this windfall on returning us from America to the UK the wrong way. I promised to pay him back on our return.

So, without further ado, we purchased two one-way tickets to Hong Kong via South Korea. Not a lot of thought went into this, but we did think to purchase a small yellow guidebook called *East Asia on a Shoestring*. It became our travel bible.

We set off on our adventure.

Several connecting flights were involved, and I made the mistake of drinking lots on the first one and being much the worse for wear. I arrived in Hong Kong with a pounding headache and little idea of where to go or what I was doing there.

We headed for Manila in the Philippines to stay with a friend, Dave, but couldn't find him, so again ended up sleeping at the standby counter for two days before giving up on him. We moved on to Singapore and Malaya, the beaches of Thailand and the temples of Burma, the Irrawaddy River, and then the old-time hippy trail through Bangladesh, India, Nepal and finally Pakistan.

We ate at cheap hawkers' stalls or street vendors, travelling on windowless buses and overcrowded trains. We slept in dollar-a-night fleapits, shacks and brothels. Our quests were monasteries, temples, pyramids and pagodas. Sometimes we travelled by night, sometimes by day, on riverboats, rickshaws, tuk-tuks and taxis.

Smithy became very ill in Kathmandu. Now, that sounds far away. As a kid my grandad Arthur used to recite a poem to me, or at least part of one, which started, 'There's a little yellow idol to the north of Kathmandu.' John Lennon used the same line in his song 'Nobody Told Me.' It was actually from a 1911 song by Milton Hayes. So, I'd always been aware of a place called Kathmandu, and now I had seen it. I'd even shared my lunch over several days with a troupe of temple monkeys as Smithy did his best to recover. He was laid up and losing a very significant amount of weight in bodily fluids in a dank flea-ridden hostel room, as he tried to recuperate from hepatitis B with me as his distracted nurse.

At the very worst, I would be a well-travelled tyre fitter on my return, and Smithy, well, he would be a whole lot thinner. He stayed alive and recovered. It was India next.

Crossing East Asia on our economy extravaganza the train journeys were the worst. Sometimes we were forced to travel on the roof of a windowless carriage that had seats for fifty but was occupied by more than three times that number. It was either that or stand inside crushed against a fellow third-class traveller and his eighteen other family members for twenty-plus hours, being a constant source of amusement, as we were the only white skinned people stupid enough to have bought a $5 third-class train ticket for a 400-mile journey, under the misguided impression that this was a bargain. It was always more comfortable to cling to the less crowded carriage roof while hurtling through the hot Indian countryside, ducking under the overhanging power cables. People would stick their arses out of the moving carriages to go about their business – it was not a glamourous way to travel.

We finally ended up at the Afghanistan–Pakistan border town of Quetta. Most of the buildings were hardened mud structures, with thriving bazaar type markets. Today it's not a place that, as a westerner, you would want to find yourself. Staring out at the arid landscape from stark windowless carriages on our journeys through the rocky foothills of northern Pakistan gave me a nagging concern at the time. The partition era steam locomotives sometimes slowed down to walking speed as they made their way through the foothills. As usual, we were the only white guys. All the other men on the trains wore big turbans, thick black beards, loose-fitting tribal garments and sandals made from goat-skin and old car tyres (the tread of which I was readily able to identify as Michelin ZX radials with water traction grip).

It didn't bother us at the time, but looking back it should have. All of them were armed to the teeth, hefting heavy silver handguns or rifles that they let us hold and point and shoot out of the glassless windows, like kids playing soldiers. Beneath their bushy black beards, they were all very friendly, spoke very limited English but were nice enough to let us out alive. I swapped a penknife for a T-shirt with one of them, and I still have my half of the trade today. It never even crossed our minds that the Mujahedeen might have been less than welcoming a few decades later to the whitey tourist boys who travelled innocently fourth class with them.

We stayed nearly two weeks in Quetta enjoying the ambience of a mud-walled hut with a very active family of fleas, fruitlessly trying to get a visa to cross through Afghanistan to Iran. We must have been nutty as fruitcakes, and someone must have seen this and decided to save us from ourselves, as the visa was refused twice. We gave up and headed back south, sleeping for a few days on the floor next to the standby desk at Karachi airport until we managed to get on an Air Pakistan plane bound for Heathrow.

To be honest, it was a joy and something of a relief to be heading home to the UK, thinner, with a tummy that would take a few months to settle down, but alive. Tyre-fitting looked like it was an absolute heaven-sent occupation at that point. For a few more months it was; then I made the decision that maybe it wasn't.

Dear Writer,
What part of 'Do not send us your unsolicited manuscript' do you not understand?
Really, DO NOT send us your unsolicited manuscript!
Sincerely.

CHAPTER 5
Time to go

I told Ken, my boss, I was no longer content to be a tyre fitter. I had seen that the world was a bigger place than Motorways and BeefyMeat. I wanted to taste that bigger world and all it had to offer. Ken took back my blue coverall with its little embroidered breast-pocket badge, I said goodbye to Aled's brothel-creeper boots, and that was that.

My worldly goods at that point consisted of a brown, very battered 'L' registration Triumph Toledo 1100 with a dodgy second gear and a grey/brown primer and filler finish. I unloaded this on to Willy, my old shoplifting pal, for the princely sum of thirty-five quid. He was desperate for transport; I was desperate to sell it and be gone; done deal. It was now or never to break from my old town and go.

My other possessions included a battered human skull, a real one repaired with masking tape. And you know what's funny? It's staring back at me today thirty-odd years later, sitting on my desk as I write this. I think I acquired it from an unlocked cabinet at college many years ago when my scruples were not as high as they are today. I also have a small stuffed jaybird from those earlier days. I retrieved it from the smoking rubble after "someone" set fire to the school annex.

Those items were among my most treasured artefacts, along with my box of vinyl albums by the Black Country boy's quartet, Slade. I love Slade's music, always have, ever since I attended my first proper rock concert, a Slade gig in June 1973 at the Victoria Hall, Hanley, a pottery town of oatcakes and Wrights Pies in Stoke-on-Trent. I'd been wowed by the glam of it all, as a twelve-year-old boy, crushed down the front, sweating and screaming.

A young Noddy Holder, looking just like he'd stepped straight off Top of the Pops, bedecked in mirrored top hat and braces, bellowing the immortal lyrics to the newly-released #1 single in the country, *Skweeze me Pleeze me* at a thousand decibels. Fantastic! Four thousand screaming northern teenage fans who, like me, had paid their £1.50 for a seat they would stand on, singing along, clapping and stomping to every word. I'm still a fan to this day, and have Noddy's framed autograph, along with those of the rest of the band, on my bathroom wall here in Los Angeles: 'To Mil, keep on Rockin,' scribbled on an old Roto-sound string packet. Pretty bloody cool.

A sidenote, fifty years on: over the last few weeks I have been illustrating a children's book by Don Powell, the drummer of the aforementioned rocking Black Country quartet. I probably should have moved on musically to Miles Davis, Winton Marsalis, Dave Brubeck and/or Mozart, Gorecki, Mahler and everything in between, and to be honest I have, though the soft spot I have for Slade and the glam of the 70s is still as soft as it ever was. Though it now competes with YoYo Ma and George Winston, Ray Noble and Glen Miller, etc.

But as Joe Strummer sort of said, London was calling, and who was I to ignore it? London was the place to be, bright lights, big-city opportunity and all that. I needed to get my arse down to the Big Smoke and leave behind my provincial small-town roots.

I said goodbye to my girlfriend, who couldn't believe her luck. I like to think she must have laboured for hours on a touching goodbye note that she ultimately binned in favour of the card she handed me, with its short unsentimental message, "Good luck in London". Then, with a smile of relief that surely masked a world of upset as I puckered up for just one more goodbye kiss, she gently closed the frosted-glass front door on our relationship. I was London-bound.

* * *

'One ticket to London please. What? Thirty-five quid! You are joking with me?'

A train ticket was thirty-five quid? Thirty-five quid! I thought, I'll be fucked if I'm going to spend all my car money on a train ticket! That's a whole Triumph Toledo. I needed an alternative method of getting my arse down to London. I managed to persuade my mother and father to help towards this end of bettering myself. Maybe I could have my inheritance early or at least part of it? They reminded me that we were fuckin' broke, and I wasn't going to get any inheritance, so I should shut the fuck up. But they said, in lieu of financial support, they would give me a ride to the nearest motorway service station. From there, I could thumb a ride down south. That's what they said they could do, what's more they would do, and true to their word they did do.

They drove me the few miles to Keele motorway services and the nearest on-ramp. We said our tearful goodbyes (sans tears) and they drove away in Dad's old Datsun 160. Standing on the slip road I watched them fade into the distance before stoically transforming my waving hand into the obligatory fist with a raised thumb.

I smiled at all the motorists going by in their cars, but after an hour it dawned on me that such a tactic was getting me nowhere. Two hours later I was still standing at the side of the road. I stopped smiling as it began to rain hard. Sod this, I thought, I might find it easier just asking people in the service-station restaurant if they wanted company on their journey. Truckers are friendly people, probably glad of a bit of conversation, I figured. I spotted my first friendly-looking trucker, a likely candidate eating on his own, bound to be in need of company. I ambled up to his table and interrupted his mealtime solitude.

'You heading to London?'

'Ay.'

'Can I get a ride with you, mate?'

'No.'

'No chance then?' I pressed.

'I said fuck off!'

'Oh right.'

This was repeated a few times before I went back out into the rain. Some bastard will give me a lift at some point, I reasoned. I usually picked people up if I had room; someone was bound to do the same for me. I was due a bit of reverse karma. But by the time I got back outside, I wasn't alone. Several other would-be hitchers now stood in a line with me, all of them looking as pathetic and damp as I did. How would the motorist make a choice? Some hitchers had cards stating their destination, some no baggage. I tried to look the best prospect I could as a travelling companion. I practised my smile.

By now, I was at the end of this motley line of hitchers that was growing ever-longer by the minute. But wait: a large yellow British Rail van loaded with workers was slowing down. They must have been choosing whom to stop for? This is it, I thought, smiling as hard as I could. Pick me! Pick me! I willed them to pick me, and they did. They slowed and the doors and windows all seemed to open in unison, and, as if in slow motion, volley after volley of plastic cups filled with wet hot porridge were ejected with uncanny accuracy from within.

Every angle was covered as a rain of cups filled with hot, breakfast cereal found their mark. Me. I had been well and truly 'porridged'.

Everything went quiet for a moment, then normal traffic sounds resumed. I stood frozen, immobile, dripping head to foot with porridgey breakfast goo. I turned my head and watched as the van roared away, the laughter of the lads inside clearly audible even above the roadside traffic. I could hear it despite having porridge in my ears, nose, eyes and pockets. It crossed my mind to make out they had missed, but that wasn't really an option. I had been wearing a little felt-brimmed hat, vaguely to be trendy but also to keep the rain off. I lifted it from my head with a sigh, folded it once and cleared my eyes of porridge as best I could. I looked back at the line of other hitchers that stood there, all shocked but thankful the van had stopped for me and not for them.

They began to smile and snigger, and some actually laughed out loud, as how could they not? Even I could see the funny side, and, from the point of view of the porridge hurlers, it must have looked spectacular. I took a few steps back and tried to get the biggest dobs off with my hat before tossing it into the verge. One of my fellow hitchers, a young woman with green hair and red rucksack, left her boyfriend's side and wandered over, obviously feeling sorry for me but amused nonetheless. She held out her hand and offered me a tiny red cotton hanky. While not ideal, it was all I had to help scrape off the Tiswas porridgey gunge.

'Oh … dear … Sorry … er … Is this any use?'

'Thanks.' I took her little handkerchief.

'No problem, keep it,' she said, stifling her need to smile and re-joining her boyfriend, who was not as good as her at hiding his amusement.

I could do nothing but grin along with everyone else. It had probably looked really funny. One of the inherent risks of hitching, I guess, a porridge-pelting in the rain. At least it keeps you on your toes. Preferable to a garrotting, but bloody annoying nonetheless.

I went about the task in hand. I would clean up first, hitch later. It began to rain harder. So, this is why people pay thirty-five quid for a train ticket and don't travel third class, or even fourth given the choice.

Eventually I did get most of it off and I did get a ride,

straight into central London, as it turned out. A lift in a big black Mercedes playing classical music – Mozart or Vivaldi, I think – from a guy who wore finely-tailored clothes and who, so I gathered during our conversation, was into high level banking and success. No dodgy second gear for him to wrestle with in this motor. I tried my best not to leave any trace of porridge on his fine-smelling calf leather seats. We left the M6 and hit the M1 for London. I felt good despite the porridge-pelting, watching the oak trees dotted in green fields sitting in the undulating English countryside as it washed by the window. As we left the north and headed south, I was struck by what a pretty country we live in. Things could only get better. The silence of the finely-engineered Mercedes running gear meant the Bosch speakered Vivaldi sounded crystal clear. Yes, things would definitely get better.

'We don't have to listen to The Four Seasons,' said the driver. 'What sort of music do you like?'

'Got any Slade?'

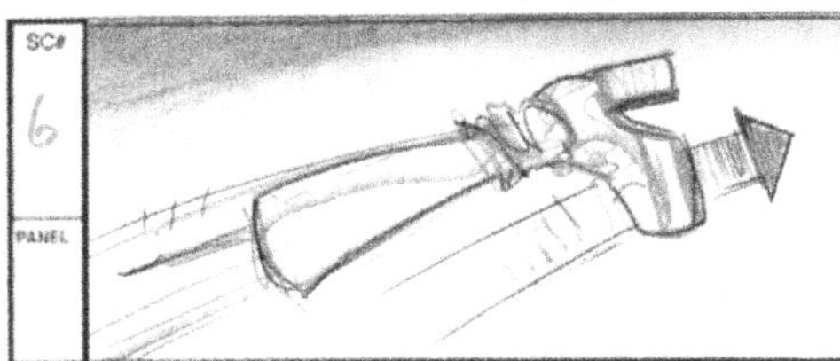

CHAPTER 6

Nearly there

A couple of my friends from college had moved to London and rented an apartment in a mansion block just off Baker Street. They'd said I was welcome to sleep on the floor and see if London held any prospects for an artistic tyre fitter. I thought, why not? It wasn't so long ago I'd spent a few days on the concrete waiting-room floor of Howrah train station in Calcutta; this would be like the Ritz. And with a stroke of exceptionally good fortune, my Vivaldi-loving chauffeur dropped me almost outside the door of my new digs in Marylebone! Porridge-pelting? What porridge-pelting?

I hadn't much of a clue what I wanted to do. I did know I was going to have to move to an environment where there were more "prospects", as they were always vaguely referred to, and in that regard, London seemed to be my best bet.

I'd been renting a room in a shared house in the Cheshire village of Mow Cop, a craggy hill that pokes up above the Cheshire plain with views towards Liverpool, Macclesfield and the Peak District. A Gothic folly in the form of a castle sits atop the peak. I had occasionally sat in one of the open windows of that stone-cold landmark under the vaulted dome of glittering stars, looking out over the lights of Cheshire, wondering what the fuck my life would bring.

My rental accommodation, a back bedroom in a pebble dashed semi on the Rookery estate, was not up for renewal, owing to a minor rodent problem. Well, the rodent was small, but maybe the problem wasn't. I had upset the landlord with the purchase of a pet brown rat that I'd wittily named Stilton. It was one of those lame attempts at rebellion at an age when I should have known better; a last gasp of youthful nonconformity in the form of a rat. Not really that bold, in fact a bit clichéd, but I thought it was a little bit radical, or maybe I just wanted a rat. The pet-shop owner had assured me that the rat I was buying was a boy, but Stilton put paid to that when "he" gave birth to fourteen little ratlets. Dave turned up for his rent to find his rental property "infested".

Infested? He didn't know the meaning of the word. I could have given him Michael White, the boy who sat next to me at primary school, if he'd wanted infested! A dozen or so years earlier, I'd been in Mrs Siva Kamara's class at Brierley Street Primary School in the backstreets of Crewe, Michael White next to me. Michael had really bad head lice that he would share around for free. As a bonus, he used to draw pictures on the desk of the little pinworms or roundworms (*Strongyloides stercoralis*) that would fall from his bottom. Michael! Now, he *was* infested! I also have an abiding memory of Michael loudly wailing one afternoon as he freely peed his pants during his infestation.

At the end of the school day, our class of eight and nine-year-olds would place our chairs on the desks, I suppose so the floor could be mopped by the cleaners. We would then face the chair, put our hands together and murmur the Lord's Prayer. Mrs Siva Kamara would get her sari in a tangle if she caught you messing about or talking during the prayer. She was a tough cookie, so nobody moved. Then one day, mid-prayer, I heard a plaintive wail.

'Thy kingdom come … Wahhrr! … Thy will be done … Wahhrr!'

I opened one eye and looked across at Michael. Pee cascaded in pale amber rivulets from his baggy grey shorts on to his Clarks' slip-ons, at the time the most fashionable shoe a boy could have. He kept praying and peeing like a leaking statue. The rest of us just watched, hands together, as the amber puddle spread wider and wider beneath him across the classroom floor.

I can't remember what happened or why he stood immobile. Nobody tangled with Mrs Siva Kamara, so maybe he felt he had no option. I'd previously been a victim of Mrs Siva Kamara's wrath for talking or breathing or something or other. She made me stand on a chair. A particularly irritating nose bogey had bought itself to my attention so, to relieve the boredom of facing the wall while standing on a chair at the back of the classroom, I tried to retrieve it. Moments later a thick Crewe accent mixed with her native Pakistani lilt screamed across the classroom in my direction.

'Mark Millicent, boy! Get your fingers out of your nose, you disgusting child, and put them in your pockets. Now!'

I slipped my hands into my pockets sharpish.

'You'll stay another ten minutes up there. You disobedient

child, you will not be picking at your nose when you should be standing up straight on that chair!'

Whether it was a very tall chair or I just got dizzy, I can't exactly remember, but the next thing I knew, I was crashing headfirst towards a hard schoolroom floor, unable to save myself as my hands were stuffed firmly inside the pockets of my baggy shorts. Head met floor with a sickening, dizzying thud. Funnily enough, when I came to from my dazed stupor, she was very, very nice and very concerned about me. All it took was a leap headfirst from a chair with my hands in my pockets, in what probably looked like a misguided suicide attempt, and suddenly we were best pals. I remember my mother's response to the ostrich-egg-size bruise on my head when I got home from school that day: 'Well, I expect you deserved it'. And she was probably right.

They bred mothers a lot tougher back then, and doctors too now I come to think of it. Around the same time, my mother Ann disciplined me and my younger brother Paul – some incident involving a squirrel from next door. She disciplined us in the age-old but time-tested manner of banging our heads together. I think she must have picked up this snippet of parenting from a *Tom and Jerry* cartoon. Then, a few hours later, Paul had sustained a more serious injury that required a doctor's visit. Doctors used to do that, actually come to your house. He arrived to see us two young boys sporting identical egg size bruises on our foreheads, and thought these the reason for his visit. I put him straight, explaining that Mum had smashed our heads together to 'knock some bloody sense into us' as she had told us at the time. I can now imagine my mother's jaw dropping and hanging limply as she envisioned a visit from the child welfare agent then the police. The doctor simply smiled and said, 'Well, I expect you two must have deserved it'. Today, we would be made wards of the court and the doctor charged as a co-defendant at my mother's trial. But back then it was all cool!

I renamed Stilton as Cindy – I felt it was more feminine – and she promptly escaped to begin a proper infestation within Dave's building. Dave went nuts, of course, and our relationship as landlord and tenant was severely strained. Cindy had gone AWOL, leaving her ratlets behind. What could I do? As Dave put it, 'Either they go or you do'. I couldn't just let them perish, so I had the idea of drowning them in a bottle of water, something I'm not too proud of now, but which seemed at the time like the right thing to do – quick and painless. It was strangely mesmerizing to see these little pink hairless new-borns all sinking to the bottom of a two-litre plastic bottle, then paddling around like that was their natural environment. They swam like tiny manatees as I dropped them into oblivion one by one, as if I was returning unwanted jelly babies to the bag. But then, one by one, their little lungs filled with water, breathing ceased, and they sank to the bottom of the bottle. It was such a strange thing to see, strange thing to do. Like something Stanley Kubrick might have dreamt up for an opening credit sequence. It's funny how some things stick with you. And, yes, I do still wonder why Michael White never raced to the bathroom but just stood there in a growing yellow lake of pee.

So, to London …

CHAPTER 7
London

I needed to spread my wings; London had seemed an obvious choice. My battered meagre portfolio did more to showcase my inexperience than any aptitude for an actual job.

After a several weeks hawking it around town and with nothing to show for it, I was down to my last few quid. Living on coffee and the odd cigarette, taking tube journey after endless tube journey to see anyone who would look at my motley collection of college sketches, I would grab a copy of the trade magazine Campaign every Wednesday and troll through the classifieds. My cash reserves were almost completely depleted when I stumbled into Domino Studios, a small advertising studio just off trendy South Molton Street, in a little mews close to Bond St tube. Central London, the heart of the West End. It was exactly where I needed to be.

Domino did 'magic marker' art for London advertising agencies. Storyboards were their main staple. I had never thought about storyboards, not even knowing what they were. But storyboards, I was about to learn, were where the money was at, and I needed money. All commercials and movies had to be broken down into a series of separate illustrations that gave the positioning of the camera, the look and feel of the subject to be filmed – the story in pictures, a visual shot list for the director, a readable plan of what the commercial would look like. In short, everything to be filmed had to be drawn first. That was where storyboards and Domino came in. After I had learned what they were, storyboards were what I wanted to be in.

London was busy, Domino was busy, everyone in Domino was busy. The well-dressed studio manager in Oxfords, pressed tailored trousers and braces introduced himself offering his hand.

'Hi, I'm Alisdair.'

'Hi, Alistair,' I replied.

He rolled his eyes. 'Oh, another one. I can see I'm going to have to write it down for you as well.' He picked up a pen, tore a page from his Filofax. Carefully spelling out ALIS 'D'AIR on the piece of paper, and handing it to me.

'Oh a 'D', eh?'

This little act of correction didn't initially endear me to Alisdair. I wasn't sure about him, but like all of my new toffee-nosed pals, he would grow on me. I would work on my 'OK, Yars,' later.

The advertising campaign that was all over the desktops, the first thing I would get to work on, was Ridley Scott's Apple computer commercials, advertising the very first Apple computers. First, I had to earn the right, and that meant starting at the bottom in the kind of dogsbody role that no one wanted but was all they had to offer to a young northern tyre-fitter off the street trying to make his break into the heady world of commercial art.

Domino was owned and run by a chap called Duncan McInnes, a flamboyant public-school-educated geezer with a staccato cough-type laugh, a sort of Beavis and Butthead snigger. He had a rakish smile, rockstar looks and a shock of unkempt strawberry blonde hair, always dressed in a baggy, crumpled, linen Armani or Paul Smith suit. Duncan ran Domino, and from what I could see, he ran it pretty well. Over the next few days I became seriously in awe of him. Duncan seemed to have all the perks that came with the job: definitely the sex and the drugs, though I'm not too sure about the rock'n'roll, even if he looked the part. He would close the doors to his office and have very private uninterrupted meetings with the attractive young secretaries or temps, involving bottles of Pimm's or Montrachet, quail eggs and French cheeses. That sort of thing would never have happened at BeefyMeat.

The first time I met Duncan, he was riding high as the king of Domino Studios, smiling brightly because life was good. The mid 80s was in full swing. Like a cartoon character and his sidekick, Duncan never travelled anywhere without Boozle, his shaggy English sheepdog, by his side. Not yet thirty years old, with a white, five-storey Regency house overlooking Regent's Park. To my mind he was a cross between David Bowie and the cartoon character Tintin. After viewing my portfolio, he flashed a smile and said I was welcome to work temporarily for no pay for two weeks and gain whatever experience I could pick up with Domino.

No pay, I thought; that's not very good. But choices were limited. I needed experience; Domino could give it to me.

I was to be general dogsbody and gofer. The dog's body I was to walk was Boozle; when he needed to 'gofer' a crap, I would be the one to take him. Central London is not a great place to take a dog for a crap, especially down a swanky crowded Bond Street! But as a junior 'gofer', I would get to do this and many other dog-related missions. A bit of a crappy job, you might think, and at twenty-two, maybe I was pushing it a bit as a junior, but taking that job despite its lack of pay was the best decision I ever made. I was down to my last twenty notes with no room for manoeuvre, and the last thing I wanted was to head back up north to resume my friendship with the BeefyMeat boys. Junior gofer sounded pretty fucking good to me. I kept my expenses to a minimum by never leaving the studio!

Some days, the missions involved finding Boozle. Duncan would go clubbing in the heady 'Loadsamoney' eighties, would inevitably get trashed and would take a taxi home. Duncan's clubbing car, a short wheelbase Land Rover, would be missing the next day. He would remember the club but not where he'd parked the vehicle containing Boozle. With the aid of an A to Z street guide – another thing that technology has rendered obsolete – my job was to find the car and the dog. Boozle had inevitably shat all over the interior of the vehicle during the night, so the ride back was never something I looked forward to.

But during those two weeks I watched and worked every hour possible to learn all I could about storyboarding. I never went home before midnight and sat on the arm of every artist who could pass on a little knowledge of this strange new world. One look at the cars parked in the mews told me storyboarding and advertising was a paying proposition. Along with his black turbo 911, Duncan also drove a convertible 1956 vintage Jaguar XK150, ivory cream to match his suits. Red leather interior, walnut dash, wire wheels; it was a car that got you noticed. I would get to drive the Jag around the West End to avoid the parking wardens who stalked the mews, looking for illegally parked storyboard artists.

Stuck in traffic, top down, outside Sotheby's on Bond Street, cruising around Barclay Square and Regent Street, people stared. Although I knew I was faking it, it felt good to be the king, even if just for a fleeting moment. One of the artists even drove a red Ferrari Dino. The ubiquitous soft-top, must-have cars of the eighties – the convertible Golf GTIs and XR3Is – were everywhere. Everyone was so sophisticated, speaking with posh public-school accents and driving something "awfully" great. Not a Triumph Toledo, Austin Maxi or Ford Cortina amongst them.

At the end of the two weeks, Duncan called me into the office. I thought crap, this is where I get shown the door, my two weeks is over and done. Duncan sat with his expensive handstitched brogues resting on the desk along with a glass of chilled Beaujolais. Shelling a quail egg with one hand, while the other nursed his permanently lit Camel. Grinning at me, he lifted what looked like a large plastic brick.

'What do you think?'

'That's great, Duncan.'

'Weighs less than three pounds.'

'Fantastic.'

'Best you can get.'

'Is it? Er, what is it?'

'It's a phone, see?' He held it up and pointed out the dialling buttons, tapped one and got a dial tone.

'Wow! A phone brick,' I offered.

He smiled, 'I'll take you on as a junior illustrator. Annual salary four grand.' Then he went back to playing with his state-of-the-art phone brick. It took a moment to sink in. I had fuckin scored! Wow! I was now officially a professional commercial London artist. I had landed the job. I stayed rooted to the spot. I hardly had any words.

'Thanks Duncan, you won't regret this'

'I hope not,' he smiled without looking up.

I spun around sharpish heading back to the studio before he changed his mind.

'Oh, Mil.' (Shit; he's pissing me about … there is no fuckin job.) 'Can you take Boozle round the square, she needs a shit.'

'Sure!' Smiling I headed back into the studio to join my new work colleagues and tell them that I was now officially one of them.

Thirty quid more a week than I'd been getting fitting tyres, and all I had to do was draw all day to get it. It certainly beat lying in blood and guts, fixing tyres on antique, offal-covered tractors. BeefyMeat's petfood-processing plant would have to do without me for good. No more lying face down in the rain, jacking up eighteen-wheel semi artics on the hard shoulder of the M6 motorway. Things were looking up.

It was the start of several years of what was to be a very happy part of my life. A year or so into the job I met my future wife, Luisa, a tall, pretty blonde girl who popped in one day, bright-eyed, bushy-tailed and smiling. To me she looked like she had just stepped from a gilded frame; you might say she was as pretty as a picture, a real-life Holman Hunt painting. Luisa came into Domino, portfolio in hand, looking for a job, wearing tight pink pedal pushers and fluorescent-green Wellington ankle boots. Duncan employed her on the spot; maybe her flowing blonde hair played a tiny role, knowing Duncan. Luisa had a boyfriend at the time, and by then I had paired up with a nurse from Camden. But I could deal with that later. I knew that persistence paid off.

Luisa was a junior illustrator, just like I had been, and her first job was to take over the dog-walking chores as I moved up within the company.

So, I had the London job now; I just needed London digs, though preferably not at London prices. I worked hard to keep learning all I could. London was a far cry from Crewe, and advertising in the eighties was going great guns. It felt like I had landed on another planet. The glamour of it all was the fun part. Up north, Maggie Thatcher was closing the coalmines, and there seemed to be this north–south divide. People thought I was an unemployed coalminer looking for work with my quaint, low-brow northern accent, and I'd thought it was posh Cheshire! But here, down south, was money. You had money, you had opportunity, you had prospects. People were buying shares in public offerings and making fortunes in a day. It was that easy. You just bought British Telecom shares one day and doubled your money the next. Heady times that were due for a fall. The miners were getting ugly, council houses were being sold off, the poll tax was introduced and things started on a bit of a slow downer. But I was making money for the first time in my life, and it was good! Who knew the stock market and the property market were about to crash in unison and that Black Monday was just around the next corner? Nobody was paying attention, certainly not me, not then. It was London in the eighties and things were good. It was Live Aid, Duran Duran, Freddie Mercury, Andrew Lloyd Webber, The Young Ones, Kenny Everett, Lady Di, big hair and shoulder pads. The technology explosion of MTV and electronic consumables: Fax machines, Walkmans, photocopiers and computers. And this orgy of conspicuous consumption was sold by endless TV ads and pop videos, and they all needed storyboarding!

Steve and Paul, my college pals who had let me share the floor space in Marylebone, were also moving up in the world, so they rented a flat in Hampstead, North London. I moved with them and rented some more floor space. It was cosy, to say the least. For a brief moment I lived in Hampstead, next to Hampstead Heath, London's largest and most ancient parkland. I didn't know it at the time but Hampstead was, and still is, a leafy village in the middle of Greater London: a prestigious place to live. Famous people like to live there, and so they should, as it's bloody nice and quite, 'Ok Yar.' I was lucky to have the chance for a few months, but it was always too good to last. With house prices spiralling ever upwards, the landlord decided to sell the house in which we were renting the flat.

Luckily, his girlfriend had a spacious four-bedroom apartment in Notting Hill, another of London's more desirable urban villages. A pal and I rented a room in her beautiful Victorian terrace house on Pembridge Crescent, W11. So once again, fate landed me in fantastic digs in a top-floor flat, minutes from the Tube and the Portobello Road. Notting Hill was even more trendy than Hampstead and practically in the middle of Central London. The kitchen window had an unobstructed view of the Post Office Tower, as it was then known, and the London plane trees that lined the street were a feast of changing seasonal colours, the leaves turning from green to gold against a backdrop of white porticoed Regency buildings. Portobello Road and the antiques market was right on the doorstep, and Saturday morning trips pushing in and out of the crowded emporiums always saw me and Luisa returning with some antique knick-knack or other. I started buying old clocks from the market, some good, some bad, some just rubbish. I also added to my stuffed-animal collection, buying a few stiff companions for my jaybird: a couple of little owls, a cuckoo, a kingfisher and two mounted dippers, a curlew and a pickled rat and a bat.

Notting Hill was close enough to Hyde Park and Kensington Gardens for those wonderful green spaces to be my own personal exercise track, with several prominent landmarks to mark the route of my daily run: Kensington Palace, the Serpentine, the Albert Hall, the Albert Memorial. The Horse Guards would exercise their steeds along Rotten Row and hold band practice in the bandstands dotted around the park. I loved it: Hyde Park Corner, Marble Arch and the Mall. Sometimes I would run further, cross the roundabout and carry on down Constitution Hill to Buckingham Palace. One night I stopped to see two guys talking to each other at a side gate of the palace wall. They were two very familiar faces: one a trainee king, the other one of the UK's most beloved comedians.

An armed police officer appeared from nowhere, then another in rapid succession.

'Isn't that Prince Charles and Spike Milligan?' I asked.

'Never you mind who it is or isn't, just you keep on running, sir.'

I kept running. It was pretty cool, though. How many people, on their nightly jog, get to see the Prince of Wales deep in conversation with one of the country's most beloved comedians? At that point I think he probably still had a shot at the throne – Charles, that is.

From Bond Street tube station, I walked down trendy pedestrianized South Molton Street every day to get to work. It was damn cool at the time, full of trendy shops and eateries where I'd spot the odd celeb. Elton John, Billy Idol and the like would come to shop at the Paul Smith boutique a few doors down from Domino. Here, if the mood took me, I could buy ridiculously overpriced shirts and trousers and then go and have a ridiculously overpriced tea and cucumber sandwiches in Claridge's Hotel at the bottom of the street. Gone were the days of a Wright's meat and potato pie washed down with a pint of milk drunk from the bottle while sitting on disembowelled car seats at a milk crate table. I started to buy nice shoes to go with my nice clocks, and that was pretty much where my attempts at self-improvement ended. You can tell the mark of a man by his shoes, his handshake and his clock (no pun intended). And, of course, his dead animal collection or his stuffed stuff!

As a boy about town, I could also meet and mingle with the odd famous bloke or lassie as well. We even joined the Hare Krishna gang for a brief moment. I'd seen them rapping along

Oxford Street in a happy conga; sporting shaved heads, sandals and orange bed sheets, they tapped their bongos and jangled their bells and chanted. I joined not in search of enlightenment, but because George Harrison was a devotee, which meant there was an open invitation to the former Beatle's manor in the Hertfordshire countryside north of London. There I rubbed shoulders with other celebrity devotees. People who until that point I had only ever seen on TV. Not counting Basil Brush, whom my parents had taken me to see at a show on Bournemouth pier years prior.

This was during my transition period from oik going nowhere to person with prospects. I never seemed to have decent socks to wear at the Krishna get-togethers, so I was always acutely conscious of my toes poking out as we sat cross-legged on the floor chanting for all we were worth. I met a several minor pop stars and TV celebrities in my holey socks. Lynsey DePaul was one of them, and if you were a schoolboy of a certain age, you will know who she is. She was dating James 'Our Man Flint' Coburn at the time, the fastest guy to throw a knife in *The Magnificent Seven*. Over Indian sweets she told me she lived in a Gothic mansion in Highgate. Spike Milligan being her neighbour, and we all loved Spike. The heir to the British throne loved Spike; I'd seen them chatting on my run the other night.

George Harrison's manor was home to lots of different people on different nights. Some nights I would be taking tea with some divorcee from one of Pink Floyd's number, the next it might be Hayley Mills or punk singer Poly Styrene or postpunk singer Hazel O'Connor. There were so many faces of the early eighties, minor pop stars I'd seen on *Top of the*

Pops, actors and dancers from various British TV shows of the time. We all had a jolly good chant every night I remember being there: Hare Krishna, Rama, Rama, c'mon!

That's what I did then. It was a world away from Crewe and BeefyMeat. It was celebrity fantasy cheesecake, real-life pop history like Willy Wonka's chocolate factory. I had won a golden ticket.

CHAPTER 8

A contract

Thank you, God! My prayers had been answered. A contract. I'd been offered a genuine we're-not-messing-about contract.

'A contract for what?' I hear you say. A contract for a film!

'For a film? What film? And who are you anyway?'

Well, I was a storyboard guy, just like I had been in London. I was still a nobody, same as you, but I had ideas above my station. I wanted to make a film. For years I'd watched other people do it, and laid out the shots and direction on paper for other people to follow. Now it was my turn. That was my idea, and, yes, it wasn't original or unique. But it's the hardest thing ever if you are, as I was, a nobody. Even for a nobody working in Hollywood, as I've been doing for years now, making headway is bloody tough going, with many a cross-wind to counter.

Poly Styrene once screamed in her 1978 punk anthem to mediocrity, 'I'm a cliché,' and I admit it: it's what I'd become.

Everyone you meet in LA is a writer/director/actor – all of us. You can't get out of an elevator without overhearing someone discussing the plot points of their latest script drama. We are all falling over ourselves to enter the euphoric state known as *Production*; it's what we wannabe clichés do. Hollywood greatness is just around the next bend. Or in my case, small indie movie satisfaction. It's a lemming-like, wildebeest kind of thing, an uncontrollable pull of nature.

So, it was for me several years ago; in fact, you know what, it is closer to twenty years and counting that I decided to join the gang of wannabes and put finger to keyboard to write my script. The heady days of the early 2000s, our C-grade president at the helm of the good ship US of A, fumbling for the words in speeches about the state of the nation while dreaming up a plan to find WMDs under Saddam Hussein's mattress. The state of the nation up until the point George W had stepped into the presidential boots had been pretty good, from what I had seen.

The world was now ready for my baby. My script, *Fizzy Days*, was the story I was trying to get produced. 'Fizzy Days?' you say. 'Never heard of it.' Well, *Fizzy Days* is my little ball of shit. It's my movie, the movie I wrote based on my experiences as a kid, an older kid, a tyre-fitting kid in part – a kid whose quest it was to own a small motorbike called a Fizzy, which was the must-have transport for many sixteen-year-olds of the day: the Yamaha FS1E sports moped. A moped complete with pedals was the only form of motorized transport available to the teenager of the early seventies in the UK.

I was sixteen years old at the time, and maybe I've taken the odd liberty in my fond reminiscence, but it was all over forty years ago, so who wouldn't get a little fuzzy about the fizzy details? Anyway, this story, the one you are reading, is not about that story. It's about trying to turn that story into a film. A movie. This is the story of the story of *Fizzy Days*.

The Fizzy Gang mid 70s

Cue the trumpet fanfare. My film, my little ball of shit, sort of "script to screen" and how it came to be, or didn't. It's taking a lot longer than I ever expected. From print to production has turned a low-key coming-of-age movie into something of an epic – From Here to Eternity – so I'm jotting stuff down as I go. So please, bear with me, as there is a point to it all.

This contract was a real piece of paper: fourteen pieces, in fact. It confirmed that someone other than my long-suffering wife Luisa, who had first suggested I write it, thought my script should be made into a proper film, a feature film, a movie. A movie with money, actors, sales and distribution, lights, camera and action! All the things those proper movies have. So now that I have given you an intro of sorts, I'm going to start right where the fun began, or should that be the heartache, which was January 2007. Yes, it was that long ago, but somehow it seems longer.

A one-page version of this contract had arrived in my email inbox a week earlier. Forecast Pictures France wanted to make my script into a film. The budget was still to be decided, but would be somewhere in the region of one and a half million euros. That was nearly three million dollars at the time, which in fact was chickenfeed compared to their last production. That film had enjoyed a budget of twenty-four million dollars. But three million was fine by me. I couldn't wait to show my new contract to people. My film, *Fizzy Days*, my little film about a moped in the 1970s, would be uttered in the same sentence as three million dollars, three million ... pretty bloody cool! This was the sort of email I had previously only dreamed of receiving. These guys were and are proper movie makers, the real deal!

Hi Mark
We're very happy and excited here at Forecast Pictures.
The contract has been Fedex-ed and is flying toward
Manhattan Beach!
I can feel it's gonna be a very good week.
Cheers,

Olivier Piasentin
Forecast Pictures
Rue de l'Echiquier
Paris, France.

'You are going to have to show that to someone who knows what it is,' came the response from the gathered acquaintances and advisers, in reality mutual drinking buddies at the local watering hole, The King's Head. The King's Head was where I liked to down a beer or two, an 'English' pub with a wannabe mock-Tudor interior, right in the heart of LA, or rather Second Street in Santa Monica. It was welcoming and reminded you of home in a crap sort of way.

Most of my drinking buddies at the time were in the industry to some extent, the industry being the film and TV production industry. Most, that is, except for Jerry, for whom things hadn't worked out as they should. Jerry now stacked deckchairs under Santa Monica pier, smiling but stacking. Not that he had had any strong vocation to stack deckchairs but it had done little to douse his ardour, and he still smiled about it – smiled on the outside anyway. We all hoped the Hollywood dream would be along shortly. Most of us were storyboard guys or production designers toiling away in the dark, the damp art departments of whatever movies were being produced in and around Hollywood. They were mostly people I had worked with in London, ex-pats who had made that leap like me across the pond in search of better things, the big time, or at least a bigger and better time than we'd been having in the UK. We would meet on the occasional Wednesday for the occasional beer and sustenance at the King's Head.

The King's Head is probably the best-known English pub on Santa Monica Boulevard, probably the best-known English pub in LA, and just a stone's throw from the Pacific Ocean. Apart from a portrait of our great British statesman Winston Churchill, the walls were almost completely covered by a celebrity photo gallery that ran throughout the establishment. It was a Who's Who of showbiz types who had visited for a quick pint over the years and had their photo taken, sitting with that same pint and the owner of the pub. It was as famous for the walls papered with celebrity snaps as it was for its Wednesday ribs! You would always see someone you hadn't recognized on previous visits staring back at you from the frame as you pried your beef from its bone. This prompted a spot of squinting and the pointing of a barbeque-covered finger at the wall while asking, 'Isn't that so and so?' Fill in the blanks and it inevitably was! As I have mentioned, Wednesday was the ribs special, so it was over the ribs that evening that I presented my barbeque-sauce-covered contract to the assembled company.

'What you need to see is an entertainment lawyer,' Jerry said over a half-drunk pint of Boddington's beer. Jerry spoke in a thick Scottish brogue, and had a strange habit of adding 'wuda-cuda-shuda' to almost every sentence. That's what people called him for the most part, 'wuda-cuda-shuda', a sort of strange aboriginal name. He'd spoken like that when we were still in London, and now we were here in LA, he still did. Reassuringly, Jerry was unchanged by the LA moxy, so there were clearly positives to deckchair stacking, and this piece of industry savvy made me realize that stacking deckchairs had not yet dulled the native Glaswegian edge.

'That's a good idea, do you know of one?'

'Ner, but this is a contract,' he said, holding the few faxed pages in front of him.

'I know, that's why I showed it to you. Not bad, eh?'

'It's got sauce on it, pal … and contracts are for stitching people up.'

'What do you know?'

'You asked me, I'm just fuckin' sayin.'

'I don't want to get stitched up.'

'No, so you wuda-cuda-shuda get one.'

I'll wuda-cuda-shuda get one, I thought.

Seeing as I was in a real-life production now, I was going to need one for this and the many more contracts and movies that would follow. But where should I look? Where do I find this attorney to the stars? After all, I'm hot stuff now, this contract proves it! More beer, please, and extra barbeque sauce. These tough and greasy ribs are especially sweet and tender tonight!

CHAPTER 9

Cuckoo Inc.

Wait a minute, I knew a lawyer already. Not well or personally, so it would probably be closer to say I knew of one. I emailed a guy named Pat. I had never actually met him, but he'd been kind enough to offer me advice online about a film-festival question. When I phoned, he remembered our original correspondence and said he'd be happy to take a look at my contract.

'My rate is usually three hundred an hour but I'll do it half price for you.'

What a guy! I knew for a fact that lawyers were apt to charge a damn sight more than three hundred bucks an hour. This guy must be in it for philanthropic reasons, a good man who had an interest in films and was having a sale! Done deal. I made an appointment! Just so happens he could see me that same day, and even I knew that lawyers were busy people you had to book in advance. The movie gods were with me.

I jumped in my old Ford truck and set off for Beverly Hills, arriving about an hour later at the address he'd given me. I was confident, cool, calm and collected. Why? Because I had a contract. I was making a film, and that was pretty big shakes. Pat's office wasn't in the most business-like district of Beverly Hills, in fact not in Beverly Hills at all, but I thought, hey, a lawyer is a lawyer, right? So, what if he was more like Beverly Hills adjacent, in fact more like Hollywood Hills, drifting towards the valley, even more sort of Los Feliz-cum-Glendale. Anyway, he was in LA, or near it, and that was good enough for me.

At the end of a badly maintained dirt road off Barham Blvd, I found The Palms, a small, drab building of rundown condo units that had seen better days. The sign by the gate said they had vacancies. I wasn't surprised. Who the fuck would want to live here? Maybe it was the wrong place. Got to be the wrong place. God, I hoped it was the wrong place. This place looked like Shitsville.

Grabbing my mobile, I rang Pat's number with some urgency to say I might be late as I was at the wrong place. A woman's voice informed me that, yes, this was indeed the right place.

'Can you see a big green dumpster?'

I stared ahead at the overflowing green trash dumpster in front of me. Shit!

'Park by the dumpster,' she told me. 'And come up to the third floor. Don't bother with the elevator. It's out of order.'

Doubt crossed my mind, then sat down and made itself comfortable, but I was here now. How bad could it be? Parking my truck, making sure to lock it, I made my way through the apartment complex. I nodded a smile to an anorexic looking lady, who had a leashed Chihuahua that she was walking around the pool as she puffed away on a cigarette beneath a wide-brimmed hat, the sort the Mexican gardeners wore. Wearing huge 'fly eyes' dark sunglasses that she lowered at my greeting, she gave me a smile. She had an odd masculine stride to her walk in her heeled cork sandals beneath her Daisy Duke denims, which were cut off way too short. The tiny dog looked like a big rat in the sunshine. She smiled vacantly and picked up her rat.

The communal pool would need dredging in the very near future. You certainly wouldn't want to swim in it. The sprinkler system had clearly stopped working. The garden around it was parched to fire-hazard dryness. The cracked tiles around the pool were covered almost entirely in fresh bird droppings, which had fallen from a jacaranda tree in full blossom where dozens of small noisy green parrots vied for position in the branches. I'd not visited the offices of many entertainment lawyers, but however you looked at it, this place was Shitsville USA and getting weirder by the minute.

I entered through an old glass fire door, wandering cautiously through the dank tired hallway of a dreary typical LA apartment building, up some tiled stairs until I found apartment number thirteen. The coolness of the dim corridors made for a pleasant respite from the oppressive heat outside, but otherwise I was not reassured. It reminded me of the nocturnal animal section of a zoo, sort of dark, but you can just about see. Gingerly, I knocked on the door.

A moment passed, then another … Then BAM!

Whatever it was rushed the door from the inside. The thud of it hitting the opposite side made me step back a pace. I heard a low growl. Visions of the Hound of the Baskervilles sprang to mind. I could see the headline: 'Excited Englishman with movie contract found chewed to pieces on doorstep of low-rent Hollywood apartment-cum-law office. Police are baffled, man is chewed, dog is satisfied.'

'Just a minute,' called a friendly-sounding woman's voice from behind the door. Friendly was good; it was the voice I had just spoken to on my mobile. I kind of knew at this point that we weren't on to a winner here, but there was always the chance that Pat was a diamond in the rough, a legal maverick, and the slobbering canine behind the door was a "legal beagle"! I knew Pat was into films because he had made a short film himself in some capacity. *Plastic Monkey*, an animated short about a plastic monkey, was probably deeper than the title might suggest. *Plastic Monkey* was how I knew of him. He was very active on one of the websites that aspiring filmmakers like myself could go to and get advice or post their films, scripts, etc. for other people to view or read, then comment on. If people said good things about your stuff, then you said good things about theirs. I'm not sure how useful that is, but the sites are popular. People who would be better off receiving advice rather than giving it meted it out by the shovelful to anyone who asked. And I had asked Pat.

Eventually the door was opened by a chubby pale-skinned woman with too much makeup, sporting those ginger-coloured eyebrows that you paint on yourself after you have shaved off or plucked out the originals. Her hair tied back in a ponytail. She did her best to smile at me while holding the collar of a huge and rather agitated Great Dane with copious slobber dripping from its maw. Dressed in matching pastel sweats, to my nose she smelled good, with lots of perfume. A Plastic Monkey baseball hat topped off the outfit. Strange attire for a law office. The straining of the dog was almost getting the better of her until she lowered her friendly voice to a surprisingly loud bass tone.

'Bob! Stop it now!'

Bob the Great Dane immediately ceased the struggle, as if he knew who was boss. The woman then returned her attention to me. Smiling through forced, clenched teeth, she shut the door and was able to release Bob to the freedom of the living room-cum-law office. Bob looked back at me before taking up residence on the couch with grudging resignation. He was like a huge Scooby-Doo, only silver charcoal in colour and without those friendly eyes that Scooby had. Sparsely furnished would best describe the living room, which also served as the reception and looked to be home to the law office of Cuckoo Incorporated. A large wooden desk looked oddly out of place, bang in the middle of the room beneath a dusty ceiling fan turning apathetically above it, doing little to make the air cooler but providing an oddly comforting background hum. The entire apartment had the atmosphere of an old wardrobe that you might have hidden in as a kid when playing hide-and-seek at your grandmother's house. Welcome to the law offices of 'planet cuckoo.' Please leave at the door any realistic hope for helpful contract advice.

'Do come in. Pat won't be a moment.'

A little stack of business cards sat neatly next to a phone; a Rolodex was positioned on the desk with a few pens. The lady dog handler told Bob not to move and then sat down behind the desk with that smile, a forced smile if ever there was one, pointed right at me. I forced one back. She now greeted me as if I'd just walked into a Fortune 500 glass-panelled office, so I tried to ignore my surroundings and go with it.

'How are you today? Don't mind Bob, he's just being friendly. Please take a seat. Pat will be right out.' She moved the pens on the desk a little to the left.

'Right.'

I had been the victim of an attack by just such a friendly dog as Bob in my younger years as a paperboy, when I used to live in the real world back in the UK. Dogs seemed to either want to hump the shit out of me or bite parts off me in those days. In fact, those four words 'he's just being friendly' were likely to instil as much fear as a vicious attack in your average newspaper delivery boy of yesteryear.

I remember vividly as a twelve-year-old kid a similar sized dog from my early morning paper round.

A big old house with holly trees and a loose gravel driveway. I had to park my bike at the gate and then crunch as softly as I could up the distance between gate and front door. However quietly I tried, my footsteps would always echo around the grounds, which must have alerted another "Bob" that his early morning shag had arrived. Resigned to my daily fate, I trudged up toward the house, as two huge paws clamped either side of my shoulders. Sometimes it was my waist, but mostly he preferred my shoulders. Resistance was futile as the dog weighed more than I did. I just gripped my sack of newspapers tightly, slowed to an awkward shuffle and tried to think of England as the amorous canine layered my jeans and parka with a fresh coat of semen.

'Oh, he's just being friendly,' the homeowner would say as I reached the front door. Sticky and damp, I held out his newspaper and we would both wait for the dog to finish. It's a good thing my parka was new and held its integrity over that time period, as otherwise I would probably would have given birth to a little set of puppies in the spring. They always tipped well at Christmas so I don't know what that makes me; a sort of canine Nell Gwynne I expect. For the price of a Mars Bar, my virtue was bought cheaply back then; something I'd rather not talk about today.

I still wasn't a dog person. The domestic canine poops on average about three quarters of a pound a day; that's 265 pounds of shit to pick up a year. Walking Boozle around the West End of London hadn't endeared man's best friends any further to me, and this fella looked as if he might deliver a pound and a half at each sitting, possibly more. I eyed Bob warily as he sat down on the opposite end of the couch, his eyes meeting mine with a frosty glare. I think he must have been like a lawyer dog, specially trained to sniff out three hundred dollar an hour suckers. I felt he had the measure of me and could probably smell me pretty good at this point. He did a dog version of rolling his eyes, as he seemed to lose interest and then ignored me with an air of doggy indifference.

'Do sit down and make yourself comfortable.'

I was already sitting down? With Bob. Bob stopped ignoring me, his eyes again met mine and he watched me for a moment, then without warning slowly he lifted one of his back legs to the vertical. I know I'm probably imagining it, but what can only be described as a doggy sneer crept across his face as he lowered his head between his legs and started to lick his balls.

Slowly at first, then more enthusiastically as he got the taste for them, all the while never taking his eyes off me. I looked away, pretending that everyone visiting a lawyer's office had to go through this, the "dog licking balls test". Bob really got into his cleaning session. I thought of blurting out the old joke, 'I wish I could do that,' whereupon his perfumed handler would reply, 'Give him a biscuit and he'll let you.' Ba boom, cymbal, crash! But I didn't, I kept it to myself and watched him for a moment, and she watched me watching him. A buzzing fly made an appearance between the two of us, so I transferred my attention to that while keeping one eye on Bob. The awkward gnawing at something Bob couldn't quite get his teeth into, deep within his scrotum, was broken as the girl behind the desk cleared her throat and said, with a smile.

'Pat is just with a client; she won't be a moment.'

She? Now, normally I would have taken this as a slip of the tongue. But without thinking I frowned heavily and said, 'She? You said "She". It's a guy I'm here to see, isn't it? Pat is a guy, isn't he?' I kind of said it because given my present company, I still wasn't sure I was in the right place. But I was sure that Pat was a guy. He had a guy's voice, didn't he? I had spoken to him on the phone. He was a guy if anyone was. But the smile on the face of Bob's handler evaporated, and I wished I hadn't opened my mouth.

With a far sterner expression she furrowed her brow and, with the same deep tone she had used to subdue Bob, said loudly and clearly,

'No!' In fact, she seemed to drag out the word 'No' for a whole sentence, so it sounded like 'Nooooowwww!' Bob stopped licking his testicles and intensified his glare in my direction. I swear that he was taking his cue from the woman behind the desk, whom I had mentally given the moniker Miss Fosdyke. Bob slowly, faintly, growled. Things were becoming a mite uncomfortable. Even the fly, sensing trouble, had settled out of sight.

'Oh,' I stammered, wondering how much pain you would feel if a Great Dane swallowed you whole. At which point, to my relief, the awkwardness was broken by the distraction of a toilet handle being repeatedly and frantically flushed several times. We all looked – me, Bob and his handler – towards the noise coming from behind the closed door at the end of the room. At some point the lavatory got the gist of what it was supposed to do and complied. The bathroom door opened and a very large blonde woman with a crewcut emerged, beaming, into the living room. She looked like a wrestler; the sort of lady you wouldn't want to tangle with … ever. I'm generally not a shallow person, except on hot Thursdays almost never make instant judgment calls, especially those based on appearance. Today, as it happened, was a hot Thursday. Not that I'm an oil painting myself, but Pat was ugly! She was wearing matching sweatpants and a tight top, and she, too, had painted-on eyebrows to match those of the receptionist-cum-dog handler. One slight difference in her attire was "Plastic Monkey" shimmering across her substantial chest. The words swayed as she moved, and I couldn't help but notice that she wasn't wearing a bra. Pat was barefooted, but a couple of toes had been adorned, or perhaps repaired, with Band-Aids. You don't see many barefooted, braless lawyers in LA. But Pat was obviously a woman who was very comfortable in business casual.

And she was indeed a woman, Patricia not Patrick. It was clearly colder in the bathroom with her "client" than in the living room, a point her nipples were now making beneath the tight material of her logoed top. The lady behind the desk glared at me as if to say, 'See, she's all woman, you freak!'

I stood up.

'Did you find us alright?' Pat said as she shook my dry hand firmly with her wet one. Yes, unfortunately, I did, I thought to myself. This lady had the same voice as Pat, the guy I had spoken to. It was also at this point I realized that the two women were an item, and as such I had just put my foot firmly in my mouth. I wanted to just pay my one hundred and fifty bucks and go; but no, I stayed. This was Hollywood, after all. And I was being lawyered for a bargain rate. What did I have to lose?

'Sorry to keep you waiting, I had to go pee.'

'With a client. I told him you were talking to another client on the other line,' said the dog handler.

Pat looked at her, confused. 'What client, and what other line?' Then she looked at me. 'Oh, don't mind Julie, she's always got one up her ass! I told you Mil was here to talk films, he's a friend, so no need to impress. Hey have you seen that *Plastic Monkey* is number one on the iTunes cell phone downloads? It just got into its seventy-first film festival, and I'm looking at a shitload of press kits to send out for the end of the week. We got fucked in the ass at that last première in Mombasa. Take a seat.'

'Thank you.' I think.

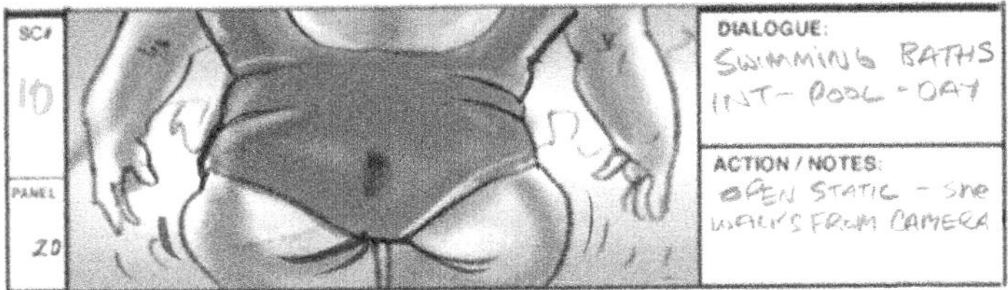

CHAPTER 10
A lawyer?

Pat didn't look or speak or dress like a lawyer, and didn't seem to work where a lawyer might work, in proper law offices. But that little pile of business cards stacked neatly on the desk proclaimed that was just what she was. Neatly printed on each card was: Drinking and driving? Then you need a lawyer who's been there! Pat Stratton. Attorney at law: Entertainment also handled.

Pat made her sizable self comfortable. She folded her arms and stretched her legs out in front of her. Several of her toes had the coloured Band-Aids. We both glanced at them. It was as if she was trying to remember why they were there. After a moment or so she gave up, and looked at me.

'Right,' she said, slapping and gripping each knee enthusiastically, before proceeding to tell me in detail all about *Plastic Monkey*, her film. It had just premièred at a festival for short films in Mumbai, its first Indian showing.

'That's great! Subcontinental exposure,' I quipped.

'What?'

Bob looked up. I smiled and cleared my throat.

Pat dismissed my interruption and continued, slowly at first, then building back up to speed. She told me where *Plastic Monkey* had been, where it was going, how it was doing and what would happen to it when it got there. She was going to get into a hundred film festivals. I kept trying to glance slyly at my watch, thinking this is going to cost me one hundred and fifty bucks and all I'm going to learn about is Plastic fuckin' Monkey's film-festival travels. What about my film? What about my contract? What about my directorial career? She probably downloaded it, I thought to myself, and read through it before I got here and has gone over it already. That's why she is not talking about it, but Pat caught me glancing at my watch and stopped in mid-flow.

'Don't worry, this is not on the clock. I just thought we'd talk shop before we got down to it.'

She gave me a friendly tap on the knee, which I don't think Bob was too pleased about. He'd stopped licking and was now staring hard at me. Pat went on and on about *Plastic Monkey*. I kept nodding my head and looking as if I was listening. Surely she had to stop soon. I could see the other woman in the room glaring at me over Pat's shoulder. Doubtless, when I left, she would spill the beans. I checked out Bob, who was now glaring and licking at the same time, his saliva-covered testicles shining brightly. He divided his glaring between me and the big buzzing fly that kept bothering him. As I was listening, not fully engaged with Pat and half-watching Bob, it occurred to me that if somebody licked my testicles for that amount of time, a certain reaction might eventually occur. And I'm sure I detected something of a lecherous sneer creep across the dog's face as he became more and more pleased with himself. I turned away and gave Pat the benefit of my full attention, at the same time as Bob was beginning to stand to his full tumescence. Bob and his boner became an item in the room, not quite an elephant, but not something you could easily pretend to ignore. Of course, I said nothing, partly because I couldn't get a word in edgeways. Then finally, she stopped. I was fully up-to-date on *Plastic Monkey*.

'So, let's take a look at this contract of yours.'

At last!

'Did you manage to take a look at it then?' I said with an expectant smile.

'Not yet, I would have done, but my printer is kaput, and I can't look at these things on a tiny screen, can you?' I glanced at the tiny laptop on the table, noticing for the first time it was the only office equipment on view in the law offices of Planet Cuckoo.

'Oh … I know what you mean.' I smiled ruefully.

I passed her a copy that I had thought to print out before I set off on this escapade. Pat took it from me only to instantly put it down on the table with the announcement, 'Sorry, I gotta go pee. Fuckin' bladder.'

I was left again with the sweet-smelling Julie glaring at me, and Bob the dog and his hard-on. I looked around and tried to appear at ease as I counted seven empty beer bottles lined up neatly by the front door, keeping company with a couple of empty wine bottles and a plastic 7-Eleven margarita mix container, also empty. The lavatory flush went again, repeatedly. We waited again, not as long as last time, and then Pat returned.

'Sorry about that.'

'No problem,' I reassured her with a smile.

'I had a procedure, an operation.'

'Oh.'

'I'm into colonics, know what that is?' she beamed.

'Vaguely,' I said, nodding.

'I recently had a real bad shit experience.'

She looked a little distant.

'Oh.' I nodded again, remembering an article on the subject that I'd read. 'The patient changes into a gown and lies on a padded table so that the "colon hydro-therapist" can insert a sterile, single-use speculum attached to a length of tubing into the anus. The colon is gently flushed with repeated doses of warmed water, which loosens waste stuck in the colon and filters it out through a closed tube system. When the colonic is over, the therapist leaves to allow the patient to use a toilet and get dressed.'

What a mental picture that conjured up! Pat saw the perplexed look on my face and felt obliged to go into more detail. 'You prepare with a weak peroxide-based enema. It's not just for hair.' She ran her fingers through her peroxide blonde, spiky marine cut. 'It's important to get the timing right, or else it can do all kinds of weird shit up there and you can haemorrhage. I got real busy and completely forgot about the time. I would have fuckin' died if Jue hadn't come home and found me. Nearly bled to death.'

I cast an eye back at the empty bottle collection by the door and wondered if "real busy" was a euphemism for passing-out drunk.

'Didn't I, Jue?' She looked past me to her partner. Bob's

handler just glared at me and arranged more pens with an intense scowl in my direction.

'Wow!' I said, and in fact I meant it.

So Pat was her own colon hydro-therapist as well? And not a very good one by her own account. Still, maybe she was a better lawyer.

'No insurance either. You'd think they wouldn't fuck with an attorney, and they'll be sorry. They think I'll be paying for it forever. No fuckin' way! Self-medication my ass.'

I could sympathize. I was guilty of being self-employed and I hated the absence of an affordable US medical healthcare system. I was fortunate enough to have experienced the UK one, the one that if you're an American you believe is the work of a socialist Satan, when in reality it's one you didn't need to talk or worry about as it's just healthcare, and why would you need to talk or worry about that? Why the words healthcare and insurance belong in the same sentence is beyond me. US healthcare was one of the things I least liked about the US. Mind you, I wasn't keen on US lawyers either, and this one was definitely giving me new cause for concern.

I was getting a lot of info from my new friend but not the info that was the purpose of my visit. She turned to the glaring woman behind the desk.

'Julie, did you offer him some water?' she said, indicating she meant me.

'No.' Julie didn't move and remained stony-faced. She just rolled her eyes and moved a pen. She glared at me one more time and went about the business of rearranging the pens on the big desk, ignoring the two of us. Three if you count Bob … or four if you count his shiny new pink friend.

Pat got real comfortable and eyed the paper contract I had handed her while I went over several visions in my head of the previous conversation.

'Hmm, Hmm, Hmm ...' She made a note in the margin. 'Well, it looks pretty good to me. What's your part in all this?'

I sighed inside and recounted everything I had already told her on the phone prior to our meeting.

'So you wrote this and you want to direct it as well?'

'Yes.' I can almost hear my apologetic tone.

'Then it's pretty dang good. You haven't done anything before, have you?'

'Not really.'

'Then you have little to bargain with. It's all up to what they will give you, as opposed to what you can ask for. I would just make sure you get it written down that you need a percentage of the budget as your fee for both the script and the directing.'

Good! I think she is a lawyer and not just an incontinent legal lesbian lady with a weak, bleach-damaged bladder and a huge dog with a taste for his own testicles. She is going to give me the full benefit of her legal mind. A diamond in the rough, after all!

'Say, have you seen *Plastic Monkey*?'

'The film or the monkey?' is what I think; but I smile and say nothing. I tried to dismiss this quick wandering off the subject of my contract with a 'No, but I'd like to sometime, if you have a spare copy.'

May as well get a free film for my hundred and fifty bucks, I thought.

'I've got a copy right here, c'mon, sit down.'

I couldn't believe it. I took up position on the couch with

Bob, who really wasn't into sharing his space. Although I was beginning to think I would come off better with Bob rather than Miss Fosdyke behind the desk, who still looked as if she was mentally disembowelling me for mistaking her wife's gender.

'Don't mind Bob, he's really friendly.' Pat insisted, and just to prove the point, she got up and pushed her face against the dog's. 'Who's a big softy, then … yes?'

She and Bob shared a big wet doggy kiss as she said something else to him in "baby dog" speak, and patted him affectionately before wiping the shiny dog slobber from her lips. (I hoped it was doggy slobber …) Bob turned to me with his dog version of that condescending sneer. Pat then popped Plastic Monkey into the DVD player; all we needed now was to dim the lights and grab some popcorn. Thinking along the same lines, Bob's handler got up and walked to the window, twisting the cord of the slatted blinds and darkening the room. I got the idea they had done this before. Bob turned towards me and cast me a 'Come hither' glance. I prayed that this was not about to get even weirder.

'I bet you don't want to see it again; you must have watched it a million times.' I stammered, while silently begging her not to say that she wanted to see it again.

'Yeah, must be millions,' Pat said, cranking up the volume with the remote.

'But you are going to watch it again anyway,' I said smiling with resignation.

'It's only seven minutes. I love watching people watch it.'

The smile on my face was interrupted by a sickly sweet-and-sour smell that joined us, obviously one of us in the room had created it. A really strong, sickly smell. As my grandmother used to say, 'Someone had let Polly out of prison.' I assumed it was Bob and looked his way. The woman behind the desk looked my way incriminatingly. I looked at Pat. Bob, Pat and the woman behind the desk all looked at me. There was an awkward moment which Pat interrupted. 'I gotta use the bathroom first, though, back in a mo.' She pressed a button and paused the DVD before disappearing through the door at the corner of the room.

I was left breathing through my mouth, sitting on the couch with Bob. It struck me how useless small talk would be at this point so we waited in silence, staring at the words 'Plastic Monkey' on the screen. The phones didn't ring. The traffic on the 101 Hollywood Freeway hummed a few hundred yards from the open, screened window behind the shaded blind, competing with the whirr of the ceiling fan. I seemed to be the only business in the law offices of Cuckoo Land's Butch and Fosdyke. Just me and a rather annoying bluebottle fly that kept dive-bombing Bob and interrupting his genital polishing. Eventually the flushing of the toilet broke the silence. Pat returned this time a bit red in the face. 'I don't know what I've been eating.'

All I could do was smile.

We all watched Plastic Monkey: me, Pat, Bob and Miss Fosdyke. At this point I can't quite recall what on earth it was about, but I do know it had a monkey in it that was plastic. The fly landed on the TV screen several times throughout the screening, but nobody mentioned it.

When the final credits were done, Pat looked at me and said, 'Did you see it?'

'What?'

'C'mon, you must have seen it?'

'Er, no. Guess I missed it.' She surely doesn't mean the fly, does she, I thought?

'Some people see it straightaway, but you missed it?'

'I must have.'

'The monkey looked like me. I got the animator to base the monkey on my features and characteristics.'

I was tempted to say, 'A really fat monkey that keeps using the bathroom every two minutes? Now that would have been funny.' But I didn't.

'They used photographs and a model. Just thought I'd see if you noticed. You weren't just being polite? I don't mind. Some people wouldn't want to look like a monkey!'

'I suppose not, yeah.' Smiling. Just keep smiling. It's only one hundred and fifty bucks.

'It was my idea. I wrote it, and I'm in it. How cool is that?'

'Pretty cool. I should probably go now. Already had too much of your time. So it looks okay to sign this then?'

'What?'

'The contract,' I pressed.

'Sign it. What else are you going to do?'

She was right, of course. What the fuck else was I going to do?

I paid my money and smiled at Miss Fosdyke. I almost went over to give Bob a friendly pat, thought better of it and left.

As I stood outside the elevator, which I'd forgotten was never going to arrive, I had the distinct feeling I was going to need a second opinion. I swatted unsuccessfully at the fly which had followed me out and was now beginning to bother me as much as it had Bob. It must have got bored with Bob's balls and was after something new.

'The elevator doesn't work.' A very raspy voice, a smoker's voice, a manly voice, joined me outside the elevator. I turned to see the old withered crone in the sun hat from the pool who'd been walking the Chihuahua when I arrived. She had now appeared at my side. Did nobody around here have a voice that matched their gender? She was smiling oddly through painted lips and beard stubble, which I hadn't noticed on our first greeting. So, there was a dong in those Daisy Dukes. The "she" was a he.

'It's a lot cooler in my apartment, if you like.'

'Oh right, thanks.' I spun on my heels and was about to depart the same airspace when she repeated her invitation, only more forcefully this time.

'I'm good, thanks,' I almost pleaded. 'Maybe next time. Thanks for the offer though.'

I smiled, and it was then I noticed that down the corridor a door had opened and Bob was now bounding toward us without the constraint of his handler who just smiled from the doorway. I didn't want to wait to see if he wanted to be friendly, so I set off at a steady jog, which by the time I got to the stairwell had turned into a flat-out sprint. It really was time to go. I knew that Miss Fosdyke had unleashed the hound on purpose. Down the stairs three at a time and through the doors, then racing across the garden, completely forgetting the slippery parrot droppings beside the swimming pool …

Everything from here goes into slow-mo, as the white noise of an imagined wind rush fills my ears. That's how I remember it. I glide effortlessly for what seems like seconds, but in reality, must only have been nanoseconds, before plunging into the murky green water of the toxic communal pool.

The last hour of that meeting still passes before me like a lifetime of images before I finally come up for air. It's wet, dark and smelly. I wonder if Spielberg had to go through all this.

CHAPTER 11

Backing up

At this juncture I need to back up a little to fill in a bit of background to all this script nonsense.

Well over fifteen years before any visit to Pat and her testicle-licking Great Dane at Cuckoo Incorporated law offices. I had come from the UK to California to try and make it in the movie business as a storyboarder. I'm not sure if I came here with the specific idea of making movies, but what better place than LA to have an exploratory expedition? Probably the same reason that a lot of people who are not directors or even in the industry at all also make their way towards Hollywood. When I was working in the UK, storyboarding for other directors, over the years people had told me on a regular basis, 'You should direct stuff. Go to America, if you are serious. That's where all the movies are made.'

These were people I admired, successful people, "director" people who knew what they were talking about. People at the top of their game. 'They make a lot of movies and commercials out there in the US,' they would say. 'You should give it a go.'

In fact, people said it often enough that after a while I did start thinking about it, though probably not as long or as seriously as I should have. I was a busy storyboard guy in London in the late eighties and early nineties. But I was also a bit bored and looking for my next new trick. Aren't we all? I had moved on from Domino by now and had set up my own small London studio operation, just off Baker Street, which was doing well. I enjoyed the bustle of the area. We would often see the odd celebrity in the local pubs, the likes of Wendy Richard or Barbara Windsor or Kenneth Williams, all Carry On heroes of mine.

The pub, 'The Duke of Wellington' was near our offices on York St. We would go there at lunchtime. George Best, Man United legend, was a regular, and we often saw him at the bar to nod a hello to. He was there one day when he was due to appear on the Terry Wogan chat show in the evening. His understated Irish lilt announced from the bar that he was going to be on the telly that night.

Luisa now worked at an advertising agency in Knightsbridge so was usually home before me. I remember getting home that day and saying, 'Hey Lu, Besty was in the bar at lunchtime. He said he was gonna be on Wogan tonight.'

We sat down to watch in our new basement flat in Notting Hill, switching on the Sony Trinitron to see the expected car crash.

Best had obviously spent the rest of the afternoon glued to the bar stool. Now at the BBC TV studio he was pissed as a fart. Hardly able to string two words together as he self-destructed on live TV while sitting next to Omar Sharif, in whose face he tried to insert his fingers at one point during the interview. I don't know why I felt so embarrassed for him. I didn't know him at all, but like the rest of Britain I felt like I did. A funny six degrees here as Besty also had his own bar, called Besty's, just down the road from our studio on York Street. On the outside awning it said 'London–LA–Tokyo'. His LA bar is here in Hermosa, the next town down the beach. I have a drink there now and again. Life's funny.

Anyhow, I moved my business to Wardour Street, London, which brought with it the temptations of Soho's many great watering holes. 'The Star and Garter,' 'The Sun and Thirteen Cantons,' 'The Coffee House' etc, the list was long. Of course, we patronized them all, but though life was on the up, I still felt that it was time for another change. By then, the early 1990s, I had worked regularly with several prominent directors of commercials on what were quite high-profile projects, subsequently attending the shoots, watching how they worked, what they did.

'You should direct instead of just boarding.'

I had heard it so many times from people I admired and respected that I thought, with this sort of backing and encouragement, I can't fail. In retrospect, I suppose I should have dipped my toe in to directing a little in the UK but … America seemed exciting! Naively, I must have believed the encouragement enough to make what would be a life-changing decision to move to America. And try to become a famous and successful director via the storyboard route. I assumed that the US film industry had to be crying out for a man of my talents over there. They were bound to need an extra director in Hollywood! It never occurred to me that most wannabe directors go to film school and learn the craft of film.

I figured I was kind of in the business already, laying out storyboards, working with producers and directors on a daily basis. So why not just direct the shoots myself and cut out the middleman? Why not indeed! I had attended as many live shoots as would have me over the years, watching the directors intently, seeing how they interacted and handled the cast and crew. I spent many hours at Pinewood and various commercial sound stages watching Directors, DPs and crew on the job, learning what setups were used and how Gaffers and Grips would do their stuff and with what, etc.

Then, without thinking about this a little more than we probably should have, I wound down the business, we sold our house in Chiswick, along with the shiny Mercedes in which I'd managed to return the favour of picking up the odd hitchhiker at service stations as I travelled back and forth up the M1 and M6 to Cheshire on many a rainy weekend. We had been lucky enough to be given the opportunity to work hard and it had paid off. But we thought we just might give London a break. Think big, then bigger – couldn't fail. Somehow, I convinced Luisa who was by then my wife to go along with my dream, telling her that this would be easy. If it didn't work out and I wasn't a successful director within the first year, we would come back to England, and nobody would even know we'd been gone.

'You are sure this is a good idea, mil?'

'This is a great idea, Lu. Can't fail. Trust me!'

By the early nineties, I was already somewhat familiar with LA, having visited it many times over the years. Hollywood was rather more down-at-heel than you might expect. Fast forward to now; like so many places, it has received its fair share of gentrification over the years.

It was not the scary place that we had seen in the riots of a few years before, when Rodney King's beating at the hands of officers of the LAPD sparked violent protest in the city's black and Korean communities. Neither was it the semi-dystopic vision of Joel Schumacher's *Falling Down*, the Michael Douglas film we just happened to watch at the Coronet cinema in Notting Hill one wet Sunday night the weekend before we were due to fly. Luisa's reaction as we left the cinema was perplexed.

'And you want me to move there?'

'This is a great idea, Lu. Can't fail. Trust me!'

Los Angeles is hard to pin down in a few sentences. A sprawling metropolis of eighty-eight cities and a population of over thirteen million people and counting. A mixture of sun-drenched suburbs all linked by a series of freeways that run like a spider's web from the coast to the San Bernardino Mountains, bathed in the kind of Mediterranean light you see in a California plein-air painting.

The coast and LA proper is bordered to the east by a place referred to mysteriously as The Valley. The big studios are in The Valley for the most part, a place called Studio City. Warner Brothers, Universal, Disney and Dreamworks, NBC, CBS, etc. all call it home. The others – Fox, MGM (now Sony) and Charlie Chaplin's studio (now Jim Henson's) – are pretty close to each other on the Westside, flanked by the waves of the Pacific Ocean and the beaches. It's funny that The Muppets (Henson Productions) now own Charlie Chaplin's studio. If Lord Lew Grade hadn't taken a chance on an off-beat primetime puppet show featuring a talking frog, a dog and a pig, we might never have heard of them.

LA and its scenery, its ocean and its cities, studios and suburbs have been immortalised on celluloid, video and digital perhaps more than anywhere else on Earth. My fond introductions to it came in old seventies TV detective shows like Columbo and The Rockford Files and Charlie's Angels and C.H.I.P.'s, all shot in and around LA. The drive-in movie theatres, the bowling alleys and skating rinks have now largely gone the same way as the Grand in Crewe, though the coves and beaches are still there. All those places were idyllic locations in the mental landscape of my youth, as if I had already lived here, if only vicariously through the TV shows.

Perhaps it helped to seed my own aspirations that Davy Jones, the lead singer of The Monkees, LA's answer to The Beatles, actually came from Manchester, just a few dozen miles from my own home town. All those fantastic LA TV shows had seemed so exotic when I was a kid that they might as well have been shot in another world which, as if by a miracle, you got to visit just by flicking a switch on the TV.

I found that LA proper, the living city, doesn't seem to have an exact centre. It just sort of sprawls from one city to the next under constant sunshine. The downtown area of tall buildings seems miles away. It's not where you'd expect it to be and doesn't feel like the middle of anything. It still maintains a sense of history, especially in the older architecture around the Jewellery District, and Broadway with old 1920s era theatres and their beautiful ornate facades. Undeveloped stores whose glory days were decades ago. It looks like Harlem or New Amsterdam in New York City – all the old movie-house marquees and façades crumbling, but still a faded majesty to them, still regal and grand.

The LA River and its famous art deco movie bridges evoked the era of film noir of the forties and fifties, in which they had featured in many productions. A time now gone, which you can still get a sense of as you cross their Deco spans towards the downtown.

The downtown itself is the copse of tall crystalline modern buildings thrusting skyward from the financial district, which appear on the right side of any aeroplane as it approaches LAX, LA's airport. If Manchester airport has the hills of the Peak District, green and inviting, LA has mile after mile of gridded sprawl dotted with baseball diamonds and backyard swimming pools, flanked on one side by the San Bernadino's as you make the descent toward LAX and the ocean and maybe a new life.

If ever you visit LA, you have to know someone who lives there and knows it well. It's an impossible mish-mash of a place otherwise. There are uncountable little gems to see and enjoy that TV or cinema has etched into our psyche, but you need to know where to find them. Besides the Sunset Boulevards and the Hollywood Bowls, more obscure landmarks litter LA: the Batcave (the real sixties one) in Griffith Park by the zoo; the Laurel and Hardy staircase from their "two-reeler", *The Music Box*; Muscle Beach on the boardwalk in Venice; the Griffith Observatory, where a young rebel without a cause, James Dean, traded blows wielding a switchblade. Go to Beachwood Canyon to see the Hollywood sign. Pee-Wee Herman lost his bike at the Third Street Promenade, just up from the King's Head, while the evil villain played by Alan Rickman in *Die Hard* fell from a tower in Century City, which also featured in *Planet of the*

Apes. Now it's just a place to shop on Saturday afternoons. A colourful patchwork of movieland locations criss-crossed by freeways that make up the twenty thousand miles of paved roads and interstate highways forming the spider's web of LA.

Our home: A city of "anomalies and tamales", a bipolar contradiction of a place. Burt Bacharach and Hal David once said, 'Put a dollar down and drive a car'. But how? It's not easy on the gridlocked, traffic-gorged arteries, the freeways and canyon roads and congested surface streets. As with every metropolis, tremendous wealth and poverty exist side by side, but here there's no welfare state to take up the slack. There is awe-inspiring natural beauty with wide-open spaces once you get beyond the city: majestic pine tree forested mountains and snow-capped peaks. Yosemite and Mammoth lakes. Joshua trees, saguaro cactus and the baking snake-filled deserts of the Mojave and Death Valley. They're all within a few hours' drive of LA. Just turn the ignition key and go.

This was where we arrived. We had seen the opportunity and just had to try and grab it! If it didn't work out, we'd be back home within the year. But until that day arrived, this would be our home, just for a while. Just till I was a movie director! It was going to be easy.

Twenty-odd years later we were still gone, or rather still here, in the city of eternal sunshine. My little kids turned into big kids, then headed off toward adulthood and beyond themselves. I wasn't a director with a dozen movies under my belt. I was many years older; not wiser, but yes, older. I'd written many scripts; all received the same underwhelming response. I'd made some short films and attended many, many festivals. I was maybe a little jaded, inured to the truism that it doesn't happen "just like that". Who knew?

But it will, it has to. The day is but young!

The realization had begun to grow that maybe the world of directing and film-making was not crying out for my creative talents and proposed projects as much as I'd led myself to believe.

The move was not without unanticipated costs. Luisa's family were not in agreement with her relocation to the US and her father never spoke to her again – they still don't speak; it was just something that was.

In the meantime, we had become Angelenos, something we'd never intended. I had got used to leaving a tip after every food interaction. I now drove on the wrong side of the road as if I always had. I'd grown accustomed to people riffling through my trashcan before the contents were collected every Monday. I'd taken to reading the LA Times with its pamphlet-like news-lite content, along with watching the polarised TV news that now just features Donald Trump-related stories. I got used to being able to turn right at a red light, and paying out lots of money every time I visited a doctor or dentist. I'd learned to call toilets restrooms and to having two prongs on my electric plug, not three. Now I buy milk by the gallon and pay a fraction of the amount I'd pay for gas (not petrol) in the UK to power my gas-guzzling V8. A few little differences and absurdities that add up to a whole new country where the sun shines pretty much every day. And I'll persist because I've started, because persistence and perseverance pay off in the end. Right?

CHAPTER 12

The short of it

Prior to Forecast Pictures coming on board, I had made a short film of *Fizzy Days* to show what the big one might look like. It began in the King's Head.

'Why don't you make a short?'

'What …? Hmm, a short, you say?' The collective thinking just might have something here. I scanned the assembled group of Wednesday-night drinking buddies.

'People would be more interested in the script if they could see what it might look like as a film.'

'Just give them a taster. Show them what you can do.'

Sage advice, in fact a smashing idea! That's exactly what the chaps who made *Napoleon Dynamite* did. They made a short and on the back of it they got funding to make the feature! In fact it was a well-trodden path to Indie movie success. I'd also read that if you can entertain people for thirty minutes, it should be no impossible task to hold their attention for a feature-length endeavour. Raising funds should be a cinch.

So, I set about making a short. A short film, something of a teaser for what the big film was going to look like. Bound to put us in the running to make the big one. Wouldn't cost that much, would it? The rewards would far exceed the outlay, wouldn't they? Like playing the lottery, only with guaranteed returns. Once a short is completed and people see its potential, a contract to direct and make the big one wouldn't be far away, a mere formality. It will show what *Fizzy* is about. I'll do it! We'll do it! We're off to the races! I needed to enlist some of my film friends back in the UK.

To make things more complicated, this short film of ours was going to be made just over five and a half thousand miles away from my LA front door. It's a story set in the UK, so it really needed to be filmed there. I boarded a plane and flew to England.

Nutty, my old pal from art college days, was working at the time at Granada TV Studios, where a lot of shows about northern types are produced by northern types in the north of England. Nutty, or Nut, was and still is a film man. He is still called Nut, an affectionate abbreviation of Nuttall, his surname. Nut had worked for years at Granada Studios on Coronation Street and various other projects, commercials and the like, and as such had access to people who could help, namely, cast and crew and equipment; all the little things you needed to make a film, even a short one.

Nut had read my full-length script and liked it enough to say he would help with the short film. Nut found Riggy. Riggy was going to act as producer and all-round point person who could get things done. Stephen Rigg, AKA Riggy, was a film-obsessed Lancashire man whose house resembled Planet Hollywood only with more memorabilia. At first glance, Riggy looked to me like a trainspotter on acid. Along with a strange twill hat and thick-rimmed glasses, he had a cheeky-chappy smile that was mostly hidden by the short stubble of a beard. Instantly likable, he was also a Manchester music buff and a former acquaintance of Sean Ryder, lead singer of the Happy Mondays, as he liked to tell us. Riggy spoke with what can only be described as a very broad Lancashire accent. An affable bloke if ever there was one.

Riggy lived and breathed the movies, so much so that he had purchased the full-size war chariot working prop from Ridley Scott's epic *Gladiator*. The one Richard Harris's character, Marcus Aurelius, died inside on screen.

All six tons of it was proudly displayed at his place of work. He ran a small sign-writing business based on an industrial estate near the Lancashire town of Colne. The walls of his house were adorned with Sten gun props from *The Dirty Dozen*, some of Sylvester Stallone's ammunition belts from *Rambo*, Robert De Niro's handkerchief from *Raging Bull*, along with countless other movie paraphernalia. At his side was his long-time canine companion Tommy, a small old black mongrel with grey whiskers and those sort of doting doggy eyes that said he loved his dad. Tommy was the inspiration behind Riggy's small production company, Black Dog Productions – Lancashire. It occasionally got confused with Ridley Scott's multimillion dollar enterprise of the same name, Black Dog Productions – Hollywood; though if truth be told, the confusion helped a little.

The first thing to do was to organize a plan, the second to find a cast. The third thing was to find some places to shoot the cast, and the fourth was to find somebody to shoot the cast in the places we had found. Lastly, someone had to pay for it. Me. None of these things were easy. Luckily, I was busy as a bee with storyboard work. I'd been able to squirrel away some film funds, and the project was a winner after all, wasn't it? How difficult could it be?

We needed a short script, preferably culled from the big script. I had a go at writing the twenty-page version, then a more manageable twelve pages, and eventually we got something that we all agreed would work. Now we needed actors. I knew this short film idea was going to take me a good deal of time and money, probably all of our savings, and a couple of trips back to the UK, but it would all pay off in the end. I initially resigned myself to a flight back to the UK and a week of casting and scouting locations up north or, rather, north of Manchester; maybe in Lancashire around the Burnley, Bacup, Colne area.

Riggy had been sending me photos via email. He'd had found some cracking spots in the Lancashire countryside This was going to be great, though the cameraman Nut had originally lined up to use had had a heart attack a few weeks earlier, so a healthy fully functioning cameraman or director of photography was another potential crew member we needed to find.

As for the actors, we had looked on several actors' websites and had about fifty enthusiastic *Fizzy* wannabes to audition over the next couple of days. Nut used his sway at Granada to get the music room, and *Fizzy* immediately gained some credibility: casting at Granada Studios, Manchester, no less. It was a proper production now. It seemed funny to walk into the television studios that had brought us iconic TV shows such as *Coronation Street* and *Stars in Their Eyes*, and even *The Bay City Rollers Show*. Hallowed hallways indeed! At 8.30 am we stuck a little sign on the door of the music room – 'Casting for *Fizzy Days*, the short – and we waited. Sure enough, people began to line up. At 9 am we let the first aspiring *Fizzy* actor into the black foam-panelled, dark and quiet music room.

He was not much to look at, a bit nondescript, you might say, but he looked as if he might fit the lead role of a late teen if push came to shove. He nervously shook hands and pulled a few folded and rather tatty pages of script out of his sweat-moistened shirt pocket. He was a stocky character you wouldn't recognize on a bus.

'We'd just like you to read the first few scenes you are in.'

(All of about ten lines.)

'Eh?'

'The part you are auditioning for. Can you read it for us?'

'All of it?' he said, somewhat incredulously.

'No, just the first scene.' I said, thinking that reading all ten lines would be fine.

'I'll try,' he said sheepishly, wiping the beads of perspiration from his brow.

He then proceeded to shout the written words really, really loudly. Nut and Riggy stood back a pace, then exchanged glances. I think our auditionee took this to be a sign that his performance was going well, so he cranked up the volume. I made a brief pencil note on my notepad: 'Number one, shouter, not good'. I stood up and waved my hand, halting him in mid-yell. That's what directors do, I thought.

'Can you knock it back a little? Bit softer, turn it down a notch?'

'Eh?'

'Not so loud, you don't need to shout.' I said as he frowned.

'I'll try,' he said, frowning more now. He carried on shouting.

Auditionee number one had set the tone for the day. The next fellow walked in and seemed uncomfortable in his own skin; maybe it was too dark or light or too something or other in the music room. He murmured, mumbled and squeaked the words really softly. The one after that couldn't string more than two or three of them together without coughing, while the next thought that he would ad-lib; and so it went on. The morning turned into lunchtime and we took a break, a little perturbed by how the proceedings had gone. Unsure if I should find this funny, I decided they would probably get better the more people we saw.

'Riggy, what do you think so far?'

'Do you want my honest opinion?'

'Yeah.'

'Fuckin' rubbish!'

'We're on the same page with this, then.'

'Nut?'

'I have to agree.'

It became very apparent that maybe we were not going to find our actors from an ad in the Barrowford Gazette or the websites we had trawled. And this was a shame, as we did need actors. Any film, even a short one, needs actors. We needed to regroup; maybe we should tighten the script? Sarah, who was helping us with the auditions, agreed. A proper actress who'd been in a commercial, she would have a more professional objective take on the morning's proceedings.

We hit the commissary and sat down to lunch. One thing I learned about the Granada cafeteria: it's divided for the people who are in *Coronation Street* and those who are not. I found this out when Nut approached me with a look of abject horror. I had taken my can of coke and sandwiches and sat down where, apparently, I had no right to be.

'This area's for Corra's staff and cast,' he stammered.

'Didn't you see the fake ivy …? You can't sit here.'

We removed ourselves to the main part of the cafeteria where the mortals sat. Sarah joined us as we contemplated the morning's proceedings.

'What did you think of those guys this morning, Sarah?'

'I have to be honest. They were fuckin', pardon my French, rubbish. None of them are actors. We need actors.'

Which sadly, of course, was right on the money.

The rest of the day progressed pretty much the same as the morning. But there was almost a bright spot in the proceedings, a reason to keep up the hope. Nut knew a fellow called Peter Kay. At the time, living abroad, I had never heard of him, but Nut assured me he was not just a fat smiley chap I'd never heard of, but was in fact "big time funny".

'Best British comic we've had in years,' he said. (I have since found out he is indeed big time and a very funny man.) 'I've told him what we are doing and he says he might help. That's, good isn't it?'

It certainly sounded good. Peter Kay, whoever he was, might agree to be in our little film. This was Granada Studios, and Peter was doing a TV show.

Nut texted him, which, I was surprised to discover back then, was what people in the UK did with their phones. It was something that eventually caught on in the States, too, to the extent that more recently we ended up electing as president an orange-haired man-baby whose idea of governing the nation was to barf out several childlike petulant tweets a day to his avid followers.

Peter Kay replied to Nut's text message and said he was free and would come down to the music room and read a part. Great! But then somewhere we had had the bright idea of asking him to wait until we had gone through all the other budding Laurence Oliviers before coming down; they had bothered to reply to our ad in the Barrowford Gazette, after all. Could he make it at the end of the day?

This was a lesson to be learned. You don't tell "big time" to wait till the end of the day while you audition every Tom, Dick and Harry who applied to an ad in the local paper.

We did a few more hours of hopelessness and the end of the day arrived on schedule. Nut's phone went off.

'It's Peter,' he said. 'He just texted me.'

He held up his phone to confirm the contact's identity. Smiling and nodding his head, he then read the text message, relaying its contents to us.

'He can't come now; he says he's busy now.'

'Oh, busy now?'

'Ay.'

At the time I don't think I was too disappointed because I didn't know who he was, having lived in Southern California for so long. I was disappointed later. But we carried on casting for another day in the music room. It's harder than you might think, listening to people crucify what you've written; it really sows the seeds of self-doubt. If we were to get this little indie flick up and running, we would need believable actors. I did feel genuinely sorry for some of the would-be Fizzers. Of course, none of them had come as far as I had, though one young lad had travelled down from Aberdeen, Scotland, to try out. One guy had come on the bus in his own costume: platform boots, fake sideburns and moustache. He actually wasn't half-bad but we had teetered on the edge of despondency and slithered over the brink by then, so it wasn't to be. Thankfully, most of them lived in or around the Manchester area, so it was no big deal. After a couple of days, it was clear that this approach to getting a cast wasn't working. Was *Fizzy* to die before it was even born?

After a week of "casting", I boarded my plane at Manchester Airport with a heavy heart and headed back to LA, harbouring the distinct notion that I may have wasted my time and everybody else's on top of a good few air miles. One last poke in the eye with a sharp stick was the driver of the shuttle bus that took me to Terminal One. I was his only passenger and I soon found out that he was a big Peter Kay fan. I guess I must have brought up the name in conversation just to see just how well-known this Peter Kay chap was in the UK.

'What? Peter Kay? Funniest bloke out there. Biggest star in Britain at the moment!'

There you have it. Bit pissed off. Bit disappointed. Bit wet. Bit tired.

Bugger.

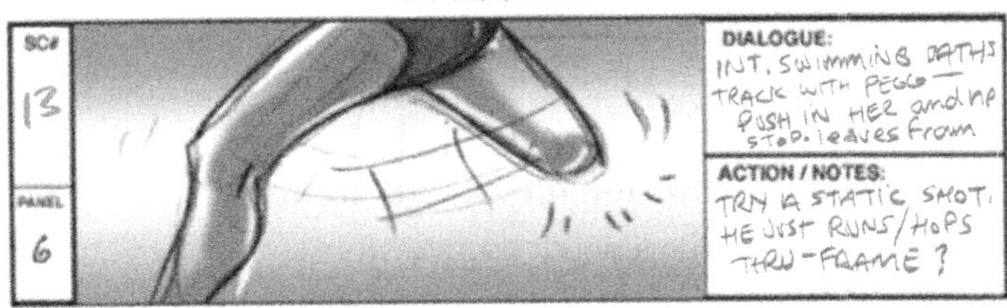

CHAPTER 13

Present

So today I'm still a storyboard guy. I map out in visual form what needs to be filmed in front of the camera. I digitally draw the running sequences, the storylines, the visual plan for what's written in the script. I'm drawing them now, pictures of what has to be filmed for a mouthwash commercial.

It's not a bad job, drawing all day and getting paid for it; certainly, I can't complain. But I'd like to have a go at telling my own stories rather than other people's. I was still a frustrated director. A director who had never directed; the worst kind. If you can direct on paper – direct the action, the visuals, the shots to be filmed the pace, the story – why not with a camera running? Like a train driver who had never driven a train but was pretty good with his toy set laid out on the living room floor as a kid. Go on, let me have a drive! I can drive. I'd be a good driver, go on … please, mister?

I had moved to America thinking the transition would be easy, or at least easier. I'd attended enough shoots, watched enough directors, read enough scripts. It didn't seem to make much difference. All these years later I was still storyboarding other people's stuff and was no closer to directing my own than when I first stepped off Virgin Atlantic flight 003 at LAX and announced to the film world: 'I'm here, so where is all this stuff that needs directing, then?'

But until this contract turned up, it just never seemed to happen. In fact, given the gap between dream and reality, a sense of frustration had me in a sort of headlock that I couldn't escape from, pinned face down on the canvas and finding it hard to breathe. Creatively, I felt I was going nowhere. My career had hit the proverbial brick wall. How I earned my living was certainly better than digging a ditch or serving fries, but it was still a way off from where I'd imagined I would be. Of course, I know that's not unique. The world doesn't owe us a living, and certainly doesn't owe us our ideal living. To a greater or lesser extent, aren't we all a little way off from where we imagined we would be? I wonder if the guy in McDonald's or the car park attendant in the booth at the shopping mall laments that creatively he's not getting anywhere. Do tyre-fitters have a yearning? I certainly did. Every year I seemed to add another tier, or maybe that's tyre, to that self-built wall of discontent. I needed to read some of those self-help manuals on how to appreciate what you've got; the ones that help you realize what you have is what you want or where you are standing is where you really want to be, or something along those lines. After all, I have a nice life; I live in the sunshine with my family. But I still I want to drive a train. Go on, please, mister, give us a go? Let me have a go at driving that train!

Some directors know exactly how they want their vision to

look. They storyboard in their head; you just draw what they ask of you. These are clever people, directors who know what they want, they have a clear creative vision; some are bloody extra-clever people. Ridley Scott, bloody clever director, does all his own storyboards, so I heard, but Ridley Scotts are few and far between, otherwise I'd be without a job. I went round to a director's house very recently. He told me how much he loved us storyboard guys as they helped him 'realize and visualize his vision.' He didn't know what his vision was until someone showed him. In our meeting, he had little to contribute other than to tell me he needed a visual draft of the script to help him raise interest and finance. I asked him the same question as I ask most of the guys I work with: 'How did you get into directing, if you don't mind me asking?'

That's a question you should never ask a director. They will never tell you. They just make a mental note never to use you again for their storyboards. A mumbled response will usually follow, like, 'Someone just asked me, so I had a go and it was alright.' Or 'The director didn't show up and I was near the camera, so I thought, 'Hey, why not?'

Everyone seems to say that, honestly. Nobody is ever going to help or offer you advice. It's a very closed shop, and the rules are you should never ever seek it, lest you be tarred and feathered and put to a slow and painful death drawing mouthwash commercials.

The director who now stood in front of me, the one I was foolishly severing any future working relationship with, was one I hadn't actually worked with before, nor was likely to again after asking the dreaded question. I knew this chap in front of me had not come up through the commercial route and was just doing features. I knew he had done at least one, and Vinnie Jones had been in it. Vinnie Jones!

'I don't know really, someone just asked me,' was his response to the question that should never be asked.

Wow, as easy as that, what the fuck had I been doing wrong?

'How did you get financing?'

'Oh, and my sister's on TV, she's in my movies.'

Tara, his sister, was a friend of Paris Hilton and inhabited the tabloid pages as a minor celebrity. She's also inhabited the Promises Treatment Center, a drug rehabilitation facility in LA – one of many such, I suppose – so she's into rehab as well as movies. Another well-trodden path! "American Pie star checks into rehab" reports the Associated Press on Yahoo as I write this.

'A famous sister? That's a bit of luck then,' I said.

The director frowned at me as he handed me the script, making that mental note not to use me again.

'Yes. Here's the script. Show me what it might look like.'

A movie can run to a couple of thousand drawings, sometimes more, sometimes less. I said I would certainly think about it, no pay at present, you say, but you'll use the boards to land the production? Then you'll use me if you get the job?

'Yeah.'

'Promise?'

'Course.'

'Hmm,' I think to myself with an interested smile on my face, masking my sceptical inner look of concerned amusement.

It didn't make much sense. At this point none of it seems to make much sense. In fact, it's hard to see why or how some people make it and others don't. But LA was Hollywood, swimming pools, movie stars. In the land of dreams, not everyone is going to make it. Tiny bits of glitter would rub off on you some days, if you persisted and occasionally mingled in the right places. You could even spot the odd star now and again, and no chanting with your toes poking out of socks at a Krishna temple involved.

If it was going to happen, LA was the place it would to happen. I had convinced Luisa of that as well, so I certainly couldn't give up on the dream yet. This was Hollywood, and we were going to try and get a piece of it; at least a small, independent piece of it. I had enough work for both Luisa and me, she added colour to my otherwise black and white boards so both of us kept busy.

You are sure this is a good idea, mil?'

'This is a great idea, Lu, can't fail trust me!'

In Hollywood, some mornings you could be having breakfast and look up and see someone fabulously famous having breakfast too. How cool is that? Admittedly, you generally had to leave your kitchen to do so, but that's what this town is famous for, fabulously famous people. A few days after we arrived here in LA we sat behind James Caan at the Broadway Deli while we and he were having breakfast. We had breakfast with Sonny Corleone, or at least we sat behind him while he had his. Cool. Then a few days later, a few doors down opposite the King's Head, another bit of glitter settled on our shoulders as we ate burgers in a small restaurant called the Crocodile Café, now sadly closed down. You would have days when your path would be awash with stars and A-list celebrities. That day we were munching away through our burgers and fries and Luisa got up to use the restroom. When she came back from her rest, she said, 'You haven't noticed who that is over there, have you?' She pointed discreetly.

'By the toilets over there?'

'No.'

'Look again.'

'What?'

'It's whatshisname!'

Wow, it *was* whatshisname! Arnie! Everyone's favourite Terminator and his family

Pre-"Governator". There is only one pre-Governor former Terminator of California, and there he was eating food like real people do. Actually, this movie thing is taking so long he's actually the former Governor now, and formerly married to Maria Shriver, with whom on that day he was sitting opposite enjoying lunch. This was way before she divorced him after he was forced to come clean about a liaison with the housekeeper and fathering a little Arnie with her who is now also a big Arnie now with the passage of time.

I went for a quick rest, too, and on the way I checked that it was him. Other kids were racing up to him to get their menus signed. I regret not having our kids do the same, but at the time we thought we were being restrained or refined or cool or just British. Now we are just regretful. Later, whenever we flicked through the TV channels and stumbled upon Arnie, terminating as the Terminator or governating as the Governor or divorcing as the Divorcinator, my boy Zack would always bring up his unsigned menu. Bugger. That was a good few years ago, so he probably won't "be back" now to sign his menu.

There was always a bit of everyday glitter: David Hasselhoff chatting with us outside the King's Head, Jay Leno parking his car across the street behind ours, Jennifer Aniston shopping on Third Street promenade, Jack Nicholson and Adam Sandler down the front at the Lakers game; a bit of LA glitter that drifted down every now and then. This was the town we had moved to. This was also the town where anything could happen. Where Arnold Schwarzenegger eats burgers in the same restaurant a few tables down from you. Where James Caan eats breakfast behind you. Where Brad Pitt sold fast food in a chicken suit prior to winning the Hollywood lottery, or so I'm told. Where Tarantino was working renting videos from a tiny video store in Manhattan Beach, which incidentally is the small beach town that we called home at the time. The place we were only going to be for a year if the directing thing didn't work out. I even know where that video store used to be. It's gone now, but when it was there it was called Video Archives. I know the owner of the grocery store next door to where it used to be.

In fact, Manhattan Beach is pretty groovy. Wikipedia describes it as a nice place to call home within commuting distance of Los Angeles, making it one of the most desirable coastal towns in which to live in America, according to Fortune magazine. Pretty bloody groovy indeed. So, if you were not going to live in Crewe, this might be a good second reserve, if you were looking for such a place. I had been a very lucky bastard.

It's a quaint little surfer town with an ice-cream shop or creamery, a pier and a bike path, seagulls and a beach. The locals include a few celebrity basketball players and sports personalities – Vince Vaughn was standing outside my dentist office last Tuesday – but by contrast, they are joined by a foul tempered and grizzled old one-legged surfer who hops daily into the surf. There is a wonderfully youthful grey-haired old lady who plays Scrabble every day on one of the benches overlooking the pier, always ready with a smile to challenge any passer-by to a game. There's a scruffy chap in a big black trench coat whose sole occupation in life now seems to be juggling change in his hand between scratching at imaginary bugs. He had lived in a bush by the former Santa Fe railway track, but the council removed his bush, so he set up camp elsewhere. But these are the less salubrious, more characterful, characters that call it home too. Me, now, being an Angeleno, I was indeed very lucky to be able to join them.

The town has been the backdrop to a few LA-themed movies: *Panic*, *Jerry Maguire*, *Tequila Sunset*, *Powde*r and more recently *Battle LA* used the beach. The old TV show *90210* was also filmed at a strand beach house, the blue clapboard beach-house location where Manhattan meets Hermosa.

Manhattan Beach does have one big movie-studio complex with huge studio sound stages, called Raleigh studios. The *Pirates of the Caribbean*, *Avatar* and a string of others were all filmed on the back lot in the South Bay, a couple of miles from our house at the time.

To stretch out this very limited tale of local glamour a little further, I have even held the Oscar for Best Original Screenplay that was awarded to Tarantino's *Pulp Fiction*. It wasn't the first Oscar I'd seen up close and personal. One of the fathers at my daughter Caroline's school used to bring his dad's in for "Oscar Day", as you do. It was Tom Sturges, whose father Preston had been awarded it for the film *The Great McGinty* way back when. The Oscar now in front of me was owned by Roger Avary. He and his wife Gretchen were, for a brief time, friends of my wife's, owing to the fact we had infant daughters of the same age who attended the same playground and lived on the next street along from ours. We were around their house for a kiddy birthday party. I knew vaguely that he was something to do with something in the film industry, as he had lots of posters on his walls, movie posters, and they all had his name on them. Over a slice of birthday cake, I made the mistake of asking if the Oscar on the mantelpiece was real?

'I got it for *Pulp Fiction*,' he replied.

'Roger, I know it can't be *for Pulp Fiction* because Tarantino was *Pulp Fiction*.'

Roger then corrected me, telling me that yes, it was him and Tarantino. He then popped a handy video into the player and Luisa and I watched both himself and Tarantino receiving the very Oscar at the awards. Wow! He was the co-writer of *Pulp Fiction*. Not many people know that.

'I didn't know you were a writer.'

'Yes.'

'I do storyboards,' I said, and that was it. End of new friendship, in fact, the end of our acquaintance with the Avarys. They told us that anyone who seemed to make their acquaintance after the Oscar arrived wanted something from them, usually somebody in the business or somebody trying to get into the business. I was now seen as someone who was "in the business" and trying to get further into the business via them. We were instantly viewed as a pair of hangers-on trying to weasel our piece of Hollywood from them. We were summarily jettisoned and dismissed. After the kind of success that *Reservoir Dogs* and *Pulp Fiction* had thrust upon them, they were always wary of new friends; we were new friends, at least for a moment.

I can't say I really blame them. He's done lots of other stuff since then, but *Pulp Fiction* is his best-known film and, despite my ignorance at the time, what most people know him for. Years later I was to see his face on the news again under the headline "*Pulp Fiction* writer in fatal DUI crash". His wife, Luisa's friend Gretchen, was also badly injured and a friend of theirs had lost his life. He managed a strange celebrity-type deal and avoided prison time until he made the mistake of Twittering about his ingenuity. Somebody made the tweets available to the press, and Roger was hauled off to a proper low-security jail to do proper low-security celebrity jail time.

CHAPTER 14

Hollywood – Hey

The movie industry, despite its reputation as a warm, nurturing place, is a fickle one.

To the movie industry you, the storyboarder, are about as important as the fish handler, the jelly setter or the pepper sprinkler. That's not to say everyone on a production is not as important as the next, especially the jelly setter. But story boarding seems to be the 'Roger Dangerfield' of production, 'It don't get no respect!' It's the storyboarders and production artists that get to work closely with the director for a great proportion of the story part of pre-production and where the look and the scaffolding of the film is put together. There are plenty lining up, waiting to be picked for the chance to work in the heady, glamorous world of advertising or the movies, all waiting for their step upwards, so it's a very competitive field. Producing as quickly and legibly as possible around twenty to forty little screen grabs a day of what is to be filmed or taped. You are paid well, but those who want to get their first break into the storyboard world will work a lot cheaper than the seasoned professional who's already had his break. It's a constant battle with people who will do it for less to almost nothing, and so it should be.

Those people whose "two weeks" are about to be given them are always waiting in the wings. The best way to inhabit the storyboard world is to be in the union. In the union there is a scale that has you paid based on the fee you received for your last job; and that's great, providing you had a last job. Being in the union also gets you medical insurance, which here in the US is often more important than the salary or wages that come with employment. A full eighty percent of commercial advertising seems to be related to pills, sprays, creams and ointments, and healthcare. Anyone holidaying in the States is always amazed at the number of medical ads that are aired and bombarded at the viewer between programming on network TV.

Sometimes I got to work on movies. One of the directors I quite often worked with on his commercials bought me on board for the Arnold Schwarzenegger vehicle *End of Days*, a Gothic apocalypse-at-the-millennium-type tale. The Arnie movie was budgeted somewhere in the region of eighty million dollars. Production offices were rented in Santa Monica, complete with a panoramic vista view of the ocean and the pier, the Ferris wheel and girls in colourful thong bikinis.

It was a union gig; I wasn't in the union at that point so I was hired as a consultant storyboard guy. Several other artists were brought in to get the storyboards done, and pretty soon we had taken over the whole second floor of rentable prime real-estate office space on downtown beachfront Santa

Monica. Yards of storyboards covering many black foam-backed display boards, they ran wall to wall, ceiling-high, as we graphically produced each scene from the script and displayed it for inspection, continuity and display. Arnold came in now and again. I looked up from my drawing board one day to see his smiling face at the door, looking tanned and fit in white shirt and slacks, an unlit cigar clenched firmly between his grinning white teeth, a tall James "Titanic" Cameron standing behind him.

'Hi fellas, do you know if the director is in?' said Arnie

'Should be in the office at the end of the corridor,' I said, trying to seem as if Arnie asked me directions every day.

Immediately, one of the story boarders behind me jumped up and said, 'Mr. Schwarzenegger, would you sign one of my storyboard frames, please?'

It was like being in the restaurant again – bigger children, but same reaction to Arnie's presence.

'It will all be taken care of later,' he grinned without removing the cigar.

Wow! Arnie again, and asking me directions … California cool! I went for lunch as the two of them disappeared down the corridor. When I got back from my tuna sandwich, Arnie, true to his word, had signed a couple of the guy's production sketches, and again I had a faint tinge of regret that I hadn't hung around. I didn't get him to sign one of mine: I was being restrained, I was English, and he was a busy man after all. I had my dignity … but no autograph. I'll get one later in the production or in my career, I thought. He'll be back … Damn!

The first time I got to storyboard a movie solely by myself was a remake of the old slasher classic *The Texas Chainsaw*

Massacre. The same director Marcus Nispel was set to direct, and this time I was the only storyboard artist on the production. Its budget was a "paltry" ten million so there was no money for a gang. I boarded at my home without having to work on site at a production office, which gave me the opportunity to do commercial work at the same time as fitting in Chainsaw's dismembered victims' limbs.

I would cover my studio walls in swathes of death and destruction graphically displayed in little widescreen renderings. My daughter Caroline, who was six at the time, would look over the drawings and remark, 'What's happened to that man's head, daddy?' or 'Where is his arm … leg … hand … etc?'

'All in a day's work.' I would mention that I hadn't finished the aforementioned body part and would be adding it later, when she had gone to bed.

'Both his legs too?'

'Both his legs too, when you're in bed.' Funny thing, I had a large action figure of Leather Face, the chainsaw wielding maniac complete with chainsaw that I was using to draw from. Caroline took to it as if it was the best Barbie ever, playing with it more than any of her dolls – despite its heavily blood-spattered butcher's apron. Over fourteen hundred drawings later of armless, headless, legless people, it was done. It was filmed in Texas and I bought the DVD and watched the "making of" in anticipation of seeing my handiwork. They, the production company, had mentioned my boards would be on the DVD that would be supplied as an extra. I never did see them.

I did get to attend the première. I was invited last minute,

'One ticket only, no guest'. My first première, on Hollywood Boulevard, at Grauman's Chinese Theatre – the big one, the Chinese one, the proper place to have a première. Luisa had to remain at home as I had practically to beg for the single ticket as it was. Grauman's, where I remember as a kid watching Saturday morning cartoons. The animated Pink Panther always started his show by arriving there in his "Panthermobile". Red carpet, crowds and Hollywood Boulevard packed with photographers looking at you trying to work out if you're a nobody or not. I trotted through the throng. Fooled 'em all!

I was invited to the after-screening party, and of course it was filled with pretty people, all those who weren't in the industry mingled with those that were. I struck up a conversation with a woman leaning against the bar. She seemed nice enough, not Hollywood at all. We chatted and gradually I felt comfortable enough with a few beers inside me to ramble on about my ambitions. I was the storyboard guy, see, but I would be making my moped film soon. I would be a "big cheese" like the producer. I regaled her with my tales from the trenches, and my contradictory aspirations of thinking everyone in movieland seemed to be such tossers yet I wanted to be one.

Maybe she thought I already was? On reflection there are probably a few that would. She brought up the filmmaker Michael Bay, who had produced this film. I don't know why, but I must have said a few less-than-flattering comments about my experience with producers, fuelled by my few pints; it's what I do. She agreed with me and kept referring to Michael as if she knew him well. How could she know him well? Our grandmothers always used to say that if you can't think of anything nice to say about someone, keep your fucking mouth shut. To this day, I wish I could follow that advice. I can't.

'Oh, he's probably a twat too.'

'Yes,' she said, neither confirming nor denying it.

'So, what do you do?' After I was finished talking about me, at some point it must have occurred to me to ask her.

'Oh, on the movie, nothing. I'm just Michael's sister.'

'You mean Michael. That Michael … the Michael *Tranformers* Bay … Michael?'

'Yes. He'd be my brother.'

Bugger!

A few weeks later, I nearly got the chance work on Chaz Shyler's *Alfie* remake. I loved the original, one of my favourite films with Michael Caine. I met Charles himself at his Hollywood Hills home, through the automatic gates, sat in the dark wood-panelled coolness of his office. I read the script that evening, stayed up overnight and boarded the first twenty-five pages – about seventy frames, if I remember. I never heard anything back.

So that's storyboarding for me in a small nutshell. Creatively, it was not as fulfilling as perhaps I would have liked, but that would be down to my shortcomings, not the industry profession. The industry was a starting point, and I would just have to try harder! Of course, being a storyboarder is to most a dream job – we get paid to draw all day – but after doing it for so long I had got the idea that I would like to try being the painter rather than the paintbrush. Sort of extend my dream. It may sound dismissive, but it's how I felt. Anyhow, painter or paintbrush, I was lucky enough to keep busy, in fact very busy. I was lucky enough to work with A list directors on a fairly regular basis. Top guys at the top of their game. Today I was in Hollywood above the old Virgin Megastore on Sunset Boulevard drawing boards for Zack Snyder, whose action films I admired and enjoyed. But today it was the banality of a toothpaste TV commercial that had me filling in my little boxes. So everything was cool, for now.

For storyboarding I have an agent, Mitch. As fate would have it, I knew Mitch had been a writer for TV before succumbing to the heady glamour of a small dingy office in Culver City representing storyboard artists like me. Mitch now spent his days sending hapless storyboarders to other dingy offices or faceless advertising agencies in and around the Los Angeles area. Some days you were downtown twenty or forty floors up, some days it was Orange County or Studio City or anywhere within driving distance. So when it came to knowing how to cultivate opportunities, I could think of no one better to ask than Mitch. He'll know what to do about this contract, I thought. He'll tell me honestly if it's a good one or not, and besides he's a member of the WGA, the Writer's Guild. Hell, he even wrote some episodes of the TV show version of the film *In the Heat of the Night*. He's bound to have seen a contract or two in his time.

'Well, I've seen a contract or two in my time, but nothing like this. Don't sign it. You need a proper entertainment attorney.'

'I know!' I said.

It seemed the more I asked the less I knew. To his credit, Mitch, who, God rest his soul, is no longer with us, gave me the sound advice to ring the Writer's Guild and get them to recommend an attorney who could help. A proper one, preferably one without a dog. For thirty bucks they will do this, promising to come back to you within five working days. I gave them a phone call, so then all I had to do was wait for them to recommend someone. In the meantime, while I was waiting, a few more script rejections arrived at my door. These must have crossed in the post between me receiving the contract that would launch my career as a storied director of motion pictures.

Dear Writer (that's me!)
Thank you very much for the opportunity to review your work, and for your patience in awaiting our reply. We apologize for our delay in responding to your submission. Unfortunately, we do not feel that it is right for us unless you have cast of note attached and some finance in place, an Oscar-winning director, etc. etc …

Sincerely

Dear Writer
Thank you so much for submitting your script idea to us. Your synopsis sounds really interesting. However, at this point we can only consider scripts that also come to us with at least half of the financing in place.

Dear Writer
I have finally read your script; so very nice. Moving and very educating.
Good job!
Thank you again for sharing.

(me) Er … thanks for looking …?

CHAPTER 15

The King's Head

What I thought I would do while waiting for the referral service to ring me back with a suitable attorney was to write another script to be a backup to the backup. I sent it out like others before me, full of hope and confidence that it would succeed. I now had three scripts in circulation.

I headed down the pub; waiting and dealing with contracts can be thirsty work after all. It was Wednesday again, so a few of my drinking-buddy advisers would be at the King's Head. They were; and remember there were always great ribs on a Wednesday. Normally I wouldn't have mentioned the Wednesday meeting again but for an odd happenstance of synchronicity that occurred over a pint of Boddington's and the aforementioned Wednesday rib special.

It is always comforting to be surrounded by walls covered in photos of showbiz royalty, to know that an entire firmament of stars has eaten fish and chips in the very seat you are sitting in: Rod Stewart, Maggie Thatcher, Ronald Reagan, Mick Jagger, Michael Caine. It's all crap really, but you miss crap when you are away from it for so long. As I said earlier, at this point I'd been over twenty years and climbing here in LA. I had made a few short films and probably should have made a lot more. It's easier today, and if I could offer any advice, it would be: just do it! Even if people say it's rubbish, it's not. Oh, and go to film school if you can … and keep your opinions to yourself!

This particular Wednesday I was to meet Trev and his pal Brendan. Trev is a storyboarding buddy I have known forever from London. Trev's storyboarding buddy, Brendan, I met for the first time that evening. Brendan was a comic artist who had sold a script for *Mad Max: Fury Road* with a budget of 150 million dollars. With a percentage point of that budget somewhere, that's pretty damn good, I thought! He told me tales of prior failure and despair and the "never say die" factor you had to have in trying to get a project off the ground. It was a concept I was becoming very familiar with. We shared a few tales of trying to get our projects off the ground, to sell our respective scripts and to deal with our subsequent rejections.

As we chatted, I couldn't believe how similar the stories were; his matched mine cliché for cliché, even down to the people we'd seen and their stock-in-trade responses. Brendan had an agent, while I didn't. He told me of a recent case where he had sat down in a Beverly Hills bigwig's office for over twenty minutes to pitch his script. Twenty minutes is like taking a bigwig's time for several days. If a bigwig gives you that kind of time, you know the bigwig is interested and you are potentially about to join the ranks of the élite. You are heading for home plate, or to use a football analogy, you have fuckin' scored! The bigwig had sat and listened to Brendan pitch his project, and at the end of his pitch, he shook my new buddy's hand vigorously and said, 'I want to be in the Brendan McCarthy business, it's the business I want to be in.' Brendan was over the moon … GOOAAAL!!! He had fuckin' scored!

The bigwig, of course, was never heard from again, refusing all calls. Brendan and his project were dismissed out of hand as soon as the door closed behind him. I said, 'Wow!'

Brendan's story brought to mind an experience I'd had a few weeks earlier, pre-contract days. Wall-to-ceiling mahogany panelling, a crystal-clear saltwater fish tank complete with corals and colourful marine wildlife built into one wall so you could see the more menial members of your entourage through it on the other side. Leather overstuffed Chesterfields and plasma screens, awash with signed Andy Warhols decorating every panel on those mahogany-clad walls. This guy was a player with a proper swanky Beverly Hills address. A bigwig! My bigwig sat and listened to me waxing lyrical about my project, even called in someone else to watch my short thirty-minute film, which I will get to later. I showed storyboards, posters, script and music. I pitched for all I was worth, as I'm sure, many others had before me. He leaned back in the overstuffed leather Chesterfield, tented his fingers, and looked me straight in the eye.

'My father could write a cheque for this tomorrow, I love the story, I love the idea, love the budget. I love it, love it, love it! And I love your energy. I'll tell you what I'll do. I will go home and have a word with my father tonight. This is a go. I'm on board.'

At my conclusion he shook my hand firmly and said, 'I want to be in the Mark Millicent business, it's the business I want to be in.'

Wow! GOAAAL!!! I'd just scored big time! He was on board!

I was really pleased at that point; it was going to be that easy, as the bigwig loved me. I loved him, too. Bigwig's Dad, it turned out, at one point had been the head of Universal Studios; the saviour I had just run out of saliva getting on board was Jon Sheinberg, the progeny of a liaison between Lorraine Gary, Chief Brody's wife from *Jaws*, and Sid Sheinberg, the former head of Universal Studios.

Needless to say, I never heard from him again. The same chap who had told Brendan how much he loved his project and had convinced me that he was fully behind mine in fact would never return my calls and had clearly dismissed me and my project out of hand as soon as the door closed behind me.

I guess it's a game for these I guys, to raise us nobodies to giddy heights of unrealistic expectation then dash them on the rocks of disappointment. Next! I do know these are busy guys, and they must hear a million pitches, but it was difficult to equate his unbridled enthusiasm in person with his palpable indifference once I was out of the building. You have to get used to this "genuine insincerity" with people who can help you; they love to play with nobodies. You can't take it personally. It's what they do.

Anyway, to distract me from yet another kick in the teeth, the Writer's Guild referral came through. They came up with a Beverly Hills attorney going by the name of Joe. It was a Beverly Hills number, a Beverly Hills office and Beverly Hills prices, six hundred bucks an hour, one thousand bucks as a retainer to sit down with Joe for an initial meeting. If he decided to accept me as a client, and the project was worthy of his very expensive time, I was on board, or he was. Joe gave me the initial thirty minutes and said he would have a look at my project, and maybe he wouldn't mind taking *Fizzy* on board. I met with him at the office on Sunset Boulevard, not quite as swanky as Mr Bigwig Producers, but better than Butch and Fosdyck's, and no bluebottle flies or testicle-licking dog.

'Would you like something to drink?'

At six hundred bucks an hour, 'Yes fuckin' please,' I think. By rights it should have been aged for about ten years and decanted in crystal, but warm water in a plastic cup was fine. I could see the palm trees swaying on Sunset Boulevard in the sunshine outside and remember thinking, 'This isn't bad, not bad at all'. An attorney who resided on Sunset Boulevard, no less, Billy Wilder's Sunset Boulevard – not bad at all.

So, I now had a proper lawyer, an entertainment lawyer. I looked around the office and saw the odd photo of the odd celebrity – old photos, faded photos. Chuck Norris and Mr T were in there, just above some fat guy I didn't recognize. The King's Head put this paltry selection of B-Raters to shame, and the beverage being served was not even close! The carpet had a couple of coffee stains, I noticed, and the desk was a bit of a mess. Again, I took it to be shabby chic. Still, not too bad a place to be on a Thursday afternoon for a lad who just a moment ago used to fit tyres in Crewe. After our initial quick chat, he took to his computer and looked up who the actual producer would be. The name on the contract was Jean-Charles Levy.

'He's French?'

'It's a French production company,' I say.

'UK film?'

'Yes.'

'You live here in the US?'

'Yes.' Does sound a bit complicated already, I thought.

Jean-Charles Levy, last production a little 24-million-dollar number called *O Jerusalem* with Ian Holm and Tom Conti. Joe started to smell the money, which was a better smell than the one that had perfumed the air at Butch and Fosdyke's place at Cuckoo Inc.

'Tell you what, seeing as this looks like quite an interesting project, I'll do it for contingency.'

'What's that?'

'Five percent of everything you make. If this project of yours makes nothing, that's what you pay me. If on the other hand it makes money, you pay me five percent of everything you earn.'

'Bollocks to that!' I thought to myself. Five percent for a couple of hours drawing up a contract – no way.

'This may not be the one, you may have many more contracts to go before it gets made,' he says.

Rubbish, I think. Of course this is the one, how can it not be? Turning him down would be another one of the many stupid decisions I was to make in my fledgling career as an indie filmmaker. I'm sure I have many more stupid decisions up my sleeve, but that one ranks up there. I wish now I had taken him up on his offer, but I didn't. I felt that seeing as we had a contract and that moving into production was just a mere formality, I would pay him upfront and be done. Three thousand wasted dollars later, I'm thinking, stupid me. Still, I'll be making a movie soon, won't I? Pass the popcorn!

My cartoon was cancelled. What cartoon? *Fizzy Days* the cartoon strip, which ran every month in the back of the UK syndicated magazine Classic Motorcycle Mechanics. For a few years I'd been lucky enough to draw a one-page comic strip that had the dual purpose of promoting *Fizzy Days* and giving vent to the sort of daft antics that moped-owning kids might have been up to, so conveying the flavour of the project. It was a great way to get it out there, but had become increasingly hard to keep going alongside my day job and working on *Fizzy*. It was time-intensive, black-and-white line drawings as a strip.

From the Fizzy Days comic strip that ran in Classic Motorcycle Mechanics

The offer to do it had come out of the blue one morning. Someone had seen the website I had recently put up promoting *Fizzy Days* the movie. The website featured examples of the storyboards I had completed so far for our proposed feature. Whoever had seen it had shown it to Rod Gibson, sadly now no longer with us, but at the time chief editor of Classic Motorcycle Mechanics. He had said the page was mine if I wanted it. *Fizzy* had built up fans with the strip, so it had served its purpose. Rod was always a fan. He had a fully restored three-litre Ford Capri Ghia that he said we must use when we made the feature. It was never to be; Rod, like Mitch, has passed on since I started writing this tome, in his case to the great Fizzy factory in the sky. But I was happy with the run it'd had. I was now free to devote more time to *Fizzy* the feature film.

I had finished writing my *Fizzy* script in the spring of 2003. Now that's beginning to sound a long, long way off from here, about twenty years at this point. Still, if I've learnt anything on life's journey, nothing happens quickly; and you might lose your hair.

Back then, several years later, I had half a dozen scripts under my belt and a couple of short films, but *Fizzy* was the one I wanted to get started. It was my "passion project" as they say. I remember thinking, when I had finished my first complete draft: wow, I've done it. Like running a marathon, you can't believe you actually did it; you wrote a whole movie. Not being a "proper" writer and all that, it seemed doubly amazing to me.

After all, the catalyst on my journey towards writing and directing a movie had been working on other Hollywood movies. It was reading the script and storyboarding *The Texas Chainsaw Massacre*, not the original, but the remake. I read the script, I read the writer's other scripts, and thought I might be able to do this. I had a story to tell. I could also visualize it and provide a working playbook, shot by shot, of the actual movie as it was going to look. I can work well with people, I thought. I think visually, I have ideas. I set about storyboarding *Fizzy*.

Some of the scripts I read seemed to be no great shakes, but they had found their way into production. I could do this. Doesn't everyone have a story to tell? So I based a story on my misspent youth, nothing too heavy; mildly amusing, I thought. I printed out all 110 pages and stood back to look at them neatly stacked on the dining-room table. Slightly too long, but it was a finished script! This bit was good, this bit was funny; others might disagree, but I was confident I could sell my vision of a teenage comedy caper set up north with moped and glam rock music.

I'd read somewhere that it's a good idea to try and win awards with your script, as people will take more notice of the project. I entered it in a competition, the Francis Ford Coppola script competition. It placed in the semi-finals, which meant it had beaten off well over three thousand other scripts to get into the top forty. I entered it in other competitions and it did well. I felt emboldened, I was on my way. I'm going to make a film, I thought. I began another script, then another. Everyone who ever completed his or her first script thinks it's the best thing since sliced bread. I was no exception. I had this hankering to be a film-maker, and to this end I printed up several copies of *Fizzy Days* and sent them out to various addresses that I found on the Internet. This was before you could just email the entire script.

Dear Writer
Thank you for submitting your script. After reading it at this time, we find it is not something we could pursue further. Wishing you every success elsewhere.

Some were relatively enthusiastic, I thought, but ultimately still "Nos". 'Mark, after reading your script and wiping away the tears of laughter, we have decided to pass on the project only because we are currently looking for something that is smaller budget. We most certainly will keep you in mind for future projects and will be in touch if an opportunity arises.'

That was a sugar-coated no thank you if ever I read one, and I wasn't too sure if they were laughing at the script in a good way or not. I tried Film 4.

'We're only able to commit to very few films each year, and so we have to be regrettably strict in our selections. Yours, being utter drivel, is not one we would consider. I'm sorry to not come back with better news despite its infectiously engaging tone … best of luck! (As you will need it!)
Sincerely.

This being the era of transition to a paperless world, a time before people would accept a PDF or a Word doc, before $4 dollar-a-bottle drinking water and Bluetooth connectivity, you were still required to send a hard copy. I thought to myself, what I need to do is to send out more copies of this script. I printed more and sent out more and more and more. The silence was, if not deafening, a little disconcerting. As well as Channel 4, I sent it to the BBC, ITV, the UK Film Council in Britain, the Film Council in LA, the New Cinema Fund and then the Development Fund, both run by the UK Film Council.

On one of my *Fizzy* trips back to the UK I looked up Duncan, my old boss from London, the man who had gifted me my two-week unpaid try-out. I found his number from my Domino days all those years ago and we arranged to meet for a coffee at a little café off Tottenham Court Road, next to the Middlesex Hospital. He had a small advertising company and was still in the game. But it was fifteen years since I'd last seen him. He was a shadow of his former self. A divorced, reformed alcoholic, chain-smoking and to my slightly disappointed eyes a fraction of the bright creative business spark he had been. An air of faded flamboyance still rested on his shoulders. He still chain-smoked the unfiltered Gauloises or Camel cigarettes that had yellowed the teeth of that charismatic smile. Vast quantities of cocaine and all the other dubious gifts that come with the good life seemed to have taken quite a toll on Duncan. He had swapped Regent's Park for a houseboat on the canal side of Little Venice in Maida Vale. I learned over the coffee that Boozle had succumbed to one of Duncan's drug and alcohol-fuelled evenings in Soho, when Duncan had staggered into busy traffic and survived unscathed, only to have Boozle loyally follow him attached to a leash, but not quick enough to save him from getting flattened by a London black cab. Good dog, sad end.

I learned that Claire, one of the "closed door" secretaries, a tall, lithe creature I had known and worked with at Domino all those years ago, was now confined to a wheelchair after a fall down some stairs while high as a kite. There's always a piper to pay.

To be honest, I saw Duncan not just to say hello again, but with a referral in mind. If the opportunity arose during our conversation, I was planning to ask if he might be able to put *Fizzy* under the nose of his friend Tim *Four Weddings and a Funeral* Beven, the very successful UK producer at Working Title Films. Duncan had attended public school with him or something like that, so perhaps his old school tie might work for me where other methods had failed. Tim Bevan was and still is "big-time". As well as *Four Weddings* he'd been involved with *Notting Hill*, *Love Actually*, *Bridget Jones*, *About a Boy*, and a slew of other great British flicks besides, not to mention *Fargo* in the US and more recently *The Theory of Everything*, directed by James Marsh, whom I had just worked with on a commercial at the last home of Stan Laurel, a hotel called the Oceanna in Santa Monica. Very Hollywood, eh? I thought, it can't do any harm to ask, can it? He's probably always on the lookout for more scripts and projects to produce, that Tim bloke.

So I asked, and without missing a beat, Duncan answered: 'Do you know how many people ask me that question?'

'No.'

'Lots. Never ask me that again.' He drew hard on his Camel.

I wished I hadn't asked him.

'Sorry, Duncan, shame about Boozle.'

'Yes, good dog.'

'Sad end,' I thought, for both of them. I wasn't to see Duncan again, but I hope he's doing well. I liked him. I owe him a lot.

I gave my script to people I met at parties, and to people suggested by people I had met at parties. I gave it to people I worked with and then to people who worked with people I worked with; that was lots of people. I gave it to Zeppo Marx's grandson, who I met at a party. He told me about a film he had been in with Walter Matthau as a child, *The Care Bears* or *Bad News Bears* or something to do with bears. I posted it on a few script websites that would have it. It placed well on Kevin Spacey's Trigger Street, one of those aforementioned websites where people said good things about it, and in turn I said good things about their scripts; it's now defunct, of course, along with Kevin's career. Out of two thousand scripts it got into the top ten; so surely it can't be utter rubbish, I thought. On top of its success in the Zoetrope screenplay competition – that's Francis Ford Coppola's screenplay competition – that was further proof to me, anyway, that it wasn't complete rubbish. In fact, objectively, it was doing well, though not well enough to merit production. I would persevere. I started ringing people out of the blue to explain I was really enthusiastically behind my script.

'And you are ...?'

Cold-calling is hard, and even harder knowing that you are maybe following someone who just made the same call, maybe with an equal amount of passionate conviction in their voice. Who was I, after all? Unfortunately, just another nobody with another bloody script to sell.

'Goodbye.'

I sent my script to Lily Munster's agent. I sent it to the

producers of several British indie flicks that had done rather well: *24-Hour Party People*, *Waking Ned Divine* and, of course, *The Full Monty*. I gave the producer of *East is East* a phone call. I sent, I phoned, I emailed. I pulled as many Brit flicks as I could carry from the local Blockbuster video rental store (also now defunct). I scanned the Internet methodically. I spoke to Simon Beaufoy's agent, Rod Hall; he had represented Simon, the writer of *The Full Monty*. Rod Hall read it, said it had an enjoyable charm but didn't really do it for him and that I might revise it. I revised it again. It still didn't do it for him. I looked up all the successful Brit flicks of the last several years and their producers and production companies. I fired off Fizzy Days to everyone I could find a contact for, Miramax, Tiger Aspect, Lionsgate and any Independent producers, dependent producers, the world and his wife.

Nothing.

I needed to regroup, get all my ducks in a row. I sat down, rewrote and revised the script and began sending it out again. This time it couldn't fail!

Dear Mark,
Thank you for submitting your manuscript that we have since had time to review. Sorry we are not able to move forward with it at this time, but we wish you every success in placing it elsewhere …

I worked on amassing as much of a *Fizzy* fund as storyboarding would allow me. I would occasionally bump into people who I thought might be vaguely interested in reading my script. If you work with people who make movies, at some point someone will give you a hand. At least, that was my original thinking. One bright sunny California day in a glass high rise in Westwood, I happened to be drawing away on a beefburger commercial when the chap from the next office noticed I was speaking with a funny accent and he popped his head in to say hello. The fool!

'You're English. I'm working on a movie in the UK at the moment,' he said, smiling.

He had my attention.

'That's great, what's it called?'

'*Corpse Bride*.'

'And what part do you play in it?'

'Oh, it's an animated feature that we are doing some post-production on in … Shoreditch in East London, I think it is. Tim Burton is the director.

'Tim Burton? That's great. How are you involved in it then?'

'Producer, Jeffery Abicher.' He handed me his card.

Bingo!!! And without missing a beat I said, 'There's a coincidence. I have a little project that I'm trying to get off the ground. I normally wouldn't ask but, you being a producer and all that, I would reproach myself if I didn't ask if you wouldn't mind having a look at it.'

His smile dropped and he squirmed uncomfortably.

'Oh … er, yes, by all means, love to.'

He didn't look as if he would love to, but he had given me his card and I was not about to give it back. Bingo! Bingo! Bingo!

I put together the smartest little project package any wannabe moviemaker could ever manage, and popped it in the post that very night. Blow his socks off, this will, I thought.

Tim Burton's producer is bound to love this stuff! But, of course, I thought wrong and never heard from him again.

Still, you've got to try, haven't you? I was sure I was just one hustle away from somebody liking my movie project. After all, this was how it was done, wasn't it?

Never give in, never surrender!

CHAPTER 16

Get it write!

Plan B was to tighten up the short script again. I'll enrol in a writing class, I thought. Learn to write scripts from a professional who writes scripts. Let's do this properly, let's find out just what a first act is, and where it's supposed to go. I needed a writing class to hone my new skills, as a writer.

Years ago, when I was more of a kid, I used to tell a joke that ended with the punchline between two people that went something like 'We're holding a monks' ball', to which another guy replied, 'Sounds to me like you're trying to twist the bugger off! So let go of it, and we can all get some sleep!' Boom boom!

Not particularly sophisticated stuff, you might sneer. The punchline in and of itself, disembodied from the meat of the preceding joke, is not that funny, if indeed the joke ever was, but the joke was about a writer. A writer who had gone off to a monastery in the secluded hills to be able to write. That was my idea of romance: a writer, a brooding soul, a Keats or a Shelley, toiling in solitude in some lonely, secluded spot. Writing was for people like Poe and Twain, Steinbeck and

Fitzgerald, Kerouac, Salinger, and so on. Writing was a gift that you could only be blessed with, and something I could never do. The kids who had left school with qualifications, the clever kids, they could write.

A commercial artist generally is not a painter, although many do paint, and many are successful and skilful at the craft. Commercial artists or illustrators don't seem to enjoy the same standing as painters and yet to my mind the skill set is phenomenally higher in some respects. Some commercial artists enjoy worldwide recognition, like Alphonse Mucha, Norman Rockwell, JC Leyendecker and the more contemporary illustrators Frank Frazetta, Berni Faulk and Drew Struzan. A seemingly small few are held in high esteem, but Joe Public is much more likely to be able to reel off ten painters than three illustrators.

But writing is different. A commercial artist is not a musician, or a poet, although I've struggled with the same three chords on my guitar for the same period of time! I have also written my idea of the odd poem, we probably all have; and that said, I do pick up a paint brush now and then, with mixed results. But to be able to write things that people would actually find interesting and want to read, that to me was a different art. It just beats the hell out of me that people are able to take words and eviscerate themselves on a clean page, lie belly-up and show your heart and soul, display knowledge, taste, morality, prejudice, ignorance, wit, humour, compassion, feelings – all the human qualities by which we judge someone. All this you could do with writing, with words. I was not academically equipped to be a writer. I didn't even get an English O level when I left school a million years ago. But to a make a movie you needed a story, and to have a story you need to be able to write. My point and reasoning was filmmaking. I wanted to make a fuckin movie so I needed a coherent story.

I enrolled at the UCLA campus in Westwood for the Beginner's Scriptwriting evening class. Westwood is a leafy college campus, a village-type place in the middle of LA. It also has the greatest little cemetery, a tranquil resting place hidden away from public view. You can go and eat your sandwiches amongst the stars without leaving earth. Marilyn Monroe, Dean Martin and Burt Lancaster, are all buried there, along with Natalie Wood, Jack Lemmon, Walter Matthau and many other Hollywood legends. Farah Fawcett is now just a few plots down from Kirk Douglas. The writer Truman Capote is there, too, along with Billy Wilder, one of the greatest scriptwriters and filmmakers there ever was. I like Westwood; it is LA "clean and nice", even though it's just a few blocks away from the hum and constant traffic pollution of the 405 freeway.

For two nights a week I sat in a room with two dozen other wannabes and listened to some of the daftest ideas for movie entertainment I have ever heard. Although in a strange way it was reassuring to be back on planet cuckoo. People pitched their crazy ideas for script outlines in front of the class, and as I listened it became apparent that, like me, everyone truly does believe they have a story to tell. We all do, we all have a story. It occurred to me that maybe I was wasting my time, that I was as nuts as the rest of the class. Each of us outlined the daft idea we'd dreamt up for a script, while the tweed-jacketed instructor listened intently before saying, 'That's a really interesting concept, I like it,' all the while sucking one stem of his spectacles in a very professorial manner.

The first class night, I had a reality check that I should shut the fuck up and be satisfied with my lot. When we, the students, all came to say what we did during the day, there were all sorts of professions covered, some actors, some restaurant workers, a gardener, a cab driver, an accountant … and a lone storyboard guy, me. When I mentioned I made my living boarding commercials and films, everyone was really interested in what I had to say.

I'd taken what I did for a living for granted for years. It was a real buzz as people turned their chairs towards me and asked me questions: how, who, when, where, etc. That was a good moment, and I think for once at least I appreciated that I was beyond bloody lucky to do what I do. It was a lot more revered and interesting to the layman than, say, tyre-fitting. Writing was something else. So was film making and directing. So was train driving.

On one of the Thursday evenings at the class, our instructor was talking about idea pitches.

'When you get inside the executive's office, they want something clean and crisp. This is how you pitch to executives; this is how I did it at Disney and Warner Brothers and several Hollywood Talent agencies, CAI, William Morris, Endeavor. I've been to them all.'

'Will they see you with just an idea and a pitch?'

'You make an appointment,' he snarled with a distant smile.

'Even if you don't have a script?' I interrupted.

'A treatment is sometimes all you need.' Less of a smile.

'So you don't need a script?' someone else asked from the rear of the class.

'You write a good treatment, then you write a great script, then pitch it to executives at a studio, like I did at Universal.'

'You sold a script to Universal?' The taxi driver asked.

'I pitched an idea.'

'Did they buy it?' the gardener enquired.

'It was a really good meeting. I had a fantastic meeting, made some good contacts. Ever hear of Sid Sheinberg?'

People shook their heads.

At this point Mr Johnson went all starry-eyed and gazed off across the leafy campus outside and beyond the Westwood window, perhaps towards the cemetery.

'It's no exaggeration to say that as I left the building, they said they wanted to be in the Chris Johnson business, it was the business they wanted to be in.'

Cuckoo!

A few classes later, I left my Westwood writing class and sent out a few more copies of my continually revised script and started working on a new short film. I needed to test the skills I had honed at the script class. I got a few more replies back, a few more responses; most went like this.

Dear Mark,
Thank you for your submission. However, this isn't quite what we're looking for.

Best of luck.

Dear Writer
We deeply regret having to use this form letter; however, the volume of scripts we receive precludes our writing to you personally. Please be assured that your work was given serious attention.

Best.

This writing thing is way harder than it seemed at first. If you write for yourself then it's probably better, but if you write to try and get other people involved, it proves to be much harder; bit of a fucker actually. You can't get an agent unless you have been produced, and of course people won't even consider your stuff for production if it's not submitted via an agent; Catch-22 if ever there was one. I checked the Internet to see who was a good script agent in Los Angeles. I found one, Victoria Wisdom, one of LA's the top talent agents. I had read about her in industry articles and thought I would give her a phone call. 'What harm can it do? She can only say no, can't she?' I phoned her office on The Avenue of the Stars in Century City, only to get through to her voicemail. Right, here goes. I spew my spiel the best way I can. I pitch my script then and there. The message left; I didn't expect a reply, but hey, I'd tried. A couple of days later she rang me back and said that she always picks just one of the many pitched messages she receives to respond to, and today it was mine. I figured it must be my quaint British posh-Cheshire accent.

I pitched again, and she replied that if I could interest her with a one-page synopsis she would read my script. I went back to the computer and brought all my new skills to bear on a one-page "blast your socks off" synopsis. I mentioned the awards and placing in the festivals and was as upbeat as a wannabe film-making nobody could be.

'Drama is such a hard sell these days,' was her one-line reply. Which was doubly annoying, seeing as it was supposed to be a comedy. And that was that. Next please.

CHAPTER 17

And back again

I checked my airline miles, took my little passbook to the bank, withdrew our "emergency" funds out of the savings account, and smiled weakly to myself. I thought: it's only money after all. I promised Luisa again that this was an endeavour that was going to pay off big time. How could it not? You can't put all this effort in and get no results, right? I'd read about people who put a lot effort into things. It always paid off.

With the last of my air miles, I jumped on another Virgin plane back to the UK, heading for Manchester. I had little choice. I'd spent so much time and preparation on this short film, I had to get it finished and it wasn't going to get finished with me sitting in a classroom in Westwood, however enthralling the fanciful tales of Hollywood near-success and interesting concepts were.

Before I arrived back in the UK this time, I had a word with Nut and Riggy, and we decided to have an all-or-nothing casting session in a local social club in Colne, up north in

Lancashire. I say "we", but the next session of casting fell on Nut and Riggy's shoulders, along with Sarah. An advertisement was placed again in the local newspaper and Sarah, the proper actress, had a word with a few of her mates. Nut and Riggy auditioned the prospective hopefuls one afternoon in a local working-men's club, and it went a lot better without me.

This was done before I'd even set foot back on English soil. A tape of the *Fizzy* hopefuls was sent to me back in the States, and on that evidence the choice was pretty obvious. For the lead role of Eddy it was Kris, the one guy who could act, versus several others who couldn't or at least found it a little more difficult. A cast was assembled via videos and email. We had the players we needed for *Fizzy Days*, the teaser, the short, the prospective festival winner! Something big was about to happen!

I met the cast of the short for the first time for rehearsals in June 2005. It was a funny thing: they sort of thought I was this geezer from LA or Hollywood, this Hollywood guy who wants to do a film about mopeds and kids whizzing about the British countryside dressed in platformed boots, deliciously quaint! They were all great. We got on, we had a laugh, and we went over the script for a couple of weeks. Nut had found Nat, the director of photography, cameraman, lighting and grip, who also arrived with James the soundman. Nat was someone else who had worked at Granada with Nut; James had worked with Nat; both those talented individuals were going help on *Fizzy*. As I write this and look back now, I got a lot of help.

I took a truckload of time off to do this and several transatlantic journeys that I just wouldn't be able to take today.

It so makes me appreciate Luisa's understanding for allowing me to gamble our savings, as I left her to manage the homestead while I went and tried a spot of train driving. It never occurred to me for a moment that this wouldn't be anything other than a spectacular success.

We rehearsed in the old working-men's club in Nelson, a small Lancashire town not far from Colne, a place of terraced streets, canals and chimneys surrounded by countryside. The club was famous for The Rolling Stones having once played there, according to Riggy. I don't know whether they actually did or not, but it was a story Riggy was selling, just to make the proceedings feel a bit more glamorous. I even managed to persuade Brian, my father, that he had what it took to take over the role once earmarked for Peter Kay, and he ably stepped up to the plate as man with dog: Brian Millicent, a fine and natural if inexperienced thespian replacement. In fact, all the actors were pretty inexperienced, just like me, their inexperienced writer and director. We were a pretty good match. We rehearsed bloody hard for that week; then, satisfied we could go no further, a timetable for shooting was scheduled and planned over a couple of pints in the Langroyd Arms. It was one of those balmy English sunny evenings that come along now and again. We were looking at eighteen-hour days ahead; more than twenty-seven scenes to get through in three days. Easy!

A local and, to my ears, phenomenally talented band called Dexterous had offered to score the short. They even did a theme song, 'On Fizzy Days', a pastiche of T. Rex and several other seventies bubble-gum tracks all rolled into a fine new musical number. To keep us in the mood, we played it all the time in the van as we travelled around the Lancashire countryside between locations. By the time we were done shooting, everyone involved in our little film was singing it.

Indie-film shooting is a very primitive business. You scramble like maniacs, guerrilla-style, to get the required shot. No permits; just try to look like you are not filming illegally while fending off every Tom, Dick or Harry who attempts to jump in front of the camera to impress his mates. Every manner of car horn is blasted as people drive past and destroy any takes that might otherwise be half-decent. Then you race to the next location for more of the same, all the time keeping an eye out for the law. Stupidly, and perhaps inevitably, the twenty-seven scenes at maybe a dozen locations began to seem like a tall order. It would really have helped had I thought about how hard this was going to be on cast and crew; but, hey, I'd never done it before! We had no permits to film anywhere, so we resorted to orange jackets on the high street and the cunning use of mobiles to stop the traffic, backed by the officious look we tried to convey of a film crew who did have legitimate permits. We even closed the road to traffic, and the motorists either accepted it or threatened violence.

'Are you the police?'

'No.'

'Oh? What are you doing then?'

'We're making a film.'

'You got permits?'

It's funny how many people asked this question. Was everybody privy to the legalities of motion-picture production in this little town? The best we could give as an answer was a blank-faced smile.

'Well, fuck off out of the way then!' They would snarl.

'Right.'

We had a scene planned in the local Co-Op after Pam, the supermarket manager, had given the OK. Head Office didn't need to know, she said, as we could film while the store was open. We would hardly be noticed as we wouldn't be there more than an hour, in and out. Just make sure we were as unobtrusive as possible, keep the upset to a bare minimum, as all she asked.

The Co-Op, which was open twenty-four hours a day, attracted a lot of customers that you don't find in your average Sainsbury's. We were scheduled to be filming on a quiet, wet Sunday to minimize any inconvenience. Besides, I figured a few shoppers here and there would add that air of authenticity.

The noise from the freezer units was the first problem we encountered, and they had a lot of units. It was a supermarket, so I guess you would expect that, but the sound was interfering with our sound, so James the soundman informed us.

'Turn 'em all off for a bit, nobody's gonna know,' suggested Andy, one of the enthusiastic crew. 'Then just turn 'em back on when we're done,' he added.

'Right.'

On the face of it this was a good idea, but only on the face of it. Of course, no problem, turn all the freezers off, just for a moment. OK.

'Can't find any switches, I'll just pull all the plugs out the sockets.'

Brilliant!

The second little problem was alcohol and the shoppers who'd consumed it. You would be surprised how many people had decided to shop while drunk that Sunday. Some, it seems, decided to drunk-shop because they saw us filming. Groups of lads were outside in the car park swigging bottles of cider, smoking their ciggies and leaning against the van as we wandered between them to get supplies of tape and cable and the like.

'Makin a film, are ya?'

'That's right.'

'Can I be in it?'

'We've got actors, lads.'

'Bet you haven't got permits though, have ya? Fuckin' wankers!'

'Right.'

The sight of a motley ad-hoc film crew was like free curry to a piss-head shopper. That Sunday everyone wanted to be a star! People shouted, hollered and whooped as soon as they saw us. Only a few attempted to get involved as they threw themselves bodily in front of the cameras, so all in all it went as well as could be expected. We even had people who were actually shopping come through our scenes: drunk people.

'You the manager?'

'No.'

'Thought not. It's not your bloody supermarket. Who are you?'

'No one.'

'You're not the manager then?'

'No.'

'Well, fuck off then, I'm shopping. I'm after a Mars Bar.'

'Right.'

'D'you wanna film me buying it?' he sneered, but kinda serious with it.

'No.'

'Wanker.' Tossing the Vs.

Several hours later, after several impromptu auditions conducted whilst filming, we finally had a supermarket scene that would do – sort of. The most trouble we had was with an old lady ambling into the middle of a scene we were filming on Colne High Street. She frowned and stood there with her pull-trolley, hat, glasses and coat. Standing in the middle of a setup, point-blank refusing to move, for no other reason than she felt like it. Staring straight at the camera. It was, after all, her high street, and she had as much right to it as we had. Probably more.

'No, I won't bloody move! You don't own this place. You're all bloody stupid. I'm not moving. I'll stand here all bloody day if I want to.' She crossed her arms and stood her ground.

'We're trying to make a film, luv,' Nut said in as friendly a manner as he could muster.

'A film?'

'Yes.'

'Have you got permits?'

We exchanged a few glances with the crew. It was uncanny.

'A film about what?' she frowned.

'Mopeds.'

'You're bloody stupid, I'm not bloody moving.'

She then stood looking as stern as an old lady with a pull-handled trolley ever could.

'You don't own the street, do you?' she fumed.

She was right, we didn't.

'No,' I conceded.

'Well, you can just fuck off then!'

'Right.'

So she just stood, unmoved and unmoving, until Nut had the bright idea of actually turning the camera on her and meeting her fuming glare with the lens while telling her: 'We're filming you now, luv, give us your best side.'

It was a stand-off – or a stare-off. We just needed her to fuck off!

She didn't like that at all, not one bit! To everyone's relief, slowly, almost imperceptibly, she moved, then shuffled off pulling her hand cart behind her. We were able to carry on. Then it rained; lots. We stopped filming, reshuffled the storyboards and script schedule and raced to the dryness of an interior scene.

About two in the morning, we called it a day. We were only two scenes behind schedule; we'd catch up tomorrow. Without going into too much detail, we spent the weekend filming frantically, but even frantically wasn't enough. Monday night turned into Tuesday morning at about half past three, our night scene started turning into a day scene as morning began to break to the sound of the dawn chorus. I had forgotten how loud an English dawn chorus of thrushes, blackbirds and starlings could be. I headed back to Mrs Lovett's B&B and my bed.

By the time I hit the straw it was half past four and we were going to need to shoot more film to get the project finished. And I so wanted to finish this project! Only problem was, I was booked on a flight back to LA the next day. The cast and crew were due back at their respective places of work; the camera, lights and gear also had to go back, along with the costumes. We were done, but not finished.

Actors Kris Scholes and Scott Whitley discuss the goal of owning a Fizzy

The author (in the beanie hat) watches the day's proceedings through the video playback

All in a day's shoot. Setting up one of the shots on location in the High Street as passers-by shout encouragement and honk their car horns as they pass!

On location filming Fizzy Days

Filming Fizzy Days

The engines of the Airbus 300 roared and again I was hurtling along runway three of Manchester Airport. Up and over the Peak District, heading north, then out across the Irish Sea. I was on my way home.

I got back to the States as if I'd never left and explained to Luisa that we had run out of daylight and seeing as I had spent so much on getting ninety percent of this little film made it would be crazy not to spend a load more and finish it. It was all going to be worth it, I insisted. Just one more weekend back in the UK should see it through. I'm not sure where we were meant to find this money, but we would find it … somehow. One small re-mortgage later, a few signatures on a few documents, and hey, I had a new source of funds! And funds were what we needed as a few unexpected expense "overages" were about to occur.

Nut phoned me to deliver a bit of unwanted news.

'Hey, Mill, I've had a bill for damages,' he informed me.

'What damages?'

'The supermarket.'

'What? We dented a few cans of peas; how much is that? A couple of quid at best?'

'No, not the cans of peas.'

'Oh?'

'You know how we turned those freezers off, remember?'

'Yes.'

'Because of the noise.'

'Yes.'

'Do you remember anyone turning them back on?'

I thought about it for a moment, then turned to an imaginary camera pointing in my direction, and smiled an imaginary smile.

'Well, we never turned them back on, did we?'

'We never?'

'No.'

'Ah.' Imaginary smile. Real damages.

We needed three more scenes that we hadn't managed to shoot in the original three-day schedule. I now had my equity line of credit on the mortgage, so another trip back to the UK was financed and arranged to shoot those last few scenes. Most of the cast and crew were up and willing for the pickup shots, despite the unpaid hours they'd already put in.

We managed to schedule another weekend in June and fortunately it was a sunny one. The wig worn by Kris, our lead actor, was finally located, and we were off to the races again. One of the other actors, James, had sported a moustache and sideburns in the footage we had shot a month earlier, but when he turned up to fill in the pickup shots, he was now sporting a clean-shaven smiling baby's face. Ah, shit! This is going to look odd with continuity, I thought. Luckily, our makeup girl was quickly on the case! With the aid of a mascara pencil and sheer willpower, a more hirsute Mr Mantle, the tyrannical store manager in our little film, was brought back to something like the character he'd played in the previous month's shoot.

We had also lost a hat, which in itself sounds like no big deal, but proved a problem we were not able to get around. You can't cut back and forth hat – no hat- if you get my drift, so planned extra singles and dialogue had to be scrapped. So small stuff turned into big stuff, and the reverse shots that we needed just couldn't be done. But we resumed as best we could where we had left off a month earlier, racing again at breakneck speed from one location to the next, picking up scenes here and there, dragging our short film nearer to completion or, as they say in film jargon, a wrap.

Another eighteen hours on Saturday, and we were ready for what we thought would be a relatively easy Sunday: the moped-riding scenes. We had several mopeds bought and donated from Fizzy Galore, a fizzy shop in Yorkshire specializing in fizzy mopeds and nostalgia. Margaret and Russell were the owners and were more than accommodating in loaning us several of the best little mopeds ever made, all running fizzies. Racing around the countryside for all the running shots, with Nat and his camera hanging out the back of Riggy's borrowed minivan, filming our every near miss, was the order of the day; a memorable sunny day as it turned out. I could almost remember doing this thirty-odd years earlier and thirty-odd pounds lighter!

I rode a little gold fizzy from the shop and Russell a bright yellow pinstriped one. Several local middle-aged lads joined us, reliving their youth, until Russell's clutch disintegrated after a few miles, and we got tired of racing up to the back of the bus to be filmed, then dropping back as another bee-like wail screamed past you as the rider made a bid for celluloid immortality. There were several near collisions as the gaggle of now-tired middle-aged men pretending to be sixteen again swarmed around the Lancashire countryside. Under the shadow of Pendle Hill, the late afternoon turned into early evening. As many hours as we could muster under our belt, we called it a day.

A good, tiring day. An all-done, we-were-actually-finished day. A fizzy day!

I volunteered to take the camera equipment we had borrowed back to some far-flung Manchester suburb with the aid of Riggy's GPS, and another very, very tiring weekend was over. We had over eleven hours of footage shot on to almost a dozen hi-def tapes that now need editing down to twenty minutes or so. Easy!

I jumped on a plane back to America, eleven HD digital tapes safely in my bag. As I sat in the plane on the runway, the beautiful weekend that we had so happily been blessed with turned into something more recognizable, a wet and windy Manchester morning. I watched the rivulets of water run down my window outside the plane, smiling in relief that we had achieved our goal and shot all the scenes we'd planned. I pictured the ten tapes on my bed in the B&B as I'd packed. All that work in a few tiny black plastic cases. How many cases?

Had I remembered all the tapes? Did I have ten or eleven? Did we take that last one out of the camera? The camera that was now in some darkened suburb of Manchester.

The engines spooled up and then roared into action, the rain began to pour, and we started to hurtle down a very wet runway. I was heading back to America, land of opportunity and dreams. How many tapes? The engines got louder as I frantically went over the tape count in my bag. Did we take the last one out of the camera? My bag in the hold had all the tapes in, didn't it? All ten, eleven. No, ten … eleven. Bugger!

CHAPTER 18

Post-production

The first thing I did after claiming my bag at LAX was check the tapes. Thank God! I had eleven tapes, the number I was supposed to have, so everything we had shot was ready for editing. And editing was easy, right? Riggy was going to have a go at the initial edit on his Apple. Final Cut was the editing software, the new innovation that every indie filmmaker had needed at his fingertips and now had. He did some rough cuts and they were good, but they needed to be tighter. With Riggy's blessing I sought out a proper editor here in Los Angeles, Mike. Mike said he was up for the task of editing *Fizzy*, as he needed a longer-format example for his showreel. Mike did a lot of commercial work and was a first-choice editor for Michel Gondry, a top-notch French director based in LA. Funny thing, I am working doing storyboards for Michel Gondry at present on the Showtime presentation of Jim Carrey's *Kidding*. Hollywood, eh?

Mike would edit *Fizzy* on his Avid, professional equipment that generally costs an arm and a leg. Mike came with a fully equipped edit suite in a darkened room off Colorado Boulevard in Santa Monica. Today you would just do it on your Mac in Premier Pro but this wasn't today. However, before Mike could get to grips with editing, another minor problem arose. Our footage had been shot using UK equipment. The UK and US use different formats, PAL and NTSC respectively. We were on the wrong format to edit in the USA. So we needed to rent a PAL deck and then play it through a rented PAL monitor, and this meant more money.

Mike managed to get a player at a discount from somewhere, along with a monitor, then proceeded to put a lot of hours into *Fizzy*. The editing process takes a lot longer than people appreciate; a lot longer than I used to appreciate. From the confines of a darkened, air-conditioned room a couple of evenings a week and sometimes at the weekend, we digitally chopped, snipped, clipped and spliced the film together. Riggy's friends, the band Dexterous, were working in earnest on the score, and the cogs were in motion for *Fizzy* the short, precursor to *Fizzy* the feature. It wouldn't take long now to get it all together, right? I was able to see just what an art the editorial process is and what a good editor can bring to a project. The ability to see just what's too much, what might be flipped, cropped, reversed and cut etc. makes a massive contribution to the finished product.

Four months later we were still editing with no end in sight! And this was just the Short. Finally, on a Friday morning in April nearly a year after we had started shooting, we had a complete edit. All that remained now was to get our thirty minutes to the sound studio then get it "onlined" (I'll come to that) and coloured, and a master produced for transfer to discs. These last few hurdles would only cost a few more thousand dollars. So, break out the credit cards, unleash the equity line, and don't tell the wife!

I made a deal with a company I had previously worked for in Santa Monica. Riot were a big post-production house where people got good stuff done. I wanted good stuff done, but damn, it was expensive! They were going to prettify our short film with the cunning use of a couple of digital tricks to get rid of period continuity errors like tax discs, the brightly coloured bits of paper which back then had to be attached to your motorcycle to make it legal to ride in the UK. A modern requirement (since made irrelevant by digital licensing), we had forgotten to take them out before filming, and they stuck out like proverbial sore thumbs.

Riot normally charged seventeen hundred bucks an hour. This was a tiny little short film. They made expensive Beverly Hills attorneys look cheap, even very cheap, but in my case were prepared to do a deal. They would do the offline and the online for six grand, though I soon realised that was six grand a piece; twelve for the two. We dealt some more!

I told Luisa it would cost us a tiny fraction of what it was actually going to cost. I assured her we could easily afford it; we had a line of credit on our equity line, it would be pennies on our payment. This was going to pay off bigtime, right?

So the film was edited, got a sound mix, got coloured and onlined and transferred to DVD. In short, it was finished and ready to go. I paid Riot all the money I had budgeted and more. *Fizzy* was transferred from a high-quality digital tape on to 300 DVDs. That was an ordeal in itself and cost another small fortune. I made a bad choice of company to transfer the film to DVD. The job was less than OK, but eventually we reached a compromise: the owner of the one-man shop promised to give me what I had asked for, and I promised not to burn his shop down. It was all complete. Luisa came along to our première showing for cast and crew in a Lancashire club space. It was very rewarding to see the fruits of all our labours come together. It was fantastic; a real high point.

I had always wondered if my first film was also going to be my swansong. These doubts only grew; not because I didn't want to make any more, but because it is just so hard. Today, of course, everything is way easier. You have far more film-making kit on your phone and laptop than was the case back then.

Anyone who stands up and says they're going to make a short film or a feature and actually follows it through to completion gets my vote and awed admiration. It's an impossible journey on which only the strongest survive. That's my take on it, anyway. But again, what do I know? I'm just a little tired.

Fizzy Days the short was now beginning to look like a proper film. Riggy took care of the artwork; on reflection, he seemed to be able to take care of anything, an indispensable film-maker. I now had a few boxes of DVDs ready to take the world by storm. There was a sense of relief, as if I'd just run that marathon again. Satisfied and with a sense of wonderment that was strangely anti-climactic, I was exhausted. But we were on our way. Unbridled indie movie-making success, here we come!

CHAPTER 19

Festival shmestival

Film-festival world, get ready, because the short is complete! Riggy had done some great artwork for both the disc and the pack, and I have to say it looked bloody professional, like a real DVD. Played like one, too. The finished thirty minutes wasn't bad. We were all very pleased with it. It had taken about a year to get it from planning the post-production to a box full of *Fizzy* DVDs on the kitchen table ready to turn the film-festival world on its head. At that point, the offer of a contract had yet to come, but I figured it couldn't be far off. Once people had read the script and seen the short film, the offers should come flooding in for finance for the feature. I even allowed myself to wonder which of the household names of UK movie-land we would approach to fill the roles. Who would we choose to be in it?

I also had to work out which film festival should have the honour of showing it first. After all, they were going to love it, as how could they not? So we sent it to Sundance, the near-legendary festival where to have your film accepted was a passport to movie success. Surprisingly, Sundance said no chance, so we sent it to the festivals in Las Vegas and New York, and then to Slamdance. Slamdance said no thanks, and so on. Unfortunately, *Fizzy* didn't get into any of these prestigious popular major festivals. So maybe a more obscure less popular festival would be a better bet.

Not likely, I thought. In fact, we needed to be bolder, more aggressive, show we could mix it with the big boys. And what bigger and better festival was there at which to show your mini-masterpiece than Cannes? The jewel of the French Riviera, the festival of festivals! Riggy as producer and a couple of the lead actors, Scott and Kris, were clearly up for the challenge. *Fizzy* was entered into the shorts section along with 4000 other films, not in the competition section but the showcase section, a sort of a film-market kind of thing, where … it faded into oblivion.

Black Dog Productions did gain a brief moment of recognition, though perhaps notoriety would be a better word. Kris, our lead actor in *Fizzy* the short film, liked a beer as much as the next man. In fact, given the chance, he'd probably like the next man's beer as well. During the weekend sortie to Cannes, he got so tanked up that at a red-carpet screening of someone else's film he collapsed right there, on the carpet, unable to speak French, or by that point any coherent language at all. He was quickly medically attended to, then physically attended to, then arrested and carted off in an ambulance, sirens wailing. The glamour of it all disappeared in a pool of vomit, and Kris woke up several hours later, minus the contents of his stomach, which had been pumped on his arrival at the hospital. He was connected to an IV drip, clad only in a paper diaper on a sheetless bed in an unpronounceable French hospital. He would be asked, or rather told, by the organizers not to show his face again at the Cannes Film Festival.

So that was Fizzy's trip to Cannes. Things could only get better, couldn't they?

I had somehow mistakenly assumed that our little film, *Fizzy Days* "the short", would fly into film festivals. After all, it had now attended Cannes. It would surely win awards and go on to garner a solid reputation as a film that would have people saying when they saw it, 'That film needs to be made into a feature-length movie!'

But the rejections piled up. What? Had we made a piece of crap? Was the film as rejectable as the original script? At thirty minutes, we had made a very long "short". This was a fundamental mistake; if a film festival can show six five-minute films instead of one thirty-minute one, it stands to reason that it's going to please a lot more people. In fact, a lot of festivals don't accept films longer than twenty minutes, something we hadn't considered when making it thirty. At about fifty dollars a pop, we entered festival after festival. It started to get expensive.

Finally, we were accepted in the Hollyshorts film festival on Hollywood Boulevard, then the Chicago Short Film Fest, then the LA Short Film Festival, then Miami until gradually it picked up steam and several others found it worthy of inclusion and confidence was partially restored. It even played at Grauman's Chinese Theatre on Hollywood Boulevard, or at least the Kodak Theatre behind it, part of the same complex. That was a feel-good day as I rode my motorcycle down

Hollywood Boulevard on the way to watch my little film based on my own experiences as motorcycling teenager on a moped, now being screened in the heart of Hollywood.

It was one of those 'Is it really me?' kind of moments; it wasn't a massive Hollywood event by any measure, quite small actually, but it wasn't half bad. Better than fitting tyres in an old cinema in Crewe, or maybe on a par. Mann's Chinese Theatre is the world-famous venue, the one with all the hand and footprints in the cement outside; proper Hollywood was just a few doors down from where my film was being shown on the big screen! This was the same complex where I'd had my first proper red-carpet event at with the Texas Chainsaw première.

One disappointment about the big-screen event at a festival is that nobody other than those involved in the film is really bothered about seeing it. Seeing as all my cast and crew were back in the UK, I attended several big-screen events on my own and was pretty lonely at most of them. By this time, Luisa had had enough *Fizzy* to last a lifetime. So I sat by myself with a couple of other filmmakers looking for their bite of the cherry. Like me, they had come for the screening of their own film, but had arrived early, and having entered the darkened cinema, seeing my look of needy desperation, felt politely obliged to watch some of mine. Bit pathetic really. Mike the editor turned up with his wife, and the three of us tried as best we could to look like a crowd. It was *all* getting a bit pathetic. But soldiering on is what it's all about, never say die, never surrender. Persistence pays off, right? You bet it does!

Fizzy the short started to be accepted into more festivals and our little laurel collection on the website grew. We had not made utter crap. *Fizzy* won its first award for "best mise-en-scène" from the Idaho Panhandle International Film Festival. Mise-en-scène? Both the festival and the award were a bit obscure, but what the fuck! It came with a nice statuette of an eagle's head in faux bronze and a little plaque on its marble base; it looks pretty impressive on my desk along with my "Carp Derby" biggest fish trophy. The film was reviewed well and won a few other awards, one on a web-based monthly magazine for short films, this one for "cinematic excellence". So, it was now an award-winning film, and I guess that made us award-winning film-makers. Would have been much cheaper just to have bought an award ourselves and had it engraved. Now there's an idea.

A small, web-based distribution company called Indieflix offered to distribute it on demand. When someone ordered a copy, Indieflix made one on demand, with artwork, box and disc. It made bestseller several weeks running, which in truth was no great shakes as the numbers you needed to make the list were pretty low. But it was something; people were buying it. I made seventeen dollars, I think. Netflix offered to take it on but that deal seemed amazingly expensive for the film-maker unless you had the backing of a studio. Even Amazon are now selling it, our little film; so a few dollars trickled in each month, seventeen in total. Better than nothing. It was getting out there. Wherever "there" was!

MicroFilmmaker magazine loved it and gave it an Editor's Choice of the Month award and a separate award for Cinematic Excellence. A snippet of the review read as follows: 'A while back, I was sent a film called *Fizzy Days* ... one of the most brilliant, professional and entertaining films I'd seen in a long time.'

In all it got fairly good reviews. Rogue Cinema gave it four stars. The review opened with the importance of getting a fully authentic look in retro films, before saying. '*Fizzy Days* is a perfect example of that. The whole look of the film from the clothes, hair styles, acting style, dialogue, props and everything else all looked completely authentic. It's the single greatest example I can think of for how to do it right.'

Shucks!

'Fizzy Days' make mopeds cool in 1975 England

by Michael Sheridan September 14, 2006 No Comments

'Fizzy Days' takes you back to England 1975

Starring: Kris Scholes, Scott Whitley, Sam Kearney
Director(s): Mark Millicent
Writer(s): Mark Millicent

In the last few years I've been obsessed with the idea of getting myself a Vespa. I don't exactly know why. It started with motorcycles, then moved into the Vespa. They're getting pretty popular here in New York City, and since I only drive around locally on a regular basis, a nice little motorbike would do me just fine.

I haven't been able to afford one just yet. So in a way, I understood the feeling of the main characters in Mark Millicent's short film, *Fizzy Days*. Mind you, it's not about getting laid for me. My wife probably wouldn't be too keen on that notion. Plus, I can't quite see myself plotting a collection of rather lame thefts to support this obsession of mine, either. But I did find myself thoroughly enjoying this 30 minute flick from England.

Fizzy Days follows a pair of teens in 1975 England, as they plot to collect enough money to buy a moped (a.k.a.. "fizzy"). This

Meanwhile, real life carried on. Thankfully, I was still making good money, enough to keep financing my film-maker aspirations. I was booked in the capacity of storyboard guy to work at a place in Orange County called Marshall Advertising, some thirty miles south of my house, a short skip down the 405 freeway to Newport Beach. Marshall Advertising has one account, which just happens to be Yamaha Motorcycles. They handle the advertising for all of North America. Yamaha produced a wacky little moped almost forty years ago, a moped known as the FS1E, the 50cc; to you and me a Fizzy, the subject of my proposed mega-blockbuster *Fizzy Days*. Interesting and possibly fruitful, I thought.

Once through the doors of Marshall, I showed my *Fizzy* project to Sam, the art director I was to work with. I showed Jon, the copywriter; I showed Roger, the creative director. I showed everyone my proposed mega-blockbuster, featuring one of their Yamaha motorcycles from yesteryear. Were they interested? Were they fuck! But then this wasn't actually Yamaha, was it? Maybe they could give me the name of the man to speak to at Yamaha. To give them their due, they actually did, but he wasn't interested either. But wait: the fizzy was a UK phenomenon. I'll contact Yamaha UK in Milton Keynes. The Milton Keynes man said without great enthusiasm, 'I know it's something we should be interested in, we just haven't got any resources for a model that's been discontinued for more than forty years. Now if it were a current model, that might be a different matter.'

'Would it?' I replied.

'No, not really, I'm afraid.'

'Thanks.'

It's tough to get a break as we forge ahead!

All solid advice said keep writing, keep writing and get better at your craft. Writing wasn't my craft; I wanted to make films. I wanted to make this one, anyway. If I had to write more to do it, then so be it. I'd write. *Fizzy* was my first script, and as time progressed, I found time to write a second. It was called *Paradise Tickle* and was set in a bakery; the third was called *The Yard Sale*; the fourth *A Bouncy Business*, the next *The Falcon's Goal*, and the one I'm working on at present is called *Love is a Fuel*. Oh, and there's another short, *Hell's Angel*, which I will talk about. All of which met the same tremendous response: a vacuum of nothing, a thunderous silence! I kept going, though, because if you try hard enough, you'll get there in the end. Right?

But back to that *Fizzy* contract! Almost a year had passed since my initial euphoria over the French contract, and there was not the remotest sign of anything happening. Well, how did I know that things take forever in movieland? Big, big mistake! Now I know things take forever!

As Cher says in her song: If I could turn back time!

Having a project in play, so to speak, gave me confidence that maybe I could write a few words and people would want to read them or maybe let me film them. Maybe I have several projects that people want to see, and this is just the start of things. I began to write more and more.

I wrote another script and was pretty pleased with it. I had always liked the Ken Loach film *Kes*, so I thought, why not write something about a falcon like Billy Casper's kestrel in *Kes*? As a kid, I'd always been fascinated with animals and nature. Just like numerous other school boys, I had wanted a kestrel myself after seeing the film and read numerous books on falconry; I never got one but I did have enough knowledge and interest to be able to write about it with some conviction. Not to rip it off in too blatant a fashion, I changed the kestrel to a red-tailed hawk – this is America, after all – and threw in a younger brother with learning disabilities, all set against the mundane dreariness of a working-class neighbourhood, not in the north of England but in Riverside County, East LA. It's the LA version of Liverpool or Manchester. It's definitely not Hampstead!

Now there's an original idea. This just might be a winner, I thought. I set about the script and within a couple of months, a few dozen late nights and some solid days later, it was done. I gave it to Luisa to read. She said she wasn't sure, that I needed to change some of it so she could be sure. I worked on it every chance I got to get it to the "Oh, I like this" category. A few more weeks and several more late nights and I had it to where I thought it was there! Luisa humoured me and said it might be there, which was good enough for me. I began to send it out into the big wide world.

After the first several dozen 'Fuck off, this is rubbish' slips and replies, and an equal number of unanswered query letters, I finally received a response that wasn't the same as the rest: from RSA, Ridley Scott's Beverly Hills production company. It went something like this: 'Interesting idea, but isn't a similar project opening in theatrical release this week?'

Similar? How similar? Can there be something similar to the most original idea since *The Terminator*? They were kind enough to even email me the similar script back. I compared the similarities and sure enough, the similarities were fucking bothersomely similar! Someone had based on or adapted another screenplay from a book I had never heard of called *The Hawk is*

Dying. What sort of title is that? Starring a red-tailed hawk, an autistic nephew and Paul Giamatti showcasing the mundane life of a seat upholsterer and his friendship with a hawk. Could this be for real? It could and it was. I was going to have to have someone or something disabled in mine, maybe my hawk is blind and missing a wing … and most of his feathers?

I emailed Peter Kay's agents. I had sent them the *Fizzy* script to see if he might make good on his offer of a couple of years ago to help out on our project, maybe second time lucky. No reply. Meanwhile, I kept on posting out my new script. Maybe I'd get lucky. Maybe the rival film would sink without trace. I first sent it to some of those wannabe websites to get some feedback, the same place I had met Pat the entertainment attorney from Cuckoo Inc. I got some promising feedback, which I decided I would use to tweak the script. After several more late nights burning the candle at both ends, I reposted my new revised script. The first review I got after my revision went something like this:

'This is a terrible screenplay. All the factors that make a good screenplay were violated. The storyline was uninteresting, the characters two dimensional and the only good thing about this script was that it finally ended.'

'Oh.'

Maybe I wasn't a writer/director. Maybe I was neither. This person must know what he's talking about, whoever he is. After all, he seemed to offer his no-punches-pulled criticism in a very forthright manner. I wasn't sure what sort of constructive criticism I was to draw from that sort of critique.

But thankfully they weren't all as bad. And perseverance pays off, right? So bear with me. I would persevere.

CHAPTER 20

Slam dunk

The AFM, the American Film Market, is a big gathering of buyers, producers and film-makers from around the world that gets together once a year at the swanky Loews Hotel in Santa Monica, California. Set on the palm-tree-festooned oceanfront, it's a prestigious event. People travel from far and wide to attend it. I didn't have to go too far as it's just down the road from me. Deals get done, pictures get "green-lighted", a lot of bigwigs mingle under one roof. Forecast Pictures were in attendance and mingling in the January of 2006, along with myself.

I made my way through the throngs of industry folk: producers, directors, actors, all as desperate as me. I scuttled between very important people and people that were probably nobodies who had sneaked in like I had. It was difficult to tell us all apart. My laptop and script and bursting folder of storyboards in hand, I strode confidently along with a sizable bag of enthusiasm and optimistic verve. I was going to meet Olivier and Nicholas, representatives of Forecast

Pictures, France: Oliver and Nicholas, two proper producers from a proper production company. We had corresponded, they had emailed me, I had emailed them, and at this point they wanted to meet me and talk about my script – my *Fizzy* script. They had read it and liked it. They had both seen the short film; they liked that, too. They thought it was funny and intimated that they may like to produce the big film, the feature. They were my new best friends. They bought me a bottle of Budweiser as we sat overlooking the ocean talking about the production elements of *Fizzy*. They told me the head honcho at Forecast was a man called Jean-Charles Levy with a great dollar pedigree. His last film had been a $24 million-dollar-budget saga starring Ian Holm and Tom Conti, two great British actors. Nicholas and Olivier told me Forecast was looking for just such a film as I had in my bag. Can you believe it? Slam Dunk! Jean-Charles Levy, the $24 million-dollar man, would be my producer. A man with a Hollywood pedigree and substantial dollar track record was on board. I was on my way! Finally, they asked me when I would like to start production.

'April, please,' I said. It was November, so I thought six months run-up would be good.

'Then April 2007 it is. It's great to be on board.'

'Cheers.'

The Budweiser never touched the sides and never tasted so good. To make it all even more real they would get their people to put together a contract as soon as they got back to France. Wow!

The contract! Yes, the contract … that one, this one, my contract! I could not believe my luck. We said our goodbyes, shook hands, and they said their people would be in touch with my people. I needed some people. Loews Hotel is just around the corner from Second Street, and on Second Street is the King's Head. Time for a celebration! The short walk to the King's Head was made with an idiotic smile beaming from ear to ear. I got to the bar and wanted to tell everyone that I was making my film. I had just got the nod. I had arrived. They, Forecast, were going to draw up a contract!

'A pint of your finest Carlsberg, please.'

I'd just been green-lit! And this is roughly where we came in.

Fast-forward to several months later, several months since I had signed that contract and nothing at all had happened. I emailed Olivier at Forecast. He told me that they would need a UK-based producer of note for the film to go ahead. As always, he was very diplomatic. He understood my frustration. To finance it would need a bigger wig to come on board, and I had thought the bigwig was already on board in the form of Jean-Charles Levy; but, hey, what did I know? A fellow called Alex was brought on board. He wanted to know where the script had already been sent; specifically, if it had been to the UK Film Council. And of course it had. They had even seen our short film, unfortunately. They really hadn't loved it. So the UK Film Council didn't look as if its logo was going to be attached to *Fizzy*'s credits anytime soon.

I figured we might well be dead in the water, because the UK Film Council seemed to be a lynchpin to getting anything made in the UK. But surprisingly, Alex wasn't put off by *Fizzy*'s less-than-illustrious past. His company was called Pistachio

Pictures, with a subsidiary satellite company called Red Sun. It all sounded very real again.

But weeks turned into months and then years or at least a year and a half. Not that I was idle. I had many more scripts and projects all ready to go. The association with Forecast that I had been so excited about initially seemed stalled, and I was unsure what to do after several more months of nothing being achieved.

Standing back now, with the benefit of many years of hindsight, I know that nothing is supposed to happen, at least not at the breakneck speed I'd expected. I was naive and had no idea these things take years – of course they do – and finances are not easy to come by, especially for a first-time director with no proven pedigree. But I got it into my head that my 24-million-dollar producer was not producing. Forecast's idea of packaging *Fizzy Days* was to send it with a one-page introductory letter to half a dozen people and producers I had badgered earlier. To my impatient eyes they weren't exactly pushing the boat out, though it turned out that I was wrong. Disappointment began to set in. I had thought I'd won the lottery with Forecast's attachment to the project, that it was all going to be plain sailing from this point. I was now beginning to feel like my foot was stuck in a hole, and it was not going to come out unless I cut it off. But I didn't want to do that, and surely, I wasn't that stupid and impatient, was I? Again, I hear Cher singing: If I could turn back time!

Nut had another buddy from Granada, Paul Abbott, a very successful UK writer, probably best known for the TV show *Shameless*. Nut sent him a letter asking if he might help. He replied by saying that he liked *Fizzy*, that they were way too busy to take anything else, but perhaps he might still take a look.

I needed to speak to Forecast and the "on board" producer Alex. I wanted to meet with Nutty and Riggy, plus I really did fancy a pint in a proper English pub, i.e. one in England. So I jumped on the Virgin Atlantic flight and headed for good old Blighty once again. I'd been told that global warming had put an end to traditional English weather and that constant rain had been replaced by constant sunshine. This rumour was dispelled as soon as I touched down on English soil. I was soaked even before I made it to the car-rental office, which is actually in the terminal building.

London seemed brighter than I remembered, but then I had been previously been getting off aeroplanes at Manchester. As I wandered through town it was a lovely sunny day, the best kind of day: my old stomping ground, through Soho Square and down Dean Street with a quick check of Berwick Street Market, past favourite watering holes like the Blue Posts, the Ship and the Fox. There were lots of coffee shops now, frequented by pretty girls and hipster guys. The surrounding streets were populated by crazy dispatch couriers pedalling frantically on kamikaze missions in front of the London traffic. Soho seemed more 'gay' than when I had had an office on Wardour Street more than a decade earlier. Indeed, the most glamorous establishment during my time in that neck of the woods had been the NatWest bank. That was now a trendy eatery, too, next to a trendy coffee shop.

I was to meet Olivier and Alex in a trendy dim sum restaurant with a name that sounded like a sneeze, just off Berwick Street Market. I wandered around for an hour or so beforehand, then met them at the restaurant. We chatted over chicken dumplings. Everyone said they would try harder, then we all went to see a man called Patrick at Box TV, who said he liked *Fizzy* very much and would help in any way he could with names of people who might help even more. One final coffee with Alex and Olivier, who assured me they were now well and truly on the case and would be giving *Fizzy* their all in the weeks to come. You can't say fairer than that. Mission accomplished, I thought. It's been a good trip. Money well spent; time invested wisely. To be honest, Olivier was always gracious and we had got on, so I don't really know how I managed to fuck it up; but I did.

I never heard from Alex again. It was to be the last conversation I would ever have with Olivier, though I didn't know it at the time.

As far as I was concerned this was a good trip, a damn good trip! We were all on board the good ship *Fizzy*, plotting a course to production and success! In fact, if truth be told, as I said goodbye, I couldn't help feeling that these guys wouldn't be making *Fizzy* any time soon. It was just a feeling, but one that proved well founded. Despite my outward confidence in my producers, I realized that I might need a backup plan, just in case things didn't work out; which of course couldn't possibly happen because I had a contract, right?

At some point earlier I had sent the script to Richard, a producer at the British Youth Film Academy, or BYFA. We had swapped emails a few times and he had been very complimentary about the project. I can't remember now but he had come highly recommended by someone whom I can't remember either … I guess it doesn't matter at this point. We had corresponded and agreed we might meet when I was back in the UK. And we did meet up, got on, and from our conversation it seemed like he would be a good backup just in case things fell apart. So things weren't quite as bad as I had thought. The trip hadn't been a complete waste of time. I had a producer who'd be in if things didn't work out with Forecast, and they had assured me they would be on the case bigtime from now on. It was the proverbial 'win/win' scenario, or so I thought.

After saying goodbye to Rich in Boston in the East Midlands, I headed half a day to Lancashire. The weather went from bad to worse, a torrential typhoon replacing the initial downpour. I met Riggy, who told me he would set up a meeting with his financial people and to see if we could get funds for *Fizzy*. Blackburn and the North, here I come. This transatlantic jaunt had indeed been worth it, after all. My long-suffering wife Luisa had said I might be wasting my time and our money, but what did she know?

I met Nut and Riggy and talked about the new film that Riggy was producing, by all accounts very well. He had secured talent and financing from the private sector. None of this new cinema fund bollocks, but proper money from proper people with proper results. He had managed to get the right people on board, which as you have probably gathered by now is no mean feat. Riggy informed me that they had managed to get a sizable sum for his London gangster flick, *Dead Man Running*, from a Manchester United footballer who wanted his name on the credits. He just had to take receipt of the monies before he started pencilling in a schedule. We would be seeing his people on Friday. Things were moving nicely.

Maybe they want to bankroll two movies, I thought. I turned up at Riggy's house in the middle of a torrential northern downpour, standard weather for the area.

'Couldn't get an appointment with the financier, too short notice. We'll stay in and have a few beers as I've got my young daughter with me,' he said. After a few beers, Riggy added, 'I can't say who it is, of course, the financier. It's top secret.'

'Who is it?'

'Rio Ferdinand. I've told you now. Keep it under your hat.'

'I will.'

So we stayed in, drank some beer and watched some films. I headed back to the States in the morning. I thought the trip had all been worthwhile. I thought I had made real progress.

CHAPTER 21

A halting interlude

A good year after meeting, and ten months since I'd signed the life-changing contract, communications between myself and Forecast were sparse. The time and effort I put into travelling to England yet again to shake up the situation and underscore my commitment to get things moving seemed to have been an utter waste of my time and had the opposite effect. I mentally made the choice to move my project to people who could move it quicker – people whom I had yet to find, of course. Like a couple in an unfulfilling marriage, we drifted apart and then severed our relationship. I say "we", but looking back it was all me being overly impetuous, not realizing in my naivety that the wheels of movie production turn very, very slowly. Nearly two years is but a blink of an eye in movieland. But hey, this is also a cautionary tale to others, so don't be so fucking impatient like I was! Things will happen when they are meant to happen and not before. I wish I could follow that advice! I can't.

Six more weeks were to pass before Forecast, or rather

Olivier, finally replied to the last email I had sent with a strange concoction of contradictory statements, which ultimately ended by stating that they, Olivier and Forecast, wanted us to go our separate ways. I received this disappointing piece of news at the end of September, almost a year after signing the contract. Nearly two years after we had met at the Loews Hotel, I had no other choice but to reply that I too wanted to terminate our agreement, not least as it had cost me over two grand just to sign it and a small fortune to make the short film. Maybe there's a lesson here?

The first contract for my little ball of shit had come to nothing, and I was two years down the road. They had paid me no money to option *Fizzy*, and by now I was considerably out of pocket and a little out of enthusiasm too. I was back at square one again. This is hard: had I been my own worst enemy? I was feeling drained and empty, with a feeling of sweet despondency that ate at my insides. I could mend this. Still, never mind, onward and upward; though in which direction? To be honest, I didn't have a clue.

* * *

Just like that, 'Forecast' were gone, my contract was gone. Looking back, the more I analyse it, if indeed I need to, it was totally my impetuous and impatient fault. What more can I say? More to the point, what could I do now? I can fix this!

But wait, yes, I did have Rich, the chap at the BYFA. He would save the day.

* * *

My phone rang. Funnily enough, I was right outside the King's Head, it being a Wednesday. It was a female voice of no discernible age.

'Hi, I have a film I'm doing and would like some storyboards done. Is that what you do?'

'Yes, that is what I do. Who is this?'

'Someone gave me your name. Would that be something you would be interested in doing for me?'

'Well, yes, it's what I do.'

For a moment I toyed with the idea of mentioning that I was also a writer and filmmaker myself, but decided against it. I would get a call now and then for work out of the blue; usually work for free on small projects where people couldn't afford a camera, never mind storyboards.

'I don't have much money, but there is some.'

At least she was honest and upfront about that. We chatted a bit and we seemed to get on.

'I will try and help if I can. You tell me what you want and how much money there is in the budget, and I'll tell you what I can do. Who is the director?'

'I am, it's my film, I wrote it.'

'Great. Maybe we could meet up and I'll have a look, and if I can help you I will. What's your name?'

'Connie.'

'Okay, Connie, I'll send you some samples because you might not like my stuff. You can tell me what budget you do have and I'm sure we can work something out.'

'I'm a singer, Connie Stevens, but I write scripts. I want to make this one.'

'That's funny,' I said. 'There is an old-time singer called

Connie Stevens, same name as you. If you can do half as well as her with a name like that, you're gonna be a winner, ha!'

I didn't think anything of it at the time. Why would the once-big-name Connie Stevens, purported net worth somewhere in the region of fifty million dollars be ringing me? I'm not sure that a boatload of people would know the name today, but I did.

I needed to get back on the horse, replace Forecast and show some restraint and be patient and send out more scripts and material if I was ever to make this film happen. So, as if nothing had changed, as if the biggest fuckup I'd made to date hadn't happened, I started over. I sent out and I received more responses, some adding a little more salt to the moment, such as this one:

'Accordingly, we must ask that you do not send us any more original creative material. If you choose to disregard our policy and you submit screenplays, creative or story ideas, creative suggestions, ideas, notes, drawings, concepts, or other information (collectively, the 'Submissions'), the Submissions shall be deemed, and shall remain, the property of Brightlight Pictures. None of the Submissions shall be subject to any obligation of confidence on the part of Brightlight Pictures, and Brightlight Pictures shall not be liable for any use or disclosure of any Submissions. Without limitation of the foregoing, Brightlight Pictures shall exclusively OWN all now known or hereafter existing rights to the Submissions of every kind and nature, in perpetuity, throughout the universe and shall be entitled to unrestricted use of the Submissions for any purpose whatsoever, commercial or otherwise, without compensation to the provider of the Submission.'

Fuck me, give me a break! I just sent them a script. I didn't kill anyone.

A few days later I received an email from Connie. Could I come in to see her at her office on Robertson Blvd? The short of it was that she *was* Connie Stevens, the one-time famous singer and movie star from the fifties and sixties. Connie owned a spa and retreat in Beverly Hills, a multinational cosmetics company, and a huge mansion off Sunset Boulevard. She also carried the sizable cachet that came with having been in the business for over fifty years! A few days later, I parked my car on a meter on Robertson Boulevard, Beverly Hills, a tree-lined street full of trendy eateries with valet parking and neatly kept sidewalks. To get to her place at the rear of the building, I had to go through a flower shop. It was like a secret entrance, I thought, an impression reinforced by the bespectacled woman behind the flower counter, who eyed me sceptically, as if she were some kind of gatekeeper. I asked if I had the right address. I told her my business.

From behind her spectacles, she eyed me over. 'What's a storyboard artist?'

'I draw pictures for movies and commercials.' Was this a test?

With a smile, she soon lightened up, and not for the first time I was surprised at how the layperson is quite interested in what a storyboarder does. After a quick chat, she pressed a secret button, a door was revealed and she bade me enter. She guided me to some stairs and I walked up to the office. Many photographs hung on the walls: Connie with Elvis, President Ford, Bob Hope, Ronald Reagan, Mickey Rooney, Bing Crosby, James Garner, Eddie Fisher and every other iconic movie personality from California and Hollywood of the 50s and 60s you could care to mention, a photographic walk of movie business fame. Even John Wayne was up there decorating the wall, arms around a young Ms Stevens.

The Ms Stevens I met at the top of the stairs in an open-plan office was older, well over fifty years older. She remained seated in a big chair at a big desk in front of a big window, going over big papers for a moment longer before looking at me over her reading glasses. Connie did indeed look like an older version of the woman in the photos on the walls. She was all business, but still pleasant enough.

We chatted, I showed her some storyboard work, and she in turn gave me the script. I read it that night, and I have to say I thought it was very good. It was an interesting story and plot, a good three acts! Based on incidents she had witnessed and experienced as a child it was a gripping tale, told well, and one I felt would be fun to block out the shots and produce the boards for.

We arranged to meet at her house the following Monday for what would be the first of our weekly meetings to go over the script and the boards. Her address? Just off Sunset Boulevard. I had to smile to myself, as my preconceived notion of Sunset Boulevard when I'd lived in the UK was this romantic, winding slab of concrete that simply was LA. Something that had seemed so far away back then was now just a route I took to get to work. Both beautiful and sleazy at the same time, the extravagant gated mansions and homes nearer the ocean at odds with the Hollywood strip malls, the cheap hotels and mobile-phone outlets, the liquor and grocery stores that occurred with increasing frequency as you covered the ground heading east. This was a time before Google Maps and GPS, so with the address scribbled on a bit of paper lying on the passenger seat and directions in my head, I found it easily; and it definitely wasn't in the sleazy part of Sunset either.

I had a sort of strange notion as I pulled into Connie's grand driveway after navigating the intercom and the huge set of automatic gates, obligatory in any Beverly Hills mansion these days, which had silently moved aside to let me pass. This was the classic Billy Wilder setup, though without the romantic interest in each other; I was an older, shorter, less hairy William Holden, and Connie was an older, dismissive Gloria Swanson. Her place was an old-time classical Hollywood estate in the style of a Southern Georgia manor, just off Sunset Boulevard. It looked like it was straight out of a movie; and as I was later to find out, it really was.

Once up the drive, I pulled to a stop in front of the archetypal Beverly Hills-style colonial mansion, with classical statues and rose bushes, a four-columned Greek portico; faded white paintwork, huge and slightly tired-looking but ... well, wow! It looked just how you would imagine a Hollywood movie star's mansion should look. The columns and ornate planters and worn steps that led up to the front doors gave the impression of slightly faded Hollywood royalty. The paintwork had flaked and cracked, a dull white; discoloured and peeling in the sunshine. A number of large citrus trees, oranges and lemons, further complemented the lush greenery of the grounds. The fragrant scent of Jasmine filled the air. The overall look was completed with a gold 1960s Rolls Royce Phantom. The Rolls had seen better days, one of the tyres being flat, and it shared space on the drive with a slightly scruffy eighties-model Jaguar

XJS. Several Mexican gardeners popped up like gophers from the jungle of rhododendron bushes, all wearing battered straw hats, each clutching some sort of garden tool. They looked me over, dismissed me as a nobody, and disappeared back into the undergrowth as they went about their business, pruning and clipping. They had their work cut out, as the gardens were extensive, to say the least.

I stood on the porch, took a look around, then rang the bell. Nobody answered the front door, so I took it upon myself to walk around the back, half because I was being nosey and half because I needed someone to acknowledge my arrival. What looked to me like a full-size Olympic swimming pool was flanked by tennis courts in front of a wooded area that shielded any traffic noise from the cars on Sunset. The place was massive!

A woman, thirtyish, trotted out to meet me; spectacles and a smile. She introduced herself as Vicky, Connie's assistant. She told me that Ms Stevens would be down presently. We went through the open side door, passing a small, uniformed, smiling Mexican maid complete with white lacy mob-cap. She was busy at a huge hob in the colourfully tiled kitchen. I was led through to the living room, then Vicky left me to sit on an overstuffed, pastel-coloured couch with loads of cushions.

I got comfortable. Left alone I scanned the walls, noting all the fantastic movie memorabilia. The house was a little tired, but obviously well-loved and lived in. It must have seen a few things in its time. It was like I was sitting in a set from *Gone with the Wind*. An original pleated costume dress grabbed my interest first, a framed, hooped underskirt with a small certificate of authentication proclaiming that it had once been worn by Vivian Leigh in that very film. Given the house, it was fitting, and like the house it was slightly faded and looked just a little sad, its glory days behind it. Big furniture, dark and carved, added to the musty old Hollywood feel of the rooms. Rugs and carpets, drapes and fringes. Many signed pictures of celebrities of yesteryear with some framed bits of an Apollo spaceship and all the relevant astronauts' signatures. Cool stuff everywhere! Friends and family portraits hung on every wall, all staring back at me. She had done a lot of stuff; she seemed to have a lot of stuff! Hers had clearly been a life well spent, and she had all these photos and stuff to prove it. As a collection it beat the King's Heads hands down.

I waited, then waited some more. Maybe she'd forgotten about me; she was a busy lady, after all. I carried on waiting, taking a full inventory of the living room's contents. If she took any longer, I figured I could always move on to the dining room. There was a lot more stuff that would be of interest to even the most rudimentary film buff.

Presently, someone could be heard making their way down the stairs while carrying on their conversation with whoever was still upstairs. Connie, or Ms Stevens, travelled barefoot down the spiral staircase to greet me. Barefoot it seems is standard "business casual" in LA. Having seen her at her office for our first meeting in far more business-like attire, I was a little surprised. She was dressed comfortably, to say the least. Not quite as relaxed as Pat at Planet Cuckoo Incorporated's law office, but a close second. After that, Connie always greeted me dressed down, baggy sweatpants and top, bare feet; not at her most chic, but who dresses for the storyboard guy? I'm no William Holden, after all.

'Sorry to keep you. Vicky didn't tell me you were here.'

She asked if I liked the house. It's alright, I thought. Are you kidding? She asked me if I recognized the staircase she had just walked down. The house had been used as the mansion location for the 1990s movie *Postcards from the Edge* with Shirley MacLaine and Meryl Streep, directed by Mike Nichols. Proper Hollywood!

I got into the routine. Every Monday I would travel across town, meet her at her mansion and show her the boards for the script as I ploughed through it, page after page, drawing after drawing blocking out the shots for Connie's approval. After eight weeks we had pretty much done the whole thing, just over a thousand drawings, and it only remained for her to go to Missouri and shoot it.

That was the last I heard. She went, they shot it, it got done. I made a few calls to try and keep the relationship going, but found that we didn't really have a relationship. I hate it when that happens. 'Hope it goes well.' 'How did it go?' 'How is post-production going?' That sort of thing. But I never heard anything back. I think it's all going well. I think post-production went well. I think.

At least I didn't end up as a floater in the pool reciting a monologue over my own corpse, so apart from that I still like to look back and think that was my little Sunset Boulevard moment, without the other bits, and I didn't have to bury anyone's monkey either!

I was back in LA. Things workwise things ticked over as normal. I was booked up on a fairly regular basis. On this particular day I found myself working at an agency in the Beverly Centre, a big pyramid-shaped mall in the middle of Beverly Hills. It housed the corporate offices of several household company names and advertising agencies. Trundling down Melrose Avenue on my way through Beverly Hills on the bright sunny morning of my booking, I noticed a building emblazoned with the words UK Film Council. UK Film Council in Beverly Hills? Who knew? Definitely worth a call! So I made an appointment to see Simon Powers-Cunningham. Very British! I put together a blow-your-socks-off presentation, a copy of the short film, a copy of the script, press articles about the film and the project, and arranged to meet him at the UK Film Council's LA offices on the next date when he was free to see me. I could regain lost ground after my Forecast fumble.

That happened to be the following week on a Tuesday. Maybe I thought the LA chapter of the UK Film Council would get the gist of what this film could be and would inform the London office of its huge potential. The London office would in turn reassess and rescind their earlier decision that it was not worth funding, and we'd be off to the races again. That was what I hoped for anyway, unrealistically. So I met Simon, we talked, I pitched, we chatted, and I said I would follow up later after he'd had time to read and look at the short film.

'I love it!' he said. 'Have you tried The UK Film Council in London?'

'Of course I have!'

'Oh well, then there's not really much I can do for you here. I'll give you a few names, though.'

The names Simon gave me were all people I had pestered previously, so that one was dead in the water. I thanked Simon for his time and effort and crossed another avenue off my list.

Work went quiet and bookings slowed for the next few weeks.

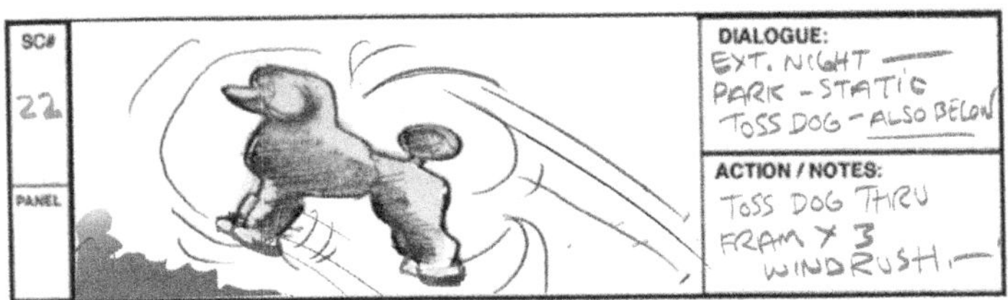

CHAPTER 22

A bit of this and a bit of that

Back at the King's Head for a drink and a rethink, I recounted my progress to date over a pint or two. Work had been uncharacteristically slow of late, so Trevor said I might do worse than call a fellow at Marvel, who were remaking *The Incredible Hulk* as a movie. I went to the offices in Beverly Hills, where it turned out they needed someone to help choreograph the fight scenes between Tim Roth and Ed Norton, who was playing Bruce Banner in the new production. In fact, it wasn't really choreographing, more mapping out the fight sequence geographically on paper.

'Who will I be working with on this?' I asked.

'Oh, Mr Norton will be here in about thirty minutes.'

'Ed Norton?'

'Yes.'

Wow, Ed Norton: *Fight Club*, *Primal Fear*. Groovy guy, I thought to myself.

'Who is directing this?' I asked.

'It's not Ed, but he has written the new draft of the script and knows what he wants to go over with you as regards the shots. He wants something to show the other director.'

Thirty minutes later, Ed and I were getting on like a house on fire. The Incredible Hulk and I spent the next four days working out who runs where, after what, how many soldiers it takes to stop him, and who shoots him when he gets there; all good fun. It turned into a sort of mapping job, bird's-eye views of who goes where. I have to say he was a nice bloke, very unassuming, clever, knew what he wanted; and then later that week he rang me from Hawaii and spent a good two hours on the phone changing everything that he had previously wanted. Nice bloke.

Meanwhile, I sent *Fizzy* off to a few more places and got back the same negative responses. So what to do now? Give in? Carry on? Carry on, of course. That's all you can do. As time passed, Riggy's gangster movie, *Dead Man Running*, ran out of puff, its production prospects collapsing with the same inevitability as *Fizzy*. Riggy, the producer, was back at square one; one moment it's all go, the next it's all no. I chatted about *Fizzy* to everyone who stood long enough in my vicinity, even to people in the local bar, one of whose patrons was Patrick Stack from Out of Pocket Films based at Sony Studios in Culver City. At that point, he was worth a try, as who wasn't? Patrick had actually been in movies. He was in the first Rambo movie, *First Blood*, as soldier number three or something or other. He told me he had once roomed with Brian Dennehy and now was a producer at Sony Pictures or at least rented an office on the lot in Culver City. I gave him a phone call and we chatted, but it was another dead end. He was kind enough to listen, which as I was finding out is as much as you can ask of anyone. I even visited the Sony lot in Culver City, sat down in the production offices of what would once have been MGM and shared another conversation that went nowhere. Then, out of the blue, I had a call from Rich from the British Youth Film Academy.

I moved my attention to Rich from Lincolnshire, my Plan B. Rich was the fellow whom I'd driven to see during a torrential downpour several weeks earlier. Was he still keen? Rich, said yes, he was! So, Rich became the new "producer". He was very spirited on the phone and seemed genuinely enthusiastic every time we spoke. Riggy and Nut agreed it was a better idea to get someone who was a proper producer on the case. Rich was our man. Rich said he was a proper producer, and that, it seemed, was good enough for me, Nut and Riggy. He was now firmly on board. Rich came with the full backing of the British Youth Film Academy. And here's something funny: the BFYA had offices based in Crewe. Yes, Crewe! Can you believe that? I move to Hollywood and end up back at Crewe. A small cuckoo clock chimes in the background.

Still, Rich was a proper producer, wasn't he? That was all that mattered, though at the back of my mind I did wonder how many blockbuster movies come out of Crewe every year.

Time began to roll, then race by, and before I knew it Rich, the proper producer from Crewe's BYFA, had been on the case for ten months and his achievements, when I stacked them against my previous progress with Forecast, were beginning to look remarkably similar. I am impatient, I know, but it seemed to take years to get nothing done. I ran an ad looking for bona-fide investors and collaborators.

The responses ranged from a Korean translator to a maimed stuntman and a monkey from Preston, to a pet shop owner from Cheadle Hulme, and of course many so-called producers who hadn't actually produced. Our inexperience began to show. I spoke to our new lead producer, Rich; he agreed with all my frustrated sentiments just as Olivier had before him and said, yes, it was time for more to be done. Time to produce the goods! Time for some straight talking and financial commitments.

'Have you actually taken any *Fizzy* meetings in the ten months you have been on the case?'

'No.'

'Have you managed to bring any of the talent you told me about to *Fizzy*?'

'Not really.'

'Have you managed to raise a penny in the form of development or production money?'

'Not as such.'

'I need you to communicate with me and let me know which avenues you are exploring.'

'Communication is not my thing, it's not the way I work.'

'Oh.'

It was going to be one of those weeks, when from nowhere I got an email from another producer who wanted to get involved with *Fizzy*. He had a midsize TV communications company based at Ealing Studios in London. Ealing Studios? Alec Guinness? *The Lavender Hill Mob*? *The Man in the White Suit*? That Ealing Studios?

This is interesting, I thought.

We chatted and he sounded a nice-enough guy. I have to

admit, they were all beginning to sound nice-enough guys. That was beginning to be a bit of a red flag, He did love the concept of *Fizzy.* He knew a lady called Lynda Bellingham or, as I would know her best, the OXO mum, as she had appeared in a popular commercial selling beef stock cubes in the UK during the eighties and nineties. He had an 'in' with her, apparently. He also talked finance and his ability to raise it.

I realized I needed to speak to someone who sounded like a complete bastard. These nice guys were just not cutting the mustard. I never heard from him again despite my repeated calls. In the meantime, my storyboarding work had gone really quiet, and for some weeks there was almost nothing. It seemed that people needing storyboards were tightening their belts.

I wrote a few more emails to people I had already seen. As usual there was no response. Quietly, I began to acknowledge I was a storyboard guy who was going to stay a storyboard guy; although if work didn't pick up, even that was beginning to look questionable. I sent a last proposal of my latest draft of *Fizzy* to an agency in London, and they did reply that they would read it. But I wasn't going to hold my breath.

Then an email arrived from Nut saying that the investor pack that Riggy had put together a few months ago had been given to his accountant, and had been passed on to a fellow called Stuart Little. No, not that Stuart Little, not a talking mouse, another one who happened to be the manager of Roy 'Chubby' Brown and Max Boyce no less. I had taken Luisa to see Chubby Brown years ago in London on the recommendation of one of my friends. I'd had no idea what his act was at all until then. Luisa must have been one of about a dozen women in a theatre of two thousand drunken blokes listening to what passed as gags about women's leaking vaginas etc. It wasn't the best night we've ever had. I wouldn't be holding my breath over Mr Little.

But thankfully some work did finally come in. I worked with an English director "Kirk" on a breakfast cereal commercial. I looked up his company and it was something to do with *Waking Ned Divine*, a smart little Brit flick of a few years ago. I banged off an email to him a week later, sent him all our info and reminded him that should he need any more boards for his commercials it would be a pleasure to assist. Would he be interested in *Fizzy*, perhaps?

CHAPTER 23

Time marches on

Time marched on. This week I was working for a fellow who seemed very nice, easy to get along with and who had some good ideas; Mark Cowen. I'd made my way that morning up the winding canyon off Sunset to sit in his office and thrash out some boards for a project in the grounds of his Laurel Canyon home.

Laurel Canyon in the Hollywood Hills, the former haunt of Joni Mitchell, Carol King, Crosby, Stills and Nash, the Monkees, Eric Borden, Jimi Hendrix and anyone who was ever a creative force in the sixties and seventies music scene, all had called Laurel Canyon their home! I was drawing storyboards for an IMAX film. I couldn't believe the number of people I was acquainted with called Mark. The early sixties had a stranglehold on the name.

'Where are you presenting these boards, Mark?' I asked innocently.

'Keep it under your hat, Mark, but Tom Hanks will be looking at these at the end of the week.'

Tom Hanks? Interesting, I think.

'What have you done before, Mark?' I ask.

'I'll send you a few examples of my work.'

And so, before I could say 'US Postal Service', I had a goody box of DVDs. What a geezer! He had sent me several DVDs, including the series *Band of Brothers*, produced by Tom Hanks and Steven Spielberg. 'I've definitely heard of them,' I thought. He seemed to have worked on everything. Interesting ...

'Would you have a look at my little film, *Fizzy Days*?'

'Er ... love to.'

'You would!' Interesting. Got to keep pushing.

Wednesday night had come around again, so I piloted my truck in the direction of the King's Head and sat down for a plate of ribs and a pint of Carlsberg with the slightly optimistic notion that if this Mark fellow was half as nice as he seemed, then maybe we would actually sit down at some point and talk *Fizzy*. Only time would tell. I mean, it was bound to be the sort of moped project Tom Hanks would be into mentoring ... wasn't it?

Meanwhile, Riggy resigned as manager of the band he was managing, or rather Virgin Records made it difficult for him to stay on, which, as with the last folding of a Riggy project, freed up more of his time for *Fizzy*. He forwarded the investor pack to Stephen Graham, who said he liked it. Stephen was the little fellow in *Snatch* who played opposite Jason Statham. He'd done quite a bit since then and seemed to keep himself very busy. He was now a successful actor with several Hollywood A list projects under his belt.

Riggy wrote back and said he had indicated that Stephen might like to be involved; he might even come "on board". I was given this little positive piece of news as I paused my second disc from *Band of Brothers*, the mini-series that Mark Cowen had so kindly sent me. There on the screen was Stephen Graham as a member of Easy Company, the ill-fated army regiment in Spielberg's serialized-for-TV epic about the *Battle of the Bulge*. This was clearly a sign. It was all falling into place.

I thought to myself that it was probably a good idea to badger Mark Cowen with *Fizzy*, so I spent the evening fine-tuning the script again. I printed out the newly tweaked draft and bradded it together, its crisp new paper making the printed words look as fresh to me as when I'd first begun this never-ending saga more than five years earlier. I then burned a CD of the music, rustled up one of my last remaining DVDs of the short, added some press articles, reviews, cartoons and a cover letter, and banged them off to his Hollywood Hills address. It was a black hole out there, but maybe this little pack would find a small ray of sunshine. Let's wait and see, I thought. A day later this was in my email box:

Mil, Thanks for sending along the *Fizzy* package. I can't wait to watch/read all of it. I'll give you a shout to set up a time to meet up. Mark

Things might just be looking up! I wrote another script and so embarked on another project, a short film called *Hell's Angel*. I had originally written it with a part for Jake Busey in mind, the son of Hollywood firebrand Gary Busey, as a friend of mine had an in with Jake. Jake was gracious enough to read a few pages that I just happened to have on me while I attended a Super Bowl party he had thrown at his house in Ventura. I got talking to his dad at some point; I don't remember what about. We had been telling jokes to a small side gathering. He didn't like the ending to one of mine and seemed to take a dislike to me for it. He ended up shouting at the top of his voice somewhat in my face:

'Somewhere a village is missing its idiot – and it's YOU!'

Staying with the motorbike theme and genre, Jake rode a bike and was a great fit for my badass biker who meets his destiny in the form of an impish little girl. Unbeknown to the biker she is an angel, but not a good one, in fact an angel from hell. I posted the script on those websites and, as before, it did better than I expected on the Frances Ford Coppola Zoetrope, garnering script of the month. If someone wanted to make it, that'd be great; I couldn't afford to, so why not let someone else have a go? At least that way it wouldn't die in my drawer of other unproduced projects. A producer by the name of Rebecca called; she came with a young director called Maks. Great!

We arranged to meet in Hollywood at a coffee shop on Third Street the coming Thursday night. The meeting was cancelled, of course. We rescheduled to meet on Saturday; no problem. Saturday arrived to find a tall mixed race woman, Françoise, alone at the coffee shop. Again, she apologised the director couldn't make it; maybe tomorrow? Françoise was nice about it all and couldn't apologise enough, so we sat and talked movies.

'This is not like Maks at all … I'll see if I can get another director …'

'I'll direct it if you like,' I say as if I'm doing her a favour.

'You?'

'Yeah, me, I've done some directing, won some awards.' I let it dangle in the air, sort of a nonchalant I-don't-care kind of thing.

'OK,' she smiled.

Score ? Goal … Goooal!! I think …

A few weeks had gone by since I'd sent off the *Fizzy* package to Mark Cowen: nice guy, Tom Hanks's producer. I bang him an email. Maybe I'll just nudge him a bit, see how we are doing. Can't hurt, can it?

'Mark, don't hate me, but I haven't read or watched it yet.'

No problemo, you join legions of others that haven't read or watched it yet! My well-put-together presentation package may have been presented to the trash can again. Shame. He was a nice bloke, and he probably is. I know nice blokes get busy, so I left it with him. I would check in again later. Well, there was always another day, and on one of those days I was off to a Hollywood casting house to listen to people read for my *Hell's Angel* script. How cool was that? A small casting studio in a proper production facility. Françoise seemed like a proper producer, certainly talked the talk, so maybe this one would get made.

I returned home pretty chuffed that a few young actors had read for the main part of the angel. My hope that Jake Busey would fill the biker role sort of went away, or rather my ability to pin him down to do it did. We could find another biker, so it wasn't too bitter a pill. We needed a crew and everything that comes with it, so we were still a long way off.

'I think I can get a crew,' says Françoise. 'Leave it with me.'

Next thing I knew, an email came saying she could lay her

hands on a guy called Jonathan Heap for DP. Oscar nominee, of course. This was getting freaky. OK, the animator from *Harry Potter* would help us with the CGI angel's wings. This was all too good to be true. I couldn't see it coming off, but if it did, well, bugger me sideways. All I had to do was to make a good job of it, then people were bound to see it and say, 'You should do something else,' and I'd say, 'How about this?', producing *Fizzy* with a flourish from my back pocket.

Françoise found another actor to play the role of the biker, then in quick succession: a makeup artist to go with our first-class animator, who came with the use of Sony Pictures facilities. I scouted out a couple of locations in the mountains to go with our promised use of a $40,000-dollar motorcycle. Blimey, it just kept getting better! I didn't perhaps feel in the driving seat as much as I had been, but Françoise seemed a producer from heaven and to have more contacts than Robert Zemeckis, so I decided to go with the flow. All the people I had met so far seemed genuine.

But things were about to change. As I was going over wardrobe with a costume designer, an email popped into my inbox which rang all sorts of alarm bells.

'Mark, hi, I'd love you to meet Raj, he's a wonderful director, he's done a short film that I would love you to watch, he's also great with actors too. He would be a perfect fit for *Hell's Angel*.'

Who the fuck is Raj? And where did he spring from? I thought I was a perfect fit. It seemed I may have been alone in that assumption. Several emails later and our lovey-dovey working relationship had degenerated into a slanging match of epic proportions. It's amazing how quickly things can unravel in movieland, and unravel they did.

CHAPTER 24

A new approach

The new plan was to divide *Fizzy* into three between me, Riggy and Nut. A few days later we registered Fizzy Days Ltd, a UK production company. The idea was to sell shares in the project and finance it that way; apparently, it had been done before with other creative projects and was a viable proposition in our case. An Enterprise Investment Scheme? We could do this thing!

I had a quick look at the Indieflix site, and *Fizzy* the short film was slowly moving up the all-time top seller list; and just to prove the point, a cheque for the princely sum of two dollars and seventy cents arrived in my mailbox this morning! Hey, I'd tell Mark Cowen, he'd want to know. I banged him off an email, to which no answer came.

'He's probably just busy,' I thought. 'I'll contact him again in a couple of weeks.'

Riggy's London gangster film had brushed itself off and was now up and running again, only at this point it was running without him. It looked as though whatever troubles people had had with the script were resolved and that Rio Ferdinand and Ashley Cole, the Manchester United and Chelsea players, had bankrolled the film, and shooting had already begun. The rapper 50 Cent had signed on, along with Brenda Blethyn – that's Brenda "nominated for an Oscar" Blethyn. It was all over the industry mags.

It beats me how these things happen. If anyone deserved a film it was Riggy; he lives and breathes film. I hoped we'd manage to pull *Fizzy* off, but boy, I now had more than a bag of doubts. To cap it all off, Tommy, Riggy's beloved dog had just died that week, the black dog that gave the company its logo identity and loyal companionship to its owner.

I was sitting in a little cubicle, my temporary home at yet another glass-clad faceless LA advertising agency, drawing storyboards for a chap probably twenty years my junior. On greeting me he remembered that a few years ago I'd made a short film about a little motorbike.

'What else are you doing at the moment? That was great. What else have you done since?'

I sighed and answered despondently, 'That's what else I've been doing. I haven't done anything else. I'm still trying to do that. I have written several others and am in the process of making another short. And you?'

'I'm making webisodes, but I have a feature that we are about to begin shooting, and another feature that we have just managed to find finance. The budget is low, but I'm keeping busy directing commercials and virials for the web at present. Done quite a few, wanna see?'

'Love to.'

Trying to get this film thing done seemed to bring out the

worst of my character traits as well: jealously, envy, petulance and scurviness. I'm usually such a well-mannered nice chap, but boy was this hard. Don't ever try it at home.

Riggy emailed me version eight of the Fizzy prospectus. We spent a couple of hours trimming a million pounds off the budget until Riggy felt that it was something he could comfortably hand over to our new saviour, John the accountant. We trimmed, we cut, we pruned, and at the end of a long iChat session, we had ourselves a very skinny top-sheet (budget). I wasn't sure at this point if a movie could be made for that money, and if it could, whether it would be one worth watching. Who knew? By then, I think I'd have put my name to just about anything if it meant *Fizzy* remained alive with even the slimmest chance that we could take it to production. I couldn't care less if I was paid or not at that point! I'd rather not have to pay any more for the privilege, but I realised that could be just a forlorn hope.

We had set up Fizzy Days Ltd and I was about to get a little encouragement as the new year got going. I actually got a positive reaction to another one of my scripts, my Kes homage, now retitled *Screech*. It was a finalist in the La Latino scriptwriting competition. I had no idea what that was, but it spurred me into picking up my pen where I'd left off a few months earlier, disheartened and disillusioned. Now, with this sudden boost to my ego, I was upbeat and enthusiastic again. I was going to finish my pike-fishing script, a rom-com called *The Fishing Lure*. May as well, could be a winner!

I was due to work on a commercial that featured a talking duck. It was with David McNally, director of *Kangaroo Jack* and *Coyote Ugly*. I got on my motorcycle and wove my way up to the Pacific Palisades to his Malibu home. I was to draw the 'spokes-duck' for an Aflac insurance ad. I left his home with my rough sketches, which I would work up then return to him as finished storyboards. 'I've written the odd script myself,' I ventured in casual conversation and like a fool he said he would love to read one. On the journey home, I was thinking I would send him a couple, and then he could take his pick as to which one to trash first!

At some point, for the sake of balance, I feel I should sprinkle these pages with a few positive but imaginary steps forward. The whole film-maker process for me is like running in glue, it really is, and like everything it has its bright spots. I can't say that some days I wasn't happy with my lot in life, driving to work along the oceanfront to be paid for drawing pictures all day!

It had been several years since I started this little note-taking exercise that was originally intended to chronicle the making of my first feature, *Fizzy Days* – to be released in conjunction with the movie – but had instead been a litany of frustrations and mis-steps as I was thwarted by either my own actions or those of others along the way. We were now in the midst of a recession, which had so gripped the nation that the idea of investing in my moped-driven 1970s comedy *Quadrophenia* seemed even more unlikely. For the last several years I'd hung on to the hope that it might happen, but finally I had to admit that it might not ever happen and the best thing was to let it go.

As things slipped into reverse here, more than a few years had passed since my life-changing contract had arrived. Work had really dried up by this time; it had got a bit scary and was getting more so, to the extent that I was seriously thinking of signing on for unemployment benefits as a last resort.

The recession had done for the business bigtime, had done for me bigtime! The Oscars were on TV. The glamour of the occasion seemed a million miles from reality, but at that moment so did reality. Riggy's communication had dried up, and I was starting to wonder if, after all these years, so had even his enthusiasm. The house in Manhattan Beach carried a large mortgage, in part because of my throwing money at *Fizzy*. I rang the mortgage people to try and get a little assistance with our payments. And I looked up how to claim social-security benefits. Unemployment! The unemployment benefits website suggested further reading, with a list of suggested titles including something called "Down and out". Seriously, why would they have that on the website? Maybe they might add "Suicide for beginners" or "So, you're now a loser!"

Making the short film *Fizzy Days* and having the money and ability to do so seemed so far away at this point. Making a feature-length film seemed like ... well, a pipe-dream. Bankruptcy seemed far more likely. The downturn in the once-abundant amount of work on offer had been so sudden; the economy had tanked, and I and many others were sinking with it. Be happy with the trick you've got.

Thankfully, I did get the odd storyboard gig. Did I say I was getting a bit bored with boarding? That I was a little discontented? That was before it all dried up and I didn't have any! Now I loved storyboarding, it was what I did best! In fact, it was all I'd ever wanted to do. Honest to God, how things take on a different perspective when you can't even afford Wednesday ribs. So off I trotted to Highland Avenue,

Hollywood. Where was my cubicle today? Lots of sandblasted, stripped redwood, cut-glass chandeliers and the fanciest sandwiches you could order! I had no cause for complaint, given my inactivity of late. And this place was great; Smuggler Films. I could even see the Hollywood sign from my window. So near and yet so far.

I waited for the director to show up, with people requesting his coffee order and organic lunchtime preferences. He arrived and we spent a couple of hours discussing the tiny details of golf clubs and sand traps, golf-course topography and cacti for the AT&T commercial set on a golf course that I was to board. Ten hours later I was on my way home, a satisfied storyboarder knowing I had done my part to further enhance the world of advertising and feeling fulfilled to the fullest extent. I looked Bennett Miller up on the IMDb and found out to my surprise he was actually a bigwig who'd been nominated for an Oscar for directing the Truman Capote biopic (*Capote*) and more recently *Moneyball*. I hadn't seen the Capote film but I knew where he was buried – that little cemetery in Westwood. Talent was getting difficult to spot without a proper label!

Next thing I knew, I got a notification asking for me to confirm my attendance at the Beverly Hills International Film Festival, in Beverly Hills! It was to promote and support my script *Screech*, as it was now an official selection of that prestigious film festival in the 'Scripts' category. I had no idea that it had even been selected. The way things had been going with my film career, I quickly sent an email back to ask if there had been some mistake as notifications were at the beginning of the month, and we were now halfway through March.

'Yes,' they wrote back, '*Screech* has been accepted into the

Festival. Out of over a thousand, yours was chosen with 100 finalists. It will come down to three winners.'

One hundred finalists? That seemed like a lot, but I'd take it! My script had been officially selected for the Beverly Hills Film Festival. Now I had a script with an official selection in the BHFF! My credentials were growing.

I also contacted a few people from my advertising days in London. London seemed almost to be going full circle. They seemed busier over there than we were over here, mired in a mighty recession. More responses to my script query letters had started to trickle in. All good stuff even if the responses were a little on the negative side: 'Many thanks for your email, but we're concentrating on TV series rather than one-offs for the moment.' 'I'm really looking for a comedy or romantic comedy with a female lead.' 'We can only consider fully developed screenplays with funding, a director and also a cast of international commercial value attached …' All in all, a sorry set of responses, but we would never give in, never surrender. It was all good fun. After being revitalized with my Beverly Hills script acceptance, I felt bolstered and confident enough that I would find further collaborators. I did get a job boarding out a Cher promo and was able to attend the shoot and watch a proper director do his stuff with my boards and the music icon at the Egyptian theatre in downtown LA. But gigs were getting few and far between.

Dear Mark,

Many thanks for letting us know about your project. Whilst it sounds very interesting, I'm afraid that it's not a story we are currently looking to tell.

This was from Simon Pegg's company, Big Talk. I love Simon Pegg. Who doesn't?

The weeks rolled by. It was getting a little scary having no work as the norm. What had happened to all my work? I used to be busy. I wasn't sure where things were heading, but my back certainly felt a lot closer to the wall. How things turn around! You put it all down to life, I suppose. One moment it's all go, go, go, the next it's all no, no, no!

I was to pick up my all-access pass for the Beverly Hills Film Festival, so a ride into Beverly Hills put me in upbeat mood. It was nice: a nice distraction, palm trees, sunny day and all that. I felt like a gunslinger riding into Dodge.

Then the Mexico International Film Festival accepted my script *Screech*. That was three festivals in a row. Surely someone must be interested now. I could tell that my enthusiasm was starting to wane a little. Maybe I wasn't a film-maker or a writer, maybe I was a storyboard artist; although the memento hanging from the black lanyard from the BHFF proclaims that I was indeed a "writer". It stated my wannabe ambitions as it dangled mockingly from the fridge; a piece of laminated card on a string proclaiming the word 'Screenwriter' for all the world to see.

CHAPTER 25

Many thanks

It never rains but it pours. Luisa came back from her six-monthly scheduled ultrasound scan with the news that she had some calcifications. What the fuck they were I didn't have a clue, and even the doctors didn't know. But they needed to do an MRI, the big white buzzing tube thing. It was probably nothing, but they were unable to pinpoint where to do a biopsy. This being the American way and all that, our insurance deductible to get back to the UK for the late summer hols had just been met, swallowed and deducted from our budget to do so. Medical stuff can get a little expensive here in the good old US of A. It dawned on me that maybe I shouldn't have spent quite so much money on our little *Fizzy* baby.

We could move to a more economical location, if need be, to free up some of the equity invested in the house.

Back at my desk I sat at my computer. I sent a *Fizzy* package to Patrick Stack, soldier number three, the producer at Sony. I had not forgotten about him. I received a response from a company in Burbank, home to Walt Disney and Warner Bros, asking me to sign a waiver and send a hard copy of *Screech* to them. This I dutifully did and sat back to await their reply.

It was another sunny work-free day. I watched the surfers do their stuff and a pod of dolphins chasing the crowded sardine shoals beneath the pier. They parted the small silver fish like oil on water. Not a bad place to be unemployed. I also rang Connie Stevens and congratulated her on the Philadelphia Film Festival première of the film I had boarded. I'm not sure she knew or even cared to remember who I was, and the conversation was very one-sidedly brief, but she thanked me for my call and said she would get a ticket to me for its LA screening, whoever I was! I wasn't going to hold my breath. I could buy my own ticket when it came out, but I don't think it ever did.

It was a glorious weekend, the start of another summer was not that far off: the girls on the beach, the lads on the beach, the sand on the beach, etc. We took a family bike ride along the strand and had an ice-cream at the creamery, a little ice-cream shop owned by an Englishman that was doing gangbusters by then. I set myself the weekend task of emailing two dozen companies with samples of my storyboard work. *Fizzy* took a back seat. I needed paying work.

I went out for a beer with an English production designer friend, Mark Tanner, and his friend Willie Patterson, another UK director. I had worked for Willie years earlier when he had his own office and company on La Cienega Boulevard in Hollywood. He was old-school and had been very busy in the eighties and early nineties directing commercials. He regaled us with some very colourful stories, as he had once been David

Bailey's assistant back in the psychedelic late sixties and early seventies. I had worked for Willie as a storyboarder and we had got on quite well. He now lived in my present hometown of Manhattan Beach. It was great to think and talk about something other than work for a few hours; things had not been easy of late. The recession was really beginning to savage my ankles. And the rejections kept coming, each with its own way of twisting the knife.

Maybe Luisa would be OK and things would get back to normal again.

Time passed. I had got used to rising from bed at about 6.45 am, having a coffee and then sitting at my computer, looking for commercials and movies in production in a flailing attempt to get some work either storyboarding or writing. At that moment, with things as they were, it seemed a Herculean task. I sent as many samples of my work out into the ether as I could. I had even started to offer discounted rates. It had no discernible effect. I sent Mark Cowen, my Tom Hanks connection, another email, not realising that he had sadly (and maybe suddenly) died the previous year. I guess that's why he hadn't got back to me before.

More replies came about *Fizzy*. One guy called Randy, at Synergy Movies, wanted to charge me a $500 consultancy fee just to read the script. It seemed just moments ago that I'd been moaning about moving my career forward. Silly me! Now in such a short space of time my career had become looking for my career, trying to re-find it or any career, or even just a modicum of gainful employment. I spent every morning at my computer as if it were my job, not leaving the house for work as there was none to be had. The response rate for written correspondence was abysmal; for every fifty unsolicited approaches I made, I got one reply. And even though the sun kept on shining, the mixture of silence and rejections kept on coming like a winter storm that just won't give in.

We attended the hospital for Luisa to have her biopsy, with all fingers crossed. The way things were going, neither of us held out much hope for an all-clear. Caroline, my daughter and teenage firebrand, was finding school and discipline shall we say *taxing* at present; there was talk of her being held back a year. We were called to the school for a discussion. The study hut that she attended after school said they would waive their fees when we tried, due to finances cancel her after-school tuition; they clearly saw her as a challenge to be overcome. So did we at that point. She has since overcome the challenge and lives in Woodstock, upstate New York, working in the topical world of social media.

We weren't going to get the results of the biopsy until the following Tuesday, so we had the weekend to fret about the outcome; which, fingers crossed, would be fine. But funny things were happening, bad karma. I bought two little glow-light tetra for the fish tank, added them, stood back and watched as they and every other fish in the tank died; about twenty of my little piscatorial pals. Then the hamster came out of his cage and had a boil the size of a quarter hanging from his fur. And to cap our animal woes, on Saturday we adopted a dog, a yappie little terrier mixture with razors for teeth. He went viciously for Zack, my boy, the day after we brought him home, biting him on the leg and drawing blood. He then bit me on the Monday morning and Luisa in the evening. We took him back on Tuesday. This being litigious America, we didn't want him chowing down on someone else's child at a playdate.

I met another producer that day and like all the rest he seemed perfectly normal, in fact quite charming. He had the unlikely name of Greg Huge and his company was called Huge Pictures, a New York motion-picture production house with a staff of one, a certain Greg Huge. I found out this last bit of information during the meeting. The name would have been a better fit for a well-endowed porn star than a movie producer. Perhaps a porn-movie producer?

Greg appeared at the appointed hour at the Coffee Bean opposite the King's Head. He wasn't huge, just stocky around the waist, sort of Greg biggish and shortish rather than huge-ish. Sure enough, one and a half hours later, it was déjà vu! It was almost like several years ago all over again, only this time my euphoria was tempered by more than a little cynicism. I was standing at the bar of the King's Head drinking my pint of Carlsberg, smiling. Was my new best buddy Greg a tosser or not? Time would tell. He said he was going to look into getting a contract together. Another one! Huge Pictures wanted to co-produce our film, so *Fizzy* once again had an interested party, a producer who was on board.

We talked contracts, we talked production, we talked bollocks. We met again, me and Greg. I gave him a *Fizzy* package to rival Mark Cowen's. Everything but the kitchen sink went in to it. I tried to be confident about my new acquaintance but by then I was tired, all fizzed out. Could this be the chap to help get it going? I didn't know. He mentioned the contract thing again, which if I'm not mistaken is where we came in. I hadn't had a good thing with contracts so far, and we are quite few pages into the story! Why should my luck turn now?

Patrick, soldier number three from the Rambo films, got back to me suggesting we had a beer, so we met at OB's Bar and Grill at the Beach. He seemed more interested in another of my scripts, *Screech*, this time round. Another producer, another day, another meeting, another beer, another dream idea; another load of bollocks!

Meanwhile Greg Huge emailed to say he'd shown the trailer to someone at Lionsgate, who had then requested the script. Whether he'd shown it to anyone was very much up for debate, but I decided to take him at his word, for now, as even the tiniest bit of interest would have been manna from heaven. Alas, all too predictably, it was not to be; Greg had got it from the man at Lionsgate (from the lion's mouth?) that they were looking for genre films and *Fizzy* didn't fall into any particular genre. I had thought it a coming-of-age comedy vehicle.

A little disappointing, as it kind of nailed the coffin shut again. We needed this one, I really needed it. But I wasn't surprised as by now it was becoming apparent that getting even a little movie made was close to impossible. I have the utmost admiration for those who can and do, but I'd got no idea where to go from here, if indeed there was anywhere to go. But I didn't give in, I couldn't. Frankly, the old battle cry, "Never give in, never surrender" sounded a bit pathetic by then. Isn't the definition of lunacy something like repeating the same act and expecting a different outcome? Something along those lines. Such a shame. I think it would have made a great little movie.

Patrick, soldier number three, came back and said he was willing to send *Screech* to two close buddies in the biz that handle Latino-themed scripts. Let's see where this goes, I thought. A week later: 'Bad news, both guys passed on the project.' Without getting into too much detail, both guys felt that it needed to either be a Hallmark movie or a tough "Boys in the Hood" movie, but not both. 'We know people who are poor have it rough, but so what?' were apparently his words.

He had liked the dialogue. 'Sorry for the bad news,' Patrick went on. 'Wish I could sugar-coat, but you know how this biz works. I guess you have to find the right creative force that can make it happen.'

That said, Greg and Patrick were my remaining two aces and without them I wouldn't know where else to take it. But it was Wednesday, so I'd take it to the King's Head for ribs and a pint of Carlsberg. By this time, I was having to forgo the ribs and make the Carlsberg last longer.

Then Greg Huge got back to me. After talking with his investors and partners (probably his mum), *Fizzy* was now too small a film for him to handle, so true to form we now had precisely nothing in his plus column. But he was still on board and keen as mustard. Well, thank heavens for that!

CHAPTER 26

Good news bad news

The waiting room at the oncology department of Torrance Memorial Hospital was as white and sterile as all doctors' offices are; vinyl seats, a few magazines and a potted rubber plant. I had been watching the small white planes coming and going from Torrance airport. The hospital was just across from the runway. The phone call Luisa had received had asked both of us to be there, but we'd been separated. After having being told I could come into the consulting room with Luisa, I now waited outside for her. I sat twiddling my thumbs, reading an article on colonics.

The consulting-room door opened and Luisa popped her head out asking if I could join her and the specialist in the doctor's office. I thought, 'This is going to be bad'. We sat down and the white-coated doctor looked over her notes and X-ray results etc. She cleared her throat, only to smile:

'The tissue we examined is fine, the test results were all clear; a benign knot of dense massed breast tissue.'

Seeing as Luisa's mother had succumbed to breast cancer,

the doctor went on to add that it was something she should be very aware of monitoring (as if she wouldn't be anyway). I didn't know whether to thank this doctor woman or strangle her. Why on earth make such a big deal of it if nothing was wrong or metastasising? I still don't know to this day why they had us both come in, only to tell us the obviously welcome news disjointedly. Both of us had the same thoughts, but relief and good news was the main ingredient of the appointment that day, despite the doctor's strange manner of delivering it.

I had my fingers crossed that the next round of outreaches might just have a little more traction. I sent the script and a treatment to Nicola Charles, former *Neighbours* star and a handsome woman if her press photos were anything to go by. Certainly, she looked great for the part of Carmen in my script *Screech*. She also owned her own production company.

Nicola got back to me asking if the option on the film was available unencumbered to her own company, Marathon Pictures. You bet it was! She had not read the script but would do so; within two days she'd come back to me again, expressing a wish to be attached as actress and producer. She also had a director in mind who was 'Known for his ability to pick winning scripts and projects, and has himself won many awards'. If he liked it as much as she did, she felt the project would become very special.

'Congratulations on a beautiful story.'

Such gushing praise; you know it's all going to end badly … and it did! The director she was talking about hadn't actually directed anything as far as I could see on IMDb. Apparently, all his directing had been for the stage and by all accounts he was very good at it. He was Ian Hart or Professor Quirrell in the Harry Potter movies and as such my kids knew who he was. He had had a long and varied career since then.

'Let me check with my assistant and we can arrange a time to meet, perhaps later this week? Santa Monica is fine,' she added.

'Check with my assistant.' It sounded very grand; how could it possibly end badly?

Marathon Pictures was the production company, with an English director from Liverpool who'd been in several big movies, albeit as an actor. This looked like it would be his first directorial feature; but I was nowhere a moment ago, and now we were meeting at the Broadway Deli on Second Street, near the King's Head, with the promise of an option agreement. She even had an assistant!

She seemed nice in her emails, but if past experience was any guide, that could mean I was off to meet Medusa! I needed to put together a package or folder of goods again, so it was storyboard time and trawling the internet for images, then off to a meeting at the deli at noon with Nicola Charles. A couple of hours later, it was déjà vu all over again. I had another contract, this time an option agreement for the motion picture *Screech*. Oh boy! Yet somehow, I wasn't feeling the buzz … maybe the buzz would come later? There was always a buzz coming along later. From what I could see, the option agreement didn't actually pay me anything, as usual. Looking up Nicola in a little more depth revealed her as not a massive player either. Now I needed another lawyer to orchestrate this negotiation. Here we go again. I managed to find one recommended by my agent Mitch, who said he would take a look at it for a flat fee. He took one look, rang me back almost giggling and said, 'This option agreement stinks. There is nothing in it for anyone.'

'Isn't it just a starting point?'

'Yes, you are starting with nothing and you end up with the same amount.'

'Oh.'

'We can build on nothing, can't we?'

'But if my starting figure is nothing, so is my percentage. I need a figure and you need an option agreement with figures on it so I can get paid. And you'll need paying, I expect.'

Hmm … I'd never had an option agreement with any money attached. Probably needed to talk to her to sort all this out. I would sort it out. I called her at five-thirty that evening. She seemed heavily out of breath, with two very loud children close by. Between trying to separate her two children from what sounded like repeated attempts at murdering each other, she went over the finer points in the contract that she had handed me the week before. I wasn't too sure how successful we were at stating our positions, but I hoped a new contract would soon materialize. The connection with the Harry Potter actor seemed to have disappeared.

Nicola had replaced her first choice of director for *Screech* with her second choice, a guy called Gary Shore who has since gone on to have a busy career as a director but at that time was looking for material to direct. She had announced she was going to have a meeting about my script with Gary later that morning, which she then emailed me about that afternoon. The gist of it was he wanted to do it as long as the following issues were addressed: the script needed a lot of editing; there were problems with the structure; there was no inciting incident, i.e. nothing that kicked off the story in the first five minutes; many of the scenes were unnecessary; there was too much dialogue; the story was mildly interesting, but it would kill it if the audience's hand was held throughout; it lacked a visual language; it was too direct and explanatory, and didactic. Despite all these negatives, he 'passionately cared about the story'.

I'd hate to see Gary's notes for a project he wasn't keen on! The story was mildly interesting and yet he passionately cared about it? Bit confused, but I decided to go with it.

A few days later a new option agreement arrived and to be honest it looked worse than the first one. She had mentioned that I should jot down a few points that were of concern to me. I jotted them down and the new option addressed them specifically: everything I had asked to be included was specifically excluded!

Nicola wrote back after I had asked if Marathon would be prepared at least to pay the cost of drawing up an agreement rather than it starting to cost me thousands in legal fees every time someone showed an interest in something of mine. I just didn't have the attorney fees at present. Nicola's response was candid and cool and final and not very neighbourly.

'Perhaps Marathon is not the best home for *Screech* if you are unhappy with the effort thus far. As you point out, we are only in pre-production on our first feature, so you may feel more comfortable with somewhere that has more experience.'

Once again I felt like shit. This seemed to have ended in another, 'Well, you fuck off then,' 'No, you,' 'No, you first'. Tit-for-tat rejections, like being in the school playground only with very young kids. I didn't even want any money this time, not a penny; just some commitment from them that I would not end up in negative territory financially, having tied up my script for three years. I had asked them to pay for the legal costs of the agreement and they'd said no. I guess that showed just how committed they were. Passionately! I would have been another couple of grand out of pocket, which was money I didn't have at that point.

It was like being on crack; I didn't seem to be able to let it go. Every morning I would get up and make it my daily mission to reach out to a dozen people, production-company houses, both here in the US and in the UK, trawling the web for any address that I could cut and paste my introductory letter into. Any production house I could get a contact for. It became something of a habit, like brushing my teeth or going to the bathroom, but with less of a result. As I kept saying to myself, 'It just needs one, it just needs one.' But there had to come a limit, and I was starting to think I'd reached it years ago.

After lots of time going by not getting anything done, we parted company with Rich, the Lincolnshire chap. The BYFA would not be featuring in *Fizzy*'s credits any time soon. A company called FruitFly Films entered discussions, another London-based company I had sent the script to.

That weekend I went to the Comic Convention in San Diego, a big annual event. I have a bat fetish that I'll admit to; have had it since childhood. Unfortunately, it's something I've never been able to shake. I collected Batman trading cards as a seven-year-old. Fifty-odd years later I was still collecting them and was able to rekindle my youth by buying the same ephemera, now vintage 1966 items, that today can be found on the pages of ebay, although my purchasing power for these increasingly expensive pieces of pop memorabilia had been seriously hit by the double whammy of work drying up and what was turning out to be the expensive dream of one day making a feature film. But no one completely leaves their childhood behind, and to this end I still attend the odd comic convention from time to time. The San Diego Comic Con is full of non-sportscard dealers with shiny, sharp-cornered wares, and for the moments that he's there, the avid collector travels back in time. Everywhere he looks there are images he first set eyes on maybe fifty years or more ago. That was not the case for me; as I said, I have a sickness, where I try constantly to upgrade my collection, getting the sharpest, shiniest, most well-centred cards to form a high-grade collection. It's a medical condition, really, one that comes with wrappers. One I must and will seek help for, eventually.

Seriously, comic cons are great fun, at least I think so; and so increasingly does my daughter. Illustration being my vocation, it was always good to keep abreast of the competition. Some of the illustrators who had made me pick up a pencil seriously in the first place were sometimes in attendance. I shook hands with Bernie Wrightson that weekend, and if you ever see his black-and-white inks for Frankenstein, you'll know what I'm talking about. There are usually a few comic cons every month. This being LA and the home of the movie stars, they didn't have to travel far to meet and greet their fans and sign 8 x 10 glossy headshots of what they'd looked like in their heyday.

That weekend it was the Anaheim Comic Con. I took

Caroline, my daughter, to meet the likes of Adam West, Burt Ward and whoever was still alive from the cast of the *Batman* TV show. Predictably, the original Batmobile seemed to have fared much better than its human co-stars. Time seemed not to have left a mark on it; it made quite a contrast with the once-nubile Julie Newmar, who'd played Catwoman in the series, now fifty years older. I sat next to her and my daughter took our photo. We shared a brief conversation. She was old and lovely; I was just old and beginning to feel older but still somewhat lovely. But the aged appearance of some of these TV icons was tempered by the nostalgic memory and affection in which all of the fans at the convention held their childhood heroes. Adam West has since shuffled of his mortal bat-cape and ascended the Bat pole to that Batcave in the sky.

These things always have a sad anoraky type of feel; Comic Book Guy from *The Simpsons* is the standard-issue comic-geek, but all sorts attend and dress up cosplay. It's like *The Rocky Horror Show* screenings, only more eclectic. But it still has the essence of weird glam; these people were once those people, massive in their time, household names. Normal people like you and me are given free rein to dress up as their favourite superhero for the day, or even meet them as they pay homage to these icons, no matter how bad the costume. It gives your average desk jockey that chance to escape. Alan from accounting or Peter from the post room can become Peter Parker or Bruce Wayne or Dick Grayson for a day, or even two days if he has the weekend pass. Stormtroopers, Klingons, Wookies, even Daleks and Morlocks wandered around as if the Land of the Lost was a real place and TV villain monster makeup was everyday attire.

The adult film stars, their silicone cleavages still in great shape, the withered, botoxed flesh around them doing the best it could to keep up. The faded TV icons, all now past their prime, but still recognizable, still lovable. Micky Dolenz of *The Monkees* TV show still smiling boyishly from beneath a large-brimmed velvet hat. Little Eddie Munster, all grown up along with little Linda *The Exorcist* Blair, again all grown up. Ron '*Tarzan*' Ely in a booth next to Captain Kirk who took time out from his constantly aired Priceline commercials of the time to do a couple of Q&A sessions about what it was like to helm the bridge of the Starship Enterprise – ably backed by Nichelle Nichols or, as she was known in her Star Trek days, Lieutenant Uhura, the couple as an item being famous for the first primetime interracial kiss! It was like a zoo for freaks, and I did love it. What else would you do on a Saturday afternoon? Then Caroline took another photo of me with Adam West, as it turned out for the very last time. She had barrelled up to him between his security, without any prompting from me saying her father was such a fan, would he stand and have photo with me? He looked at me and laughed.

'Hey cute kid you got here.'

Wow! Batman thinks my daughters cute! All was well with the world. We had a quick break in Yosemite as a family for the weekend, as we sometimes do. That was great, a time to take walks, sit and reflect, etc.

It was time to reconsider what else I could do to earn a living. In the thirty-odd years I'd been doing this, I'd never known it this quiet, and it didn't look like getting better anytime soon.

CHAPTER 27

Fruit Flies to the rescue

'Is it possible you can take a meeting here in London?'

Fruit Fly, an English company on Wardour Street, came back with a hint of an interested response, so just maybe that would mean a meeting in England. One last chance was worth the risk and we could also combine it with a family holiday. One of their emails had come back as a request for the short award-winning promo film, then a request for the script, and finally:

'In terms of potential financiers and sales companies, distributors, etc., we would be looking to bring in a named director and cast with possible production in late 2010. It would be produced under the Fruit Fly Vision label ...'

It would be produced! That's what I'd been trying to do for years, get it produced! I didn't need to direct. My new best friend was Matthew of Fruit Fly Productions, Soho, London. The last four-plus years had seen England, or maybe London, get back on its feet. The economy here in the States was still in the doldrums, work had dried up to practically nothing, and the days of bemoaning that you were only a storyboard artist seemed so long ago. Now my only ambition was to be an *employed* storyboard artist … please? How things turn around.

England in the summer is like no other place on Earth. It's bloody lovely and can't be beaten; A choral version of "Jerusalem" or "I vow to thee my country" playing in your ears as you look over acres of golden corn, skylarks ascending, ash keys, blue skies, wood pigeons, jackdaws, jays, ploughed fields, magpies and crows. To a background peel of ringing church bells.

The idea was to combine the meetings with Fruit Fly in London with a quick break for the family in the UK. As there were no cheques coming in we were eating the house; that is to say, drawing down on the mortgage using the equity line on the house as a source of salary and funds. I wasn't sure how long that would be a good idea, but we'd reached the point where there was little choice. I needed to rethink the situation and combine some meetings with a change in the game plan. Maybe it was time to seriously consider going back to the UK. It couldn't be any quieter than here, and with the equity in the house we could make a sizable down payment on a UK property and move back to Planet Earth. The vacation was easy enough to book; the meetings were another matter. So, Matthew at Fruit Fly Films was interested and wanted to make my film, like so many before him. With 'production' scheduled in 2010. Wow! Another opportunity! He emailed me to set up a meeting on Wednesday afternoon at Soho House. A proper *Fizzy* meeting!

I seized the moment with both hands and prepared for the arranged meeting at the end of our family vacation. Soho

House, the venue Matthew had chosen, is a swanky members' club in the middle of Soho. A place where film-industry types meet to do deals. I was going to do a deal. Fruit Fly had offices in London, LA and Dubai. That's what their company listing said; and they, at present wanted to get on board! This time it couldn't fail! It was deal time. But first, before any meeting, the Millicent family charged around the UK countryside having our vacation, introducing the kids to places we had talked about, seeing old friends, even attending an old pal's wedding in Durham. The meeting with Matthew was hovering all the time in the background.

The end of the vacation arrived and with it the date of my deal-clinching meeting. I stayed up late and put a mean presentation pack together ready for the event. I headed out early in the morning to present it. With the confidence of a man who was going to wow the Fruit Fly team, I jumped on a train from Bedford, where we were staying with my still good friend Smithy, and headed for King's Cross St Pancras. I had time to kill; the meeting wasn't until the afternoon. I didn't want to be late. I would take a saunter around Soho for the morning and relax. I stopped for a coffee in a bar just off Gerrard Street. The sun was shining; at least that's the way I remember it. Sitting down with my coffee, I flipped open my laptop as I finally had some Wi-Fi and I checked my emails.

Dear Mark,
I'm so sorry but I cannot do tomorrow's meet as planned. I've been called out of London. Sorry for such short notice.
I'll be in touch. Apologies.
Matthew.

A black cloud appeared from nowhere and settled about a foot above my head, releasing a small bolt of lightning and showering me in a torrential but localized downpour. At least, that's the way I remember it. I could see Soho House from where I now sat. Why hadn't I checked my emails before I set off? Why? Because I was on a roll, wasn't I? Bastard! I was less enthusiastic about the journey back to Bedford. I must say, England in the summer is crap.

The well-thought-out presentation, the spiel I'd planned, was all binned. Never mind, what doesn't kill you makes you stronger. I wished I could still believe that. We had looked at some houses for sale in Bedfordshire before heading back to the US, but they were all expensive, especially where we would have liked to live and what we would have liked to live in. Isn't that always the way? Castles and Tudor mansions don't come cheap. I imagine everyone has the same sentiments. I couldn't seem to catch a break here. Several years had passed and I'd come close but no cigar.

The plane touched down again in LA and we made the short taxi ride from the airport to Manhattan Beach, warmed in the pink evening light. Never mind the English summer, the LA summer is not too bad either. Jetlag seemed to last for several days this time, and maybe it was tinged with a modicum of depression or disappointment or a little of both.

The recession hadn't just touched my doorstep; it was now beating on the door very loudly with both fists, threatening to knock it off its hinges, demanding to come in. A number of friends had given up on LA in recent months, or it had given up on them. A few more might be forced to as so many people were now finding it difficult to meet their mortgage payments.

The job that had always promised to provide until I no longer had the strength to raise a pencil was looking decidedly precarious. People were relocating to cheaper areas, and it was becoming a luxury to be able to use the house and its second mortgage as a source of income.

There were big brush fires at present just over the mountains and a huge plume of white smoke hung over the LA basin, making for spectacular sunsets and sunrises. (Side note: a couple of years from now our home was to fall victim to the Woolsey wildfire but that's a whole 'nother story!) Today I actually had a day's work while this was going on, so was able to watch this fire's progress from the thirty-first floor of a glass-fronted office building downtown. The smoke was thick and milky and cast a weird light on everything. I was working on a burger commercial with Kathy, a groovy new age vegan type in downtown LA, an illustrator I had worked with now and again. We went for lunch and over the kimchee salad she explained how Jesus came and physically visited her one night recently.

'You can laugh, I knew you would.'

'I'm not laughing.' (I was.)

'The epiphany was indescribably real and could not be denied.' She fixed me with a frown. 'I'm sure it was'

'Cuckoo-cuckoo,' chimed in the distance. I replied that I too had had an experience with Jesus a few years ago when we could afford a Mexican gardener and you pronounced his name 'Hay-zooz'. Hay-zooz, who drove a '72 Toyota and killed our lawn and subsequently our guinea pig, probably wasn't the same chap who had come to Kathy in the wee small hours in a euphoric Biblical encounter. Basil, my daughter's guinea pig, was left on the lawn and ingested whatever bad fertilizer Jesus or Hay-Zooz had used to destroy our grass.

'I don't know why I bothered to tell you,' she snarled.

I'm not sure I knew why either, but these are the kinds of conversations that can brighten up your day. I had submitted my script *Screech* to the Yosemite Film Festival, expecting it to get in, given it was about nature and all that. A few weeks later, 'Not Accepted' stared at me from my submission's webpage. Ah, well, it's all subjective, though it would have been nice to go up there and have my film script in a festival, especially as Luisa always liked a trip up to Yosemite. Still, no harm in trying, but you would have to think I was due some kind of break somewhere along the line.

So back in LA I banged out another batch of emails before my morning run. A French producer got back to me saying she would read the treatment, but that she was ideally looking for a comedy. I quickly sent her two scripts, the sum total of about six months' work. She must have been very good at what she did as she was able to dismiss both of them within the hour. It was amazing how she could spend a few minutes on something that had maybe taken me half a year and say with clarity and surety that these really weren't any good.

Strangely, though, as before with the Beverly Hills Film Festival, I got a notice saying my script *Screech* had won the John Muir Gold Award for Screenplay in the Yosemite Film Fest –that's the festival it was rejected from. Go figure. What should I do? Well, what I usually do, which was to send my "Is this a typo?" email. I found out it wasn't: *Screech* has indeed won the John Muir Gold Award in the screenplay section. Wow! The script whose only good point "was that it ended" seemed to be doing alright as regards awards. I just needed someone to say they would make it, and then we'd be doing really alright!

Simultaneously, another chance arrived in the email inbox. A London producer liked *Fizzy*, said it needed some work, but liked it anyway. He wanted to talk about it, and I was always up for talking about it. That's what I do!

Gary Sinyor was the man. Magnet Films was the company. He'd made a few films, and directed. When I googled him there was a photo of him sitting in a director's chair, talking over a script with Renée Zellweger and Chris O'Donnell. I decided to go with it and see where it went. I knew I had to call the other "interested" party, Fruit Fly, in London to see if they were interested or not.

I had sent Gary the script and he had read it in less than a week and got back to me, bloody marvellous by the usual standards. He'd made ten-million-dollar movies too. I managed to talk to him on the phone, actually talking rather than just emailing. 'It needs a clearer sense of its target market.' It was 'cute and very funny' and with 'a budget low enough to get it off the ground' as he put it.

He seemed like a proper producer; but then again, they all seemed like proper producers, especially the ones that weren't. He told me he had submitted the script to Freddie Highmore's agent already. Freddie had been in some high-profile productions – *Finding Neverland* and *Charlie and the Chocolate Factory* to name a couple. Besides which, he was ranked quite highly at the time on IMDb's scale of bankability and so would be a good fit if it ever got to the point of someone wanting to put money behind it. Freddie's mother ran a casting company in London – ARG, the Artists Rights Group – so that was good, wasn't it? ARG represented quite a few high-profile names, Liam Neeson, Daniel Radcliffe, Alison Steadman. This Gary bloke had an "in" with them, and that was good enough for me.

Another week with no work. That followed the previous week, also without any work. The dent in the equity in the house was getting bigger, but at least we still had equity! Meanwhile, Gary Sinyor got back to me and we spoke again for over an hour. The casting agent, Sue Latimer, mother of Freddie Highmore, liked the script, so now Gary felt a little more like he just might go out on a limb and maybe purchase a little option on *Fizzy*, as he put it. Maybe?

I sent one last email to Mathew Bobbs from Fruit Fly films, who replied:

'I'm actually sitting in an airport waiting to board, hence the early start. Your enjoyable script has been read by all, and sorry, but until I have consensus at this end then it's potentially a waste of your time discussing the project's merits. Let us get back to you formally first, then let's discuss.' And so on in the same noncommittal vein.

Then Gary Sinyor sent me an email outlining his terms. He needed a 12-month exclusive option on the script, with an automatic 12-month extension if there was clear progress towards production. He wanted to be able to rework the script without my input, or else hire someone to do that 'in order to quickly get it into a shape I feel comfortable with'. He assured me that at the very least I would get a shared writing credit, or a based-on-an-idea-by credit, payment from the budget of

2% with a floor of say £20,000 sterling plus a 1% of net profits. Should the option revert, I would have the opportunity to take the project back, with suitable recompense for the writer responsible for the revision. Complicated …

He liked that there were some great set-pieces, '*but a range of opportunities need to be beefed up to make them more credible and funnier. There are also too many fat jokes.*' The email ended by saying he needed to be sure he had the ability to control the movie so that it could get made one way or another. Okay …

So back to the luck of *Fizzy*. I now had two companies interested in *Fizzy*. I ran the risk of choosing the wrong one, Fruit Fly or Magnet.

Each had a similar track record, each wanted an exclusive option, neither wanted to work with the other. Fruit Fly was talking about minimal tweaks to the script, no rewrite, they liked it as it was. Magnet was talking major rewrite and sharing the credit. Sinyor was talking about Freddie Highmore and somewhat realistic goals. Bobbs was talking Richard Curtis, Ricky Gervais, Tom Felton. To me that sounded a ludicrous, unrealistic cast of A-listers that he wanted to get involved. Both also wanted an exclusive twelve-month renewable option, no money involved. What's a girl to do? No buses forever, then two at once; but buses aside I still had no offer of any money or paperwork.

Meanwhile, I had not worked solidly for months. I heard nothing further from either Fruit Fly or Magnet. I felt like I'd spent 2009 running around in circles, though at least I could still run! How things had turned around.

Then a fourteen-page option agreement arrived from Fruit

Fly. Gary also got back to me at the same time, saying he was still interested. But ... *'If the other company are offering commitment, then you may be best advised to go with them, just because I am so busy over the next few weeks. My positive view hasn't changed, I like the project a lot, but with a rival offer, if they are more committed and you think you can work with them, I would consider them seriously. Not trying to talk you or myself out of this, but I am terribly busy.'*

I liked Gary. I pressed him again for the one-page attachment agreement he'd originally promised; it never arrived. So that left me with the contract option from Fruit Fly. I was retracing old ground. A contract but no lawyer.

I rang my old lawyer from a few years ago on Sunset and the company were actually quite nice about it all. I said I needed a contingency deal this time as I was low on funds. They looked at the players involved – including me – and agreed to work for five percent of all the money I potentially stood to make. Well, at the time I was making nothing and I did need a lawyer, so they were welcome to five percent of it. This time I would take that deal!

The law offices were now based in Beverly Hills, they had moved: a new glass-fronted high rises, proper Beverly Hills on Beverly Boulevard and Olympic, somewhat reassuring. I looked up my new attorney on Google and found that, one, he was also Oliver Stone's lawyer and two, he had just competed in the senior Olympics and won a medal for the senior parallel bars and the rings. He could kick my ass if he wanted! The conversations all went well and they promised to look over the agreement and get back to me with a revised draft.

The lawyer came back with a few minor points, which I didn't even look at, and we sent off the revised contract and the deal was done.

One week later, as far as I could tell, *Fizzy* was properly optioned with a contract again. This brought a sense of relief, maybe even achievement. And that again is where we came in. I touched base with Matthew, he said of course, it was great to be on board.

It all sounded very positive. Maybe Fruit Fly could be a good fit after all. Maybe they really did mean to make my film. I bloody well hoped so. They had a couple of pages of changes, most of which I fully agreed with, and we were off to the races again. I revised the script as per the instructions submitted by my new producer, Matthew, and settled back to await further instructions. And in the blink of an eye it was 2010, a whole new year to see if *Fizzy* was going to go anywhere or run out of gas. What were the odds that maybe this would be the year it got made?

CHAPTER 28

In Development …

Fizzy Days was now marked on the Fruit Fly website as "in development" along with several other projects. We were alive again. I had received another contract. If only they were worth the paper they were written on. I had been working with Lance Acord, a director of photography who also did his own commercials. I'd been drawing his storyboards and we had seemed to get on, so I did my usual thing: I thought I might ask him to take a look at my script. Lance was Sophia Coppola's DP. He was the Director of Photography on *Lost in Translation.* That would have been a coup, I thought, to get Lance on board, a real help in raising finances.

Then Fruit Fly cancelled our script-notes meeting for the fourth time in succession; but no worries, as Ed Speleers, the producer at the company, was now here in LA. Ed was also the twenty-one-year-old CEO of Firefly, and the star of the 100-million-dollar dragon flick Eragon and, more recently, *Downton Abbey.* I sent an email offering to meet and he replied that he was a very busy man and would rather meet on Skype the following week when he'd be back in the UK. They'd had the new draft for over a month.

I couldn't believe how hard this all was. I sent twenty script queries for my new pike-fishing script, which I was quite pleased with. I even had some storyboarding work at the Sunset Marquis, the rock 'n' roll hotel and landmark just off Sunset Boulevard, which ranks among hallowed Hollywood hotels with the Chateau Marmont a few blocks away. Then a few days storyboarding in Malibu.

Rob Cohen, the director and producer of *Fast and Furious*, had been involved with several other high-end productions along with the TV series *Miami Vice.* I'd make a mental note to bother my new contact later; perhaps he would be interested in a slow-moped version if the current producers fell through? He wasn't, of course, but you have to keep trying, don't you? That was a little spate of me being busy for a day as paying work had again dried up.

Then Fruit Fly cancelled the next arranged meeting. Again! That was six times in a row and counting. They obviously felt very comfortable with treating our creative partnership this way. We eventually managed a Skype meeting. We thrashed out some notes, some more changes, and I promised to get another revised script back to them within a week. I wasn't doing anything else.

One week later I had what I thought was a good revision and, and fingers crossed, sent it back to no acknowledgement, another tiring delay.

We took a quick family break in Big Bear, our local mountains; snow, cold and skiing. Very winter-like up there; it almost seemed as if Christmas wasn't finished, and it smelled a little stale, like Christmas several months after the event.

I managed to wrangle an interview at 20th Century Fox for a forthcoming feature, *Caesar, Rise of the Planet of the Apes*, to meet the director Rupert Wyatt, who was on his own in what looked to be a pretty empty production office, stabbing away at a laptop. The film was a remake of sorts of *The Planet of the Apes,* a prequel with a modern CGI twist. I couldn't care less; I just wanted to storyboard it for him. I just wanted to storyboard anything at this point. We got on like a house on fire and he hired me on the spot. I had got the job at Fox after all. The production office contacted me the next day. Would I sign a non-disclosure? Sure! Would I read the script? Sure, of course! Would I give them my union details? I was union, right? What was my card number?

I didn't get the job. I wasn't in the ADG Union at that point. It seemed as the recession was biting everyone, they were not about to let me use the 'consultant storyboarder' title when they could give one of their own members a job instead. Bugger.

Meanwhile, Fruit Fly had been quiet for the last few weeks. I wasn't too sure whether the winner we were on to here was actually a winner at all. Nothing had happened in the last four months, so we were nowhere again. And then an email came in from Ed, saying 'Congratulations on the latest draft, very happy with the changes and additions,' which they felt would 'solicit the response we are looking for.' He promised to keep me updated.

Work got sparser. Unfortunately, you can't pay the mortgage with updates, and financially we were getting closer and closer to rock bottom. I went across to Burbank to visit Matt, one of my storyboarding buddies, who'd actually made the transition to director, not that I'm sure he fully embraced it. He was directing movies for the SiFi Channel. I caught him editing a scene of his latest movie, *Morlocks*, in a small nocturnally lit editing suite just across from Warner Brothers. Matt was happily divorced and playing at being a Hollywood geezer. But even Matt, perennially young at heart, seemed a little older; faded like his jeans, like so many Hollywood dreams dreamt by all of us Hollywood geezers. It was such a cliché, but that afternoon it fitted like a glove.

Lunch at the watering hole of Morton's Steakhouse, by NBC, was pleasant enough, all mahogany panelling and filled with the studio people. I admit to being a bit shocked when he ordered sparkling water, as the Matt I knew never drank less than three pints at lunchtime. Still, I guessed he had a film to edit, which was more than I could say for myself. The best he could offer me was six weeks as a second-unit director in Poland, me who had never actually second-unit-ed before. No pay, but as much food and drink as I could force down my throat, which was the kind of package a single, wannabe director might go for, but not for me at that juncture. Matt had mentioned that he might be looking for a project to produce, and as usual I had put together my script package, version seven, passing it to him over lunch and running through the pros of becoming attached to a Mark Millicent project. As we left the restaurant for the car park, the pretty waitress who had served us raced after us, waving the package that Matt had left in the booth where we'd just eaten. Bugger!

'You forgot this.'

Matt smiled and apologized, saying it wasn't intentional.

Jen, one of the reps at Famous Frames, rang me to ask if I would colour or draw in another artist's style. Not my style but his, and seeing as he seemed to draw in a more rudimentary fashion, to put it mildly. I said yes. Then she said, 'It will be for a reduced rate.' OK … 'And you need to prove to them that you can do this.'

I was in no position to turn anything down, but I balked at this and turned it down. One of the youngest actors, who played the part of Titch in the short film we'd made all those years ago, appeared on my Facebook page. Facebook; another thing that hadn't even been invented when I started *Fizzy*, and now it seemed no one could get along without it. Titch, the little thirteen-year-old squeaker, had become a strapping youth who had grown up into a tall, stubble-faced young man and was now playing the role of fully fledged burly adult, judging by his photos posted on his Facebook.

Then some rather ominous news came down the wire. Apparently, Shane Meadows was making a film with a fizzy gang in it. Really? Oh, fucking hell! His vehicle co-ordinators had sent an email to the Fizzy Club, of which I was a member. That's the same Fizzy Club that was going to supply us with bikes … once we were in production. I had received the call for bikes, the same as every other enthusiast, only I was the one supposedly making the movie. The newsflash included the request that 'ideally your fizzy would need to come with a rider who looks sixteen years old' to appear as an extra in the film.

That left me scrambling through the copious folders of old correspondence I had filed away over the years. Warp Films, who were making the Meadows film, had also read my script;

I had sent it to them. There seemed to be something of a similarity; it had Fizzies in it, didn't it? And they were filming the very next day, not on this make-believe day that might never arrive.

I'd heard no more from Fruit Fly, so I was guessing that everything was OK and we were moving along in 'development'. But I also suspected that this was going to be a rerun of Forecast's involvement with me and the BYFA; I even found out from the tabloids that my young producer Ed shares the same birthday as me, only mine was twenty-seven years before his. I wished him a happy birthday, but it made no difference; communication with my producers seemed to have basically dried up. The odd job trickled in. I attended a shoot that I had boarded near Santa Monica airport. Michael Caine was doing an insurance commercial and I thought I would go along and watch the man at work. My storyboards were all up on a board and being ticked off as the sequences were shot. I thought I might meet him to say hello. That's what I had thought … but I just watched from a distance as he did his stuff on a pretty elaborate set that was made up to be a lighthouse. I went home and pondered the next up and coming meeting with my producers.

Yet again I was sitting in the departure lounge at LAX, London-bound (and gagged). *Fizzy* meetings again. Another year, another frustrating and predictable outcome, but maybe this time it would be different. It wasn't on the cards, though, as the last email from Fruit Fly was asking me for a couple of brief synopses for promotional purposes; which begged the question: what had they been using for promotional purposes up to then?

Soho House was again the chosen venue. A beautiful sunny day, rooftop terrace, the dark chimneys of Soho eateries and Centre Point staring down on you. Matthew and Simon, my producers, were shaded under an umbrella table and media deals were in full swing all around. A breeze. I ordered a pint of the finest shandy, best not start off on too strong a libation as deals needed to be done with a clear head and all that. We sat down to talk. At this point Matthew stood up and made his excuses. He had another deal to do and just wanted to meet me to shake my hand then disappear. OK, fair enough. A prior meeting with the Weinsteins, he said, so he "had to dash". I was no Weinstein – frankly, who would want to be now? – so we shook hands and he dashed. That left me and Simon, the younger half of the partnership, to go over *Fizzy*. After a few more pints we got around to the subject of my script, and Simon told me it was already being read by their first choice, Kathy Burke.

Now this struck me as a bit odd and, lubricated with more beers than was probably prudent by now on that warm and sunny afternoon, I made a point of saying so. Kathy Burke as far as I knew was the funny chick off the Harry Enfield show Waynetta Slob; she'd never directed anything before as far as I knew. Simon said she'd directed a short. But, yes, she would be a first-time director. The Matthew conversation I'd had several months earlier had involved Richard Curtis, Ricky Gervais and, yes, Gary Sinyor, who'd directed multimillion-pound movies, and yet they'd told me he was too low-profile. But Simon insisted he could raise financing if Kathy was attached. And what did I know? I just wanted Fizzy made. Kathy was a good actress. I knew she had been in the Gary

Oldman vehicle *Nil by Mouth* and the spy drama *Tinker, Tailor, Soldier, Spy*. She didn't seem an instant choice for *Fizzy Days*, but by now whoever was at the helm was fine by me, just so long as there was a helm to be at! Please, Kathy Burke, say you would like to help make my script your first feature!

CHAPTER 29

C'est la vie

I jumped on the M1, heading up to Cheshire on a hot sunny day. I made a quick detour and visited my Nan in Christ Church cemetery: beech trees, wood pigeons, gold-lettered rows of dark-grey marble headstones denoting a past life. The church that my mother and father had got married in, the one I might have if I'd remained in the "hood"; but of course, I hadn't, so it wasn't. Nan would have been 100 years old if she had still been around. I could talk about anything with Nan. She had listened to Slade music with me. Nan had loaned me the money for my first "proper" motorcycle, a Suzuki GT 250. I wished she was still around. I wished the GT was still around. She had a plot next to Gramps, my granddad, who'd laughed at Laurel and Hardy films with me as he smoked Players unfiltered cigarettes. Always dressed smartly in pressed trousers, shirt and tie. My grandparents' plots were just a few yards from my old school, the comprehensive I'd attended as a kid.

One of the names on another of the stones was David

Rhodes. I had watched David in a school yard fight in 1973 over by the soccer fields. In front of the goal mouth, he had battled it out as a twelve-year old with my pal Willy. David had swallowed his tongue during an epileptic fit one night soon afterwards. He was the first person I remember dying in boyhood, someone I knew, so I guess that's why I remember his name when others have faded. I had the morbid notion that his twelve-year-old bones lay a few feet below my feet in a box beneath the soil. His bones rather than mine, for no other reason than it was his number that was up that day and not mine. All the things that I'd got to do and he hadn't; sombre stuff. Remember the first person from your school who'd died? I'm sure you do, announced at a morning assembly then forgotten by lunchtime.

The churchyard cemetery had expanded over the years since I had left school. It was now home to a lot more residents and butted right up to the school wall. Just for old times' sake, and as the sun was shining, I had a walk around the school grounds, which I seemed to have left as a teenager just moments earlier. I stood where the old school pond had been, now filled in with concrete, just the rough outline of its shape discernible, and the memory of Mr Berry the environmental science teacher's silver shubunkin fish and the koi it used to hold. I peered into some of the classrooms and remembered some of the kids and the teachers: I could hear them.

My time at school was also part of the reason for this trip. It was the first reunion in thirty-three years. I saw my parents; I walked the hills and the Cheshire Sandstone Trail around Beeston on a balmy English afternoon. My parents still lived close by in the market town of Nantwich. I missed home and imagined that one day I would get back here. But things never go quite as you imagine they will, do they?

The school reunion was an event best described as traumatizing. I had talked my brother Paul into attending it with me. Being a couple of years younger, he had less chance of recognizing anyone he'd once known, so the evening was a complete washout for him. The venue was Radway Working Men's Club on a sprawling estate of flat-roofed former council houses. The estate was a place that my parents had lived on and Nan and Gramps had once called home, so I knew it well. The club had snooker tables, Formica furniture, orange plastic chairs, a tiny dancefloor and a bar with a white plastic roll-down security grill. Oh, and a disco ball. Fantastic! Someone had taken the trouble to organize this gathering, so the least we could do as the former class of '77 was attend and fuckin enjoy it!

Time-worn, their joyous teen years well behind them, some a little defeated and tired, best describes the attendees. I so understand now why we use name tags at these things. I was one of these former schoolboys and girls, standing with a name sticker that labelled us as our former selves; people whose races had long since been run. The finishing tape was now firmly in tatters, shredded around blistered feet and swollen ankles. I stood there with them, no better, no different, and thankfully no worse. To begin with, I thought I looked pretty good compared to some of them. I wasn't overweight, I still looked like the sixteen-year-old that left school with all of them in the hot summer of 1977, didn't I? Just with less hair?

Then it occurred to me that maybe I was fooling myself. I was just the same as them, the photographs and the mirrors in the bathroom proved it. I was just as old and bald and fat and finished; well, maybe not as finished and maybe not quite as fat, but everyone thinks they are better than the next guy after a few beers, don't they? We are all just doing what we do, for better or worse, fatter or thinner, faster or slower, more successfully, less successfully. We all get to where we're going in the end. It stands to reason. And the cemetery is where we're all going; we'll all be joining David Rhodes' twelve-year-old bones at some point in the not-too-distant future. Half of us have the same luck, the same opportunities; we either take a chance or we don't. If we choose not to, we can hardly complain that things might have turned out better. It's how we capitalize on any situation, how we deal with situations, both good and bad, how we make our own situations or chances, or don't. Money makes a difference, but you can still be sick or ill, or hit by a truck, or swallow your tongue just the same as anyone else, with the same potential to change those chances as everyone else.

That night I met friends from the past, people who at one time were as close as brothers, now just name tags in the same room for an evening, the same as me. The conversation that sticks in my mind and which probably best sums up my school reunion experience was this one:

'Hey, how are you doing, Steve ? What you up to now, these days?'

A glazed moment of uncomfortable recognition followed as the chap I'd addressed gripped his pint of lager and tried to place my wrinkly face. But he couldn't and gave up trying.

'Nothing,' he sneered. 'It's just a fuckin' shit life, isn't it?'

I'm not sure if he wanted me to agree with him or what. Maybe it is, I thought, but we were all here tonight at this little get-together, this shindig of alumni, to rekindle old friendships and enjoy ourselves and to reminisce on what were, for me, some of the happiest times of my life. I was one of those weirdos who loved school, though I never learnt a damn thing. But learning wasn't high on our list of priorities when I was at school. We wanted to burn and steal stuff, joke around, revel in the odd schoolyard fight, have amorous encounters with young teenage girls' breasts and virginal furry parts, nick bicycles and raise hell like James Bond did. School seemed to interfere with these goals rather than to serve any worthwhile purpose. So school was great for me because we had fun.

Every day was a complete waste of time for us idiots at the back of the class. I guess we, my class mates and I, must have been streamed in the lowest level for a reason, maybe not lack of intelligence but low application being high on the list. Me, Fos, Ginge, Tom and Beaver, along with Les and Little Wills, had not the slightest inclination to learn anything. But I don't think I would have changed a thing, and I'm not sure any of us would. The memories sustain me to this day. What a riot! Setting fire to Ginge's hair in the drama room, swimming in our underwear in the local mere at lunchtime, fighting on the soccer fields while kids formed a circle and chanted "scrap!" The flooding of the new science block, the science lab's mysterious subsequent fire – all fantastic! Predictably, I left school with no qualifications; fuck all, except for 'O' level art. I then had to retake all my exams over the next couple of years. But boy, I still wouldn't change a thing. I loved it.

At the reunion, my peers and I exchanged stories of our fruitless and mercifully brief academic careers, and the generally pointless but fun times we'd had all those years ago.

High on the list of shared memories were the bashings we would get from the brown-suited Mr MacPherson, the deputy headmaster. A sinewy and balding, ginger-haired cross-country runner in his mid-forties; large black-rimmed spectacles. He had a habit of inhaling through his nose with his lips closed, drawing phlegm loudly to his mouth, a sort of snorting, sucking, snoring noise that some people do. I think it's called hocking? Well, he hocked a lot, did "Macky". He also knocked seven shades of shit out of us disruptive little oiks. The headmaster, Mr Andrews, would administer the cane, which was infinitely more desirable than the "slippering" in which Macky had developed a special skill. The cane was easy to survive; just make sure your thumb was tucked beneath your palm and grit your teeth; easy. But a slippering was a whole different ball game. It was something of a rite of passage to be slippered by Macky and not be brought to tears. The first time, I actually remember stupidly and literally asking for it when for some misdemeanour or other I found myself before him in his office. He asked me:

'What do you think I should do with you, Millicent?'

'Slipper me, sir,' was my response. Let's see what all this fuss is about. And with that, I was about to find out. He would take you to the boys' toilets and empty it of any pupils who might be using them. The last boy out he would post outside the door with orders to let no one pass for fear of the same punishment. Telling you that he was going to hurt you so as to gauge your reaction and then beginning the proceedings.

Macky then produced a size ten tennis shoe. In the quietness of the empty bathroom, he would hock loudly and repeatedly to prepare.

'Hold on to the radiator and don't move until I tell you to.'

It was hot, that radiator facing the wall. Pulling your shirt from your trouser top and asking you to unbuckle your belt he then smoothly slipped his hands down the back of your trousers and gently pulled your underwear up and into the cleft of your buttock cheeks, something which today any teacher would have a difficult time explaining, but at the time we didn't think anything of it. We just assumed that this sadistic maniac wanted his full unfettered power to be felt through one layer of clothing rather than two. He then would back up his steps several yards and run full pelt waving the gym shoe like a madman. This he then brought down in an arcing blow on your arse, with all the full force that a fit grown man who loves his work can muster; as hard as he could, and I mean fuckin' hard.

It was so strange the first time. My lips moved uncontrollably on their own, the blood vessels in my arse cheek exploding, as I froze in a state of shock at the pain a seemingly benign piece of gym kit could inflict. And he was going to do this until I cried? As a thirteen-year-old boy, I'd seen sixteen-year-old lads a lot bigger than me red-faced and teary after receiving the slipper.

There was no way I was going to give this twat the satisfaction of tears. Again and again, I looked over my shoulder to see that Macky had gone to the far side of the bathroom and was now running like a berserker at my arse. Again, that weird lip-quivering thing and his frantic, almost manic questioning: 'Are you going to cry?'

I was not going to cry, but I did make a mental note to self; never willingly suggest this punishment again!

'No, sir!' I screamed in reply. I wanted to add the words, 'Fuck you: you ginger haired cunt!' But that sort of bravery only extended to the thoughts inside my head.

There were no tears, though this only served to piss him off more, so he would do it again and again. Hocking between bashing, getting redder and redder at his exertion! The red, green and black state that my arse was left in was a badge of honour, a testament to this sadistic cunt's idea of discipline, a temporary scar to show my mates. It took weeks to disappear and left red thread veins for months. Happy days, school days, far-away days now. Just like a good slippering, a school reunion is not for the faint-hearted.

I could never agree it was shit life because it wasn't and it isn't; just ask David Rhodes. Steve supped more beer and carried on trying to get me to agree what a shit time we'd had, but I really couldn't agree, I had loved it.

I moved on with my beer, but it was sad, as I remembered him as a younger version of the same person, the youth, before he needed a name tag. Obviously, neither of us knew it at the time, but just ten short months on from then he would be dead; an undiagnosed brain tumour or aneurysm, as I found out from his younger brother, who had been my Woolworths shoplifting pal in those formative years long ago. Someone else I now no longer kept in touch with despite him having been the best man at my wedding.

So, shit life or not, at least Steve didn't have to put up with it anymore. I was saddened when I heard the news and remembered a day out I'd had with him and his brother. A day trip as teenagers to Lytham St Annes, the posh part of Blackpool with nicer B&Bs and neat gardens with bright wallflowers and cut lawns with colourful gnomes, fishing in tiny ornamental ponds. Home to George Formby and his little stick of Blackpool rock.

I can so clearly remember hanging around the penny arcade on the old pier, the rattle of the dodgems, the smell of fresh candyfloss. There were all the old school attractions of a northern seaside town's pier to tempt three young lads on a day trip to invest a couple of hours. A typical teenager's day out at the seaside. Donkey rides, Punch and Judy, fish and chips. A lifetime ahead of us, a lifetime to go; a lifetime ago; when he was just a laughing lad not waiting for his cancer or emphysema or aneurysm to put him out of his misery, remove him from this shit life.

Not everyone was a defeated weirdo. Some bright sparks remained, some people who seemed smiley and comfortable with themselves. But as far as I could tell those people were in the conspicuous minority.

I don't think I'll be going to many more reunions any time soon. I'm sure most people enjoyed it. Maybe I did? Maybe I'm the weirdo? But I'll take my chances. I liked school; no, I loved school. I'd prefer to remember my old school pals as they were when we all looked young, because we *were* young, and Slade, Sweet and T. Rex had number ones in the charts, the lads dreamed of marrying a girl like Lynsey de Paul, and the girls were looking for a boy like Donny Osmond. We all had bright and burning futures ahead of us – well, if not burning, at least ready to set fire to!

CHAPTER 30

Moving on

I landed back in the US. I heard the old lady who used to sit by the pier playing scrabble had had a fall while I was away. She didn't recover and was no longer part of the unchanging scenery on my morning run. People had been leaving flowers at the bench where she used to sit. She'd been a fixture at that bench for as long as I could remember living here. It would be strange not to see her with her parasol and her smile and her little box of wooden letters. Catherine Matthews was her name, I later found out; pretty name, pretty lady.

The recession was biting deeper. Everything was getting a little tougher by the week. I hadn't worked since coming back from the UK. But I still had Fruit Fly. But boy, did I need Kathy Burke to rescue me now.

Of course, no one got back to me. Another week passed, then Fruit Fly emailed to say they were giving Kathy Burke another week. Suffice to say she was never heard from again. So, they sent it to another director, Jim Field Smith, who apparently was in LA at that moment, "knee-deep in post-production" on a feature he was making. Where on Earth a guy that busy would have time to read a moped script, I didn't know. Then Edgar Wright's name cropped up and we waited; nothing further was heard. Weeks turned into months, as they do, and there was no work on the horizon or anywhere near it.

The next idea would be to move back to Cheshire in the UK or to down-size here. To that end we started doing up the house and preparing for the huge upheaval that must inevitably come if work didn't pick up before long. Luisa had always helped me with the colour storyboards, but they came in less frequently, so she started looking into shop work as and when it became available. Her watercolour paintings were selling steadily but not enough for us to live on. With no decent income source, we were just not going to be able to keep haemorrhaging the money each month to remain on this side of the pond. Fruit Fly got back to me saying that they had sent the script out to three directors since it was first placed with them nearly a year earlier; three in a year! In fact, they were making the kind of progress I had made with Forecast, such as it had been, look positively fantastic.

Fruit Fly then wrote to say, 'Kirk Jones is currently in possession of the script.' That's Kirk "just did a film with De Niro" Jones. Wow. I had worked with Kirk on a commercial months before.

Curiosity was getting the better of me. Had they sent it to Kirk Jones or not?

One way to find out. I rang Tomboy Films, spoke to Kirk's producer, Glynis. I asked about prospective up and coming commercial storyboard work that I might be considered for as I had worked with Kirk before, then segued gently into the question of whether Kirk had maybe had time to look at my project. She told me she had absolutely no recollection of Kirk being sent the script, but I could ask him myself as he was in the office. I talked to Kirk. He remembered me, and said that from what I'd told him it really was a little writer/director passion project like his *Ned Devine*, and that no one was going to be more invested in it than me. Because of the small budget it would be hard to get a more high-profile director to do it. 'Go for it yourself' was his advice.

So there we were, red flags raised and billowing in the wind. How should I best approach this one? Again, I didn't want to piss them off. I was about to lose that all-important contract, the contract that gave me nothing but which I'd coveted so madly. I saw the partnership of Millicent and Fruit Fly heading in the same direction as Millicent and Forecast, or Millicent and the BYFA, or Marathon, etc … Bugger! When will it begin? When will it end? I questioned Matthew on this contradictory situation. I think he was pissed off that I had the temerity to inject myself into the conversation at all as he replied:

Dear Mark,
I'm sorry to report that Fruit Fly will NOT be pursuing FIZZY DAYS any further and will not be seeking another year of the option.

Thank you for the opportunity to work on your project for the last year, and we sincerely wish you all the very best finding a home for it elsewhere.

All best
Matthew

* * *

So square one had just punched me in the face again. How many places were left on the planet that I could approach? I was left with a flight booked to England and not really a whole load of reasons to go. I had planned to sit down and have a chat with my producers again. I took a motorcycle ride along the coast road, taking a moment to stop at the lookout over LAX. There is a high bluff that at some time was probably a sand dune, where you can watch the planes one after another taking off for God knows where. It looks over Imperial Highway on to runway three and puts you level with the ascending aircraft at around 300 feet. As the latest Airbus 300 noisily flew by my face I thought to myself: I may have to stop all this nonsense soon.

At least I had another day of gainful employment: a Christmas commercial, working out of a casting house in Hollywood in ninety-degree blazing sunshine. If the collective power of the brightness of the smiles on display could have been harnessed, it might have powered a small city block. What a collection of desperate, good-looking humanity, all hankering for the same as me, that bit of the Hollywood dream: the vegetarian producer, the moody director, the young and pushy PA making countless trips to Starbucks for a double autoimmune latte with almond-milk and extra shots.

I was locked in a room storyboarding, watching all the call-backs re-audition through the monitor feed; each one of them giving their all as they eagerly announced their names and interests: 'I love hiking, dogs and the great outdoors.' 'Next!' All of them looking to be cast for a tiny part in a cable commercial, every one of them brilliant and beautiful. I kept wandering out amongst the throng to take a break from storyboarding what they were to do in front of the camera. Every time, they looked up expectantly thinking that I was part of the team that might help them make the leap to stardom. I gave them the look that I hoped would disabuse them of that idea. Sorry, I'm just a nobody like you, but thanks for the attention. I also love hiking, dogs and the great outdoors …

I did still have great confidence that by the end of the year we would be looking at another interested party, maybe even production. The end of another year was nearly upon us. I was hoping to have found another home for *Fizzy* by Christmas. I had sent it to several companies, one called Shite House Films, which had shades of Fruit Fly. They sent me a couple of lines expressing interest after reading the script.

I sent out my short script for *Screech* with a few storyboards and got a few responses. They loved my artwork and were looking forward to reading the script, etc. Of course, I heard nothing more from most of them after the first response. Meanwhile, Alex from Shite House Films got back to me, sounding as if he might even be keen on *Fizzy*, praising the 'humour and the flavour' as well as 'an honesty and innocence (despite all the larceny)', as he put it. So he'd not only read it but asked me to put together some more info, which he would read over the weekend, and then, 'Let's chat next week.' Cheers, mate!

Alex cancelled the chat – no surprise – though eventually we did speak, and he confirmed that he liked *Fizzy* enough to be getting a contract from his company to me after Christmas.

A contract, eh? Hmm. So, as we stood at the end of the year, I had a couple of irons back in the fire. Better than a few weeks earlier.

But just when things were looking up, my young daughter was admitted to hospital with a suspected, then confirmed, ruptured appendix. We were all relieved when the operation went well, and she looked like being discharged home on Christmas Eve, but I was dreading the bill. It turned out to be $51,800 for three nights in hospital, so our planned trip to Yosemite looked medically doubtful. The insurance-based healthcare system here stinks on ice. Of course, we only pay a percentage of that, along with the deductible, but it still runs to thousands of dollars. Ultimately, she more than fully recovered, but the bank account was now on serious life support.

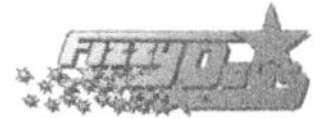

CHAPTER 31

Déjà Vu

The New Year started with two of my scripts hopefully moving forward. Alex from Shite House wanted to make our film! *Fizzy*! He even managed to send a contract, and I sent it back with my amendments. I didn't bother with a lawyer. What was the point? Honestly, it all sounded very grand, but by now I knew it meant nothing. Alex would use very grand financial terms in the same sentences as three million dollars. We were hooked!

If he could really lay his mitts on three million dollars, that gave me the opportunity to go back to Sue Latimer at ARG to see if she would be up for reading the script again. She got back to me, inviting me to send the updated material so she could take another look. She'd liked it before, so I hoped she would like it again. And what do you know, she did! This top London casting agency was on board again, with its stable of talent.

I did now have another new contract. ARG were actually London talent agents rather than casting agents. They were looking for us to furnish them with contracts, which was something we weren't yet able to do. They were looking for money for their clients, the actors, and of course we had nothing for the likes of the people they had put forward to use; all great actors, but not possible within our present budget of nothing. Bernard Hill and Alison Steadman and John Hannah would have to wait. Alex, our "top-notch" producer, was several months in and looking a little dodgy at this point; he had done nothing. We were still looking for money to finance *Fizzy* and again we were coming up with nothing.

We so wanted Alex to be the business, the goods, the real McCoy, but was he going to fill that vacancy or not? He kept heading all his emails with, 'Hey, mates,' but I was feeling as I did with everyone else who talks the talk like he does. Recently, some of Riggy's outreaches had started to get some momentum going with more people who seemed genuinely interested in the project. They wanted to speak to our "man at the top" about this finance plan of his. But as time passed, it appeared from his studied indifference that Alex was not that keen on talking to them.

I had an acquaintance at a junior school another lifetime ago; he lived on the Radway estate. He bought my friendship with an imaginary motorbike using a similar technique. A particularly unpleasant boy; Lionel. We stomached him for a week or so in our gang of ten-year-olds, the spurious friendship based on the hope we might ride his invisible motorbike that he didn't have because it didn't exist. Lionel kept his imaginary motorbike in his coal shed. In exchange, he was in our gang. The ruse continued to work as long as he kept dangling this invisible old motorbike that he had been given by his dad and would let us ride if he could just find the key to the coal shed door. Like the coal shed that held no motorbike, I think Alex's finance plan might have been distinctly lacking in funds, and he had also woefully mislaid the key. But we were more than happy to let him play with us if he let us use the promise of his invisible finance plan!

Riggy had sent all of the project information out, and several people had come back at least with a willingness to take a look at *Fizzy*. Maybe 2011 was going to be the year.

Alex sounded solidly committed, and mentioned he had access to a hedge fund. Wow! What the fuck was a hedge fund? It sure sounded pretty grand. Both Riggy and I did the best we could to sound convinced by that. He used words like 'redacted' and 'tranches' and 'recoupment', territories and hard and soft money … and I think we succeeded in talking ourselves into some kind of warm, fuzzy, fizzy "we can do it" feeling by the end of it. We agreed to try and find anyone else who might be interested; producers, sales, talent and crew. A few weeks passed, and Riggy must have forwarded to Alex well over a dozen very promising emails from various UK film people – financiers, distributors and sales agents – all asking for more info about our current project and its state of finance. From Alex there came only a deafening silence; no budget or plan or ideas or anything at all. The shed remained locked, the invisible engine of the invisible motorbike unheard and unseen.

I worked with Lance Acord again on some Lincoln car commercials. I wonder how many thousands of these thirty-second TV ads I had yet to work on and how many thousands I had drawn up to that point? Lance asked me how my film was going, I told him no change except for new producers, though "producer" would be more correct; even more correct would be "another producer who isn't producing anything". But seeing as I seemed to be in constant resurrection mode, I thought I would try and get my short film *Hell's Angel* going again, this time by myself. I would produce and direct it; wouldn't cost more than a couple of grand, and it would set me up for the task of directing *Fizzy* in a few months when the finance came through from Alex. But by year's end, Alex was starting to become a real thorn. A case of déjà vu!

We needed him to follow up after our initial pitch, a kind of one-two punch. He replied insisting that he had been following up the contacts he'd been sent, but he was, as he put it, "a busy man" – too busy to have achieved anything. He was jolly well not going to let us ride his invisible motorbike if we didn't watch it!

Of course, as I found out later when I asked them directly, he had in reality contacted none of the names we had supplied. Nobody had had a follow-up email despite Alex's affirmation to the contrary. He had done nothing, bugger all, nada, zip. What is it that makes grown adults act this way as soon as you mention the word "movie"?

He kept up the pretence for a few more weeks. I called him and left a message. He replied with what was the closest to honesty we came; in the email he called it "full disclosure". He wanted to come clean. Apparently, the hedge-fund finance that had generated some much-needed confidence among various people, not least me and Riggy, could not be counted on. He had misread the signs. The deals were off but he was still hopeful. So much for the invisible motorbike! Someone had dynamited his coal shed. Our man couldn't get the money now from his DCES hedge-fund, hard money soft money pool.

'Oh really …'

Give us the key to your coal shed, give it to us now, you bastard!

Alex blamed his inaction and confusion on his internet server, and an accident with a wild deer that he'd had while driving. He used his big financial words again and also talked about finding several more million in another secret coal shed, easy as that; recoupment this, redacted that, executive summary et al.

So, as expected, Alex eventually denied that he had ever said anything of the sort with regard to financing *Fizzy Days*. I had it all wrong. I must have misunderstood what he'd written, even concrete things like dates facts and figures and contracts. So ultimately, after another two years, he had brought nothing to the table; the same as everyone else we had spoken to or dealt with throughout this whole sorry saga. I have no idea why I might have expected otherwise. He talked the talk and could write a good letter, and we were very good "mates". But talk is really just that – talk. So as usual we were in exactly the same place. Well, not quite the same. From what I could gather, he had used the contacts we'd provided him for *Fizzy* to submit another of his projects for consideration instead. Gotta love these people! Our partnership with Alex ceased.

CHAPTER 32

Buggery Skullduggery

Would *Fizzy Days* ever make it to the big screen? I didn't know anymore, although perseverance pays off in the end, right? With this thought in mind I banged out several more queries, a bit more carpet-bombing along with a few well-researched and well-aimed shots at some genuine players. Maybe someone would be interested this time? Just one more go.

A few years had passed and I had somehow rekindled my connection with Françoise, the lady who was to have produced my film, *Hell's Angel*. She was going to be my new "script agent". We met in the afternoon for coffee at a little patisserie-come-coffee-shop off La Brea in Hollywood. I don't know how or why Françoise had become my literary agent. I didn't have an agent for scripts or writing; I had one for storyboards. But what harm could it do? I sipped my coffee and made small talk. Her Afro had grown in much more fully by now and she cut quite a striking figure, in her tight jeans and knee-high boots, looking like a scene-stealing extra from *Foxy Brown*. I thought that, seeing as we were getting on a more friendly footing, I'd ask her about her day, what she did to occupy it.

'I do a lot of therapy.'

'You do, really?'

'Yes, I was a bit suicidal.'

'Oh …'

'I guess I can tell you now, I'm bipolar.'

'Really?'

'I was diagnosed, so most of the time I'm in therapy, it's what I do with my time and my money.'

It'd be nice to think my new agent was out doing deals and talking scripts and finance and such; but no, this is LA.

'Bipolar? Wow, how did that manifest itself?'

'It was the alcohol addiction that brought it to the forefront. The alcohol, and also the drug problem.'

'Yes, I guess that would … er … do it.'

'Yes,' she smiled sweetly.

Oh boy, and she was now my script manager!

Cuckoo …

One of the more recent outreaches came back with a positive response, a company called Grand Pictures. They were based in Ireland, had actually made movies and said they would like a little more info, which I duly sent them. Ireland was offering tax incentives to people who filmed there. Maybe we could film there, and Ailish confirmed that Ireland could indeed double for Lancashire, for sure, and with a very tasty 28% tax credit to film there on offer as well. She said she would read the script that afternoon. She had just helped produce the Andy Serkis vehicle, *Death of a Superhero.*

A long week later, Grand Pictures Ireland rejected *Fizzy.* It really was a last-ditch attempt but it would have been fitting, as the Grand was also where we came in, where the romance of the movies first swept me up in its cruel and tender arms.

The next Tuesday morning my leg gave way. I was out jogging on the Strand in a losing battle to keep fit. One moment cool and looking good, listening to Sting belt out “Roxanne” through the earphones; the next sprawled on the concrete pavement with torn ligaments, yelping like a little girl asking to use a passer-by’s phone. My leg was put in a full leg cast, all very immobile, but I guess it could have been worse. The bank account took another hit.

* * *

I was able to shoot my short film, *Hell’s Angel*, in the Santa Monica Mountains. The raw footage was looking good and the performances from my two lead actors worked. We had overcome the shortcomings of my replacement badass biker actor not having any idea how to ride a motorbike. He had originally convinced me to cast him in the role because he had ‘grown up on motorcycling’. A massive fabrication. I had watched his eyes glaze over and his subsequent slump to the ground beneath the stalled and heavy Harley Davidson we had given him to ride. He couldn’t have ridden a motorcycle if his life had depended upon it.

But with the canny use of green screen, leaf blowers for the close-ups and a friend standing in with a long-haired wig for the long shots, it got made. The motorcycle scenes got filmed – again, hanging out of the back of a minivan whilst traversing Tuna Canyon in the Santa Monica Mountains. Things could be worse! It got finished. It got into several local festivals in and around LA. Even won the odd award.

I thought that now would be the time to stop with *Fizzy*. When a couple can't conceive, eventually they "let it go" and then hope maybe a baby will come along on its own without really trying. No more fuss and no more worries. No more pain. Time continued to pass, as it does. It was another January, another year had come and gone, so like a man on crack I sent out a load more queries. Might as well start the year as you mean to go on. I began to think that this was the year we would get things done. I just had the feeling, that's all; I had it every year. I had no work except the prospect of another pizza commercial soon. But don't ask me why I just thought this year was the one.

Another London company LadyBeard Pictures (not the real name), got in touch. They said they loved the script of *Fizzy Days*, and a week later, after laying out their terms, I got – wait for it – another contract, another option. I showed it to Riggy. It looked benign enough and at only one page I thought, fuck it, I'll just sign it again without an attorney. It was only one page after all.

One month later we had lots of budgets and schedules and breakdowns. All the right noises that people in the movies make when they're actually doing something. I had spoken several times to Latifa, the new "producer". Some casting companies had even sent headshots and ideas, and we were also getting offers from prospective crew – cameramen, grips, gaffers – so it seemed my chick was still alive.

A casting page was added to Facebook and people could download sample pages of the script to read from as audition pieces. Kenneth Branagh's agent read the script and forwarded it to him. Seriously. We were told that now and then he did do small parts in small films to support the local British indie scene, even though I felt more "outie" than indie at this point. His agent got back to us and said they would see if they could make it work. He had to do a $100-million-dollar Jack Ryan studio movie, and we didn't even have a hundred quid in finance yet. But Wow! We sent the script to Peter Kaye again and Peter said no again. Disappointingly, Noddy Holder came back to us and said no too. Noddy Holder, boyhood hero and lead singer of Slade, whose songs were to populate our proposed movie soundtrack! I'd even had a "Please have a word with your dad," conversation with his daughter Charisse at Granada studios; not that I was stalking anyone – it was a chance meeting at Granada, honest! How fulfilling that would have been to have the great man from the great rock combo from Wolverhampton driving the tractor and playing the part of a grizzled, disgruntled farmer from hell in our production!

There were lots more no's to come. The casting page had been up three weeks and already had a few hundred members, though just a dozen people had posted auditions. Several months went by. We worked furiously on pre-production. There was no cast as yet, no money; but still, this was way more progress than anyone else had made to date. As I had a few air miles racked up, I nipped home for a meeting to have a chat and get the ball rolling. Always worked before!

The new producer crafted a letter to Sir Ian McKellen. It laid the deal out nicely, and Riggy added a reminder that Sir Ian had contacted him before in support of a short film he was making about homophobia a few years back. But Sir Ian said no, then James May said no; he had showcased a fizzy in a Top Gear article, having owned one himself as a youth. Again it was that running-in-treacle type of feeling, as if I was up to my boots in it.

By now, my short *Hell's Angel* had got into a few more film festivals. I had a few laurels to add to the posters and DVD cases. It had been an arduous task from start to finish; but that's another story! In fact, it's a bloody miracle it got finished at all. The editing process was painful. I could afford a thousand dollars, but that amount does not buy a top-notch editor, so it was rushed and quickly finished and the best I could do. But at least it got finished, and like I said earlier finishing a short film is no mean feat. *Hell's Angel* was a good distraction for me as work had predictably been dead again for weeks. Scary dead.

Around that time, a commotion on our street one night brought me and all the neighbours out to see what was going on. A lot of blue and red flashing lights. It turned out the occupant two doors down had unloaded a gun into his mouth several nights earlier. He'd apparently left instructions as to what the finder of his body might do about his financial affairs on a series of post-it notes on the wall behind him. It'd been several days before he was found and then only because of the smell. A hazmat team went in and began the clean-up. But this rather disturbing occurrence was soon dispelled by some fantastic *Fizzy* news: Mr Ewan McGregor said he could well be on board. He loved it. It was the best chance we'd ever had, because Ewan was a motorcycle buff too, whose involvement would hugely raise our profile and the chance of raising some proper money. He'd been sent the script and apparently, he liked it and was seriously considering the project. His part would be four days' work playing the supermarket manager. We could certainly raise the money now, if he was attached. Fingers crossed. Things were actually looking up!

Helen Flanagan said yes for a non-speaking role in *Fizzy*. I was told she was a busty bird from the soap *Coronation Street* and subsequently a celebrity reality-TV contestant on *I'm A Celebrity Get Me Out of Here*. On a slightly less encouraging note, Ewan McGregor's agent got back: he loved the project and would have loved to do it but couldn't fit the dates into his schedule. He wishes us the best of luck … Bugger.

One last trip to the UK would sort it all out: lunch at Kettner's, an old-school London eatery I'd visited many times in my previous life, a white-tablecloth Soho establishment and a warm and comfy place to shelter from the rain. I had a sort of disenfranchised feeling as I didn't live there anymore, and walking the streets of a wet and dreary Soho in late November only seemed to add to it. It was early morning, and with a little time to kill before my meeting, I walked down Baker Street across Manchester Square, past Bond Street and through Soho and Chinatown to the National Gallery, whose doors weren't due to open until 10 am. So I headed off across Trafalgar Square and down Whitehall to the Thames. By then I was soaked to the skin, and the dankness of the grey early morning was dampening my bones. I walked back to the National Gallery smiling. It was striking and sombre how many images there are where some Maximilian or other is being shot, or a Lady Jane Grey is having her head cut off, or a Saint Sebastian is pin-cushioned with arrows and hanging from a cross staring back at me. I know how they feel! Morbid stuff. The quiet hallowed halls allowed time for me to dry and get my mind in a good place ahead of the meeting. I had a quick pint at the Dog and Duck then headed off for Kettner's.

Latifa, our new "can do" producer arrived. She was punctual, dark, attractive, early forties, perhaps ethnically Middle Eastern. We introduced ourselves, then sat down to lunch. We shared our experiences in the movie-making world before getting down to how to move along with *Fizzy*. I was more than impressed with her work on it so far and the momentum she seemed to have injected. Even if there was nothing concrete yet, she'd made more effort than any of the other collaborators and producers I'd been involved with previously. She seemed to do stuff, not least of which was the budget and constantly updated schedules. She asked if I would be prepared to go to Berlin to support *Fizzy*. I said, 'Of course, I'll get my coat,' though sadly that would be the last I heard of this idea.

Another Christmas came and went and we still didn't have a cast. Still, as 2013 approached, I was quietly confident that this could be the year. Just like last year! But the lull continued, with no forward momentum as we headed into March and the Oscars again.

It was around this time that a friend passed me the name and contact details of a Mr Nick Yarris. My friend told me Nick had a story to tell. He was a former lifer and convicted killer who continued to protest his innocence and after twenty-two years on Death Row had been exonerated and released. Wow! Apparently, he needed a writer in the US to help him get his story out. He was at the time living in the UK and his story had been heavily featured in the British press. I spoke to him, and he was somewhat intense; I guess twenty-two years in solitary confinement on Death Row does that to you. He wanted to get his story of wrongful conviction and incarceration up on the big screen. He said I was more than welcome to take up the challenge of getting his tale told and out there. He sent me an email of several thousand words asking me to collaborate on a script based on his book *Seven Days to Live*. This was my chance to get something off the ground! He sent me a few notes and I wrote a screenplay over several months as it was an opportunity not to be missed, or so I thought.

It took me a few months just to digest the stacks of legal material and wade through his book and numerous news articles. I didn't know of many people who had had to endure such hardship, so this story should've kicked doors down on its own without me even raising a sweat. I worked on it all told for over a year, taking it to pitch meetings and refining the script. All of which was a complete waste of time, as Nick moved back to the US and ditched me almost as soon as he got off the plane. He moved to Long Beach where I met him and his very young wife. He loved the script, but didn't see any reason not to now try and sell it himself and sell his story alone.

'Thanks for all your work, Mark, but I really don't need you now.'

'Oh … bugger.'

I had of course expected this outcome. We had a contract; it was just for a year initially so we were done. Again, there was little I could do. To be honest I had found it compelling to talk to someone who had managed to escape from a US high security prison, been on America's most wanted list, had their teeth knocked out on a daily basis, and was incarcerated in the next cell to Ted Bundy. An interesting if somewhat strange man.

I heard he even went so far as to wear a sandwich board outside Warner Brothers Studios in Burbank advertising his movie worthy plight. I again regret I didn't get a lawyer on our handwritten contract. It was another bad idea. But my experience with lawyers and contacts by then was; well, y' know!

At least Helen Flanagan had agreed to be in our movie. A publicity shoot was undertaken, girl and bike sort of thing, which seemed to go very well. Helen and our little film got national coverage across the UK. It seemed she was a popular girl. I had promised the shoot to a London rock photographer friend of mine, but I wasn't organizing it, so I wasn't in a position to argue – my position being some 5000 miles away. I got a mention as a by-line in the Daily Mail and the Daily Mirror beneath a photo of the hot blonde temptress from *Coronation Street*, pouting and smouldering as she straddled a shiny popsicle-purple fizzy. In fact, we made the national press several times over; the Sun, the Daily Mail and several UK publications all ran the pictures. Things were moving. Hot Helen and her new movie, *Fizzy Days*. Though as ever, there were still a few chinks in the armour. The shoot, we were told, had been a great financial success. National papers had paid for the images and ran articles about our project. How much of a financial success we were not told, as apparently it was nothing to do with either me or Riggy.

Not that we were looking for any money, but the very fact we had our faces slapped like naughty schoolboys for having the temerity to ask did rather take us aback. It was clear that egos would need to be massaged to maintain any sort of relationship, and already the word "relationship" was beginning to ring a bit hollow. Past experience told me this wasn't going to work.

Latifa's manner became increasingly jarring and abrasive. She took to riding a broomstick, cackling loudly, while dressed all in black with a pointy hat and a cat called Pyewacket riding pillion. At least I thought she did. Our working relationship disintegrated.

I got a new attorney, Dean. I hoped that Dean would work out that we were not chained to this awful arrangement, as *Fizzy* would be pretty much dead if we were. I asked for his assessment of the one-page contract that we or rather I had signed fourteen months earlier, which I hoped had now run its course. It hadn't. We were chained for two years. Damn! By this point it had all gone pear-shaped again. We were soon only talking via the lawyer, which was a bit odd for a team supposedly making a movie. Two more years had passed, again going nowhere!

Then it went from bad to worse; my head producer fired Riggy from the project. Even my lawyer, Dean, seemed afraid of her at this point. Her manner and tone left me in no doubt that at the first opportunity she would do her damnedest to remove me from "her" project. Riggy was obviously upset that this was even possible. Dean worked in a big smoked-glass office on Beverly Drive in Beverly Hills, so I was trusting that he didn't get there by accident. He kept telling me that things would be fine. Things had a habit of going from fine to crap very quickly!

Then I too was fired from *Fizzy*, which I had kind of expected. It seemed that because I was "in collusion" with Riggy, my fellow co-producer, that ruled both of us out of further work on *Fizzy*. It didn't seem to matter to Dean; he only got paid if the movie got made. So at this point my script had been hijacked by a woman who thought it was absolutely none of my business. I was no longer a part of *Fizzy Days* and neither was Riggy, while she had full control, and apparently the contract gave her control for two years. Bugger.

For respite from these shenanigans, I attended a script speed-pitch-fest in Burbank to pitch *Screech* with lots of other desperate wannabe characters all looking to make their mark in Hollywood and find homes for their projects. It was like speed-dating hell; five minutes to give it your best sell to attending producers and see if they are interested in your fantastic idea for a screenplay. In reality, those behind the desks that you are pitching to are as desperate and useless as you are and have as much chance of making a movie as your Auntie Carol!

Somewhat frustrating, but wholly predictable: for weeks after the firing and hijacking I heard nothing from my "producer". I could do nothing more than wait as I no longer had control over my property for reasons that were still unclear. Then, one evening, I found she had deleted our access to the project folder and removed it and all files from the dropbox, thus in effect absconding with several years' worth of work. She no longer responded to any communication, but my attorney said we must honour the "spirit of the agreement" I had so foolishly signed in the hope she would deliver for us all. I set up another appointment with another attorney as it really seemed that Dean was incapable of taking any stand against this woman other than to let her have whatever control over the project she wanted. It kind of stuck in the craw that I was now having to pay someone else to remove her, but nothing surprised me at this point!

So not only could I do nothing with my script until she said so, I was left with the feeling she would queer any deal that was even half-secured. The lesson is never sign anything without an attorney taking a look, no matter how trivial the agreement or expensive the attorney. If only I had stuck to that idea!

Dean kept assuring me that she was "very credible", as he put it. She had threatened to "take him to the mattresses" over this, a term I had never heard previously, but that was obviously somewhere he didn't want to go. It seemed like I was back to square one once again, where we came in, only going backward.

Another Christmas approached. I had just finished work storyboarding a movie gig, *Ouija*, that I had managed to secure. It would see us through for now: five million dollars' worth of indie feature, first-time directing team Juliet Snowden and Stiles White looking to make their way in a career that few are ever lucky enough to try. I hoped it all ran smoother for them than it had for me. For so long I had looked for someone to help make my film. It seemed odd to be so passionate about wanting to get rid of someone who had the same stated goals, someone who at first we'd been excited to have on our team. What we hadn't expected was that she would act like a psychotic cuckoo, expelling first Riggy and then me from the project. And then the utter stupidity of signing an undated and oh-so-innocent-looking one-page agreement kept coming back and slapping me round the face like Moe giving Curly a "what-for" in a Three Stooges short.

To make matters worse, either Dean was avoiding me or I had genuinely used up my contingency goodwill on this woman and her contract. He stopped answering my emails and was no longer available to take calls. Several months and another round of Oscars passed.

I would get occasional emails from the cast and crew of *Fizzy* the short, mentioning that it had been many years since we'd made the thirty-minute promo. How was the feature coming along, they wondered? Fine. Just fine.

The year sort of went along like this and the contract ran its two years and nothing came of it. It finally reverted back to me. I sent it out again.

I was offered another option from a company called One Eyed Dog Films. I was getting very wary of contracts; I didn't like the look of it so I didn't sign it. There was no money on offer again. Dean let me know he was no longer willing to work on contingency as my entertainment attorney after the last shenanigans with Latifa, and to be honest I didn't blame him. I was in my eleventh year of trying to get this done and it looked like placing *Fizzy* somewhere before yet another Christmas was just not going to happen.

Mitch, my storyboard agent, died on Christmas Day. Jerry, my "wuda-cuda-shuda" Scottish buddy from the King's Head, died a few weeks after. No more ribs, beer and advice from him; he had no family, he had no money, he has no grave. Nobody claimed his body and I think his ashes were scattered on a Friday with thirty or forty others in an unmarked area within a cemetery in Chatsworth near the 405 freeway. LA and the US and the Hollywood dream hadn't really worked for the smiley curly-haired Glaswegian.

As time goes by, so many of the people I'd written about in the process of trying to make this happen seem to have shuffled off this mortal coil. Hardly surprising; I guess that's a measure of how long it's been. Well over a dozen years and still essentially no closer than I was at the start! But at least I had another meeting soon with a lady called Sara. She liked the script …

CHAPTER 33

Playing Soldiers

It was a new year, 2015, and this would be the one. I was on a roll again, this time with Sara at Toy Soldier Films. She liked the script and according to her IMDb profile she had already produced a couple of films in the UK. One of the features Sara had her name on was voted a top UK indie film of 2011 and even got a full theatrical release. I introduced her to Riggy and we all got on like a house on fire, so it was off to the races we go again. We had reconnected with ARG and had some letters of intent from proper actors; nothing for the lead roles, but it was beginning to look like a movie production … again.

In the blink of an eye, Sara threw together another set of budgets and schedules for *Fizzy* and without missing a beat took several meetings. There was no talk of a contract this time, but who cared? Not me.

It all started to move rather quickly. We pulled together as strong a promotional package as we could muster and out into the world it went. Might this finally be the one? We didn't have any meaningful finance ideas yet. Sara's emails came thick and fast. Pretty soon we had some splendid news: *Fizzy* had garnered an offer of sales by not one London company but two. The first came with a percentage of sales guaranteed, which apparently is called a minimum guarantee (MG), basically a figure against which we could borrow against projected sales, and wait for it … the budget being set at around two million, the MG was £300,000 pounds. I was not a hundred percent sure how this worked, but the sales "contract" had these figures and global projected sales worldwide and recoupment for the monies likely to be expected with *Fizzy Days* the motion picture! Get it? This was fantastic news … The contract looked very legit, several pages of legalese and figures that ultimately translated to an offer of funding. I thought.

Kaleidoscope had been the sales agent for many successful UK films and had a strong standing and reputation in the UK film industry. They liked my previous short films and would love to see what we might do with a longer format. For the next few months, we were sustained by the thrilling belief that, yes, we were moving to places hitherto untrod by *Fizzy*. We sent off a package to the BFI and even enrolled in the EIS tax schemes as we trundled ahead; but still we had no solid finance behind us; just another contract, none of this had worked too well up to now. The *Fizzy* fan club was behind us and chatter began on the web and in the motorcycle world. Magazines and internet sites began to carry articles.

We had a Twitter account and a Facebook page, and some national newspapers – the Sun, the Daily Mirror, the Guardian and others – had now reprised their interest, running features on us and the proposed movie, *Fizzy Days*! James May of *Top*

Gear fame, who had had a fizzy himself back in the 1970s, declined our offer of a cameo role but ran a much-read article in Top Gear magazine about the Fizzy or the Yamaha FSIE, though there were still no actual solid ideas for finance. This was really affecting any logical move forward, as without it we could not issue any serious promissory notes to actors. I met with Jeremy Zimmermann Casting in Covent Garden; they cast for all the high-profile UK films. I was back in London taking meetings all over town. All the copyright owners who would need to be approached for music licences for the soundtrack were outlined. We were wined and dined at the Chiltern Firehouse restaurant, by the licensing company; superb treatment. It seemed like it was really happening! People were actually showing interest in *Fizzy Days* the proposed motion picture, my project, our project, our film.

In a proactive move, we were now going to do the thing that I really hadn't wanted to do with *Fizzy*: embark upon a crowdfunding campaign to see if we couldn't get a few quid to add to the sales offer, which actually translated to almost half a million dollars of the proposed two-million-pound budget. We broadcast the fact; we shouted it on Facebook, Instagram and Twitter. At first, we thought of setting a realistic goal. Somehow that got changed and we were looking for £500,000 on the crowdfunding site Indiegogo. Half a million quid; not much at all in the world of film-making. But we didn't have to stop at that figure. We could just carry on as the funds poured in, right? Not sure which part of Planet Cuckoo this idea had come from, but current outreaches were not presenting any solid funds at present, so the consensus was we might as well have a go. After all, what harm could it do?

I could hardly say no, seeing as it was my film, and in theory it was a positive move. I had little to lose and lots to gain. I was doubly reassured on seeing the groovy informative music-laden campaign. It featured clips from the short and of course my smiling self as the "can-do" director confidently espousing the virtues of backing the proposed movie. It featured all that '70s glam music that just makes you smile and tap your feet. I got Mike, my DP cameraman pal, who had recently helped me shoot a small film about a dragonfly at the lake in Malibu, to record my film pitch. Riggy duly edited it all into shape, complete with music, stills, clips and me.

It looked great. It looked very polished and backable. I'd back it! We were looking for a total budget of two million quid, so a cool half a million would be a helpful down payment. Writing this figure down now seems, well, a little optimistic. The campaign, coupled with the MG, the EIS schemes and the BFI application, was bound to see us through. With great enthusiasm the script was submitted to several more casting companies; we seemed very confident that we could raise the money. I was informed that there had been lots of dinners and drinks with prospective investors, who were a shoe-in to contribute. We had opened another *Fizzy Days* bank account, so all was looking good to receive the expected crowd funding cash influx about to pour into it. Very Good!

Three, two, one … We launched the crowdfunding with an internet fanfare and several press releases in national publications. The Daily Mirror ran another feature on us, and so did the Guardian newspaper. We sat back to await the torrent of funds for our efforts. The crowdfunding did its thing for one month. After all the donations were tallied and committed monies counted, pledges logged and offers computed: the total funding raised was just £498,500 short of our goal of £500,000.

Yup, an absolute disaster. We'd raised 1500 quid! It was a winding gut punch to the stomach. My sceptical reluctance to go down this route seemed to have been proved well founded. People had seemed keen, *Fizzy* certainly had fans, they loved the comic strip, they loved the short promo, they loved their own fizzies; but sadly, save for a few, not enough to donate any money to the movie project. Times were tough, so who could blame them? Conversely, we did now have dates for rehearsals and shooting, we had dates for postproduction, and we had actors tentatively attached. We were talking about a serious production; organizing a second-unit team, the amount of stunt work needed, and set construction as an alternative to location work in Lancashire. Which sound houses we might get deals with. My seasoned producer assured me it would all be fine.

'Don't worry. Concentrate on the creative aspects of production.'

So many people seemed to be involved at this point it seemed completely unwarranted to be doubting its success. Like a fool I kept tweaking the script, the storyboards and my shot lists and working out what lenses might work for what shots. What sort of lighting, hard light, soft light, key lights, back fill … but £1500? All the music tracks I had worked out over the prior years, of course. What particular excerpt married with what particular scene? What mood would certain tracks convey? I blocked out what worked as a dolly or a pan on paper. What might work as a locked camera or what might naturally lend itself to a tracking shot? I talked with production designers and exchanged ideas for set design. Trawled through alternative music tracks and incidental style composers' websites. What style tracks evoked the best feel for the many scenes we would be filming soon?

Fast-forward a few months – well, several actually – and Sara still seemed as keen as ever. I had tweaked the 1300-frame storyboard plan, sorted out the details regarding the costuming I'd like and liaised with the vehicle people and production designers as to what I would like to see in front of the camera. Style and costume guides for all interiors were completed. Prop availability, and days on days off for crew, what sort of sandwiches for catering. Who should have a centre-parting and who should have a side, who should have butter on their sandwiches and who should not, who should wear red socks and who should wear blue. I had tweaked all I could fuckin' tweak. I had no more tweak left in me.

Sara re-presented the script to Ewan McGregor's agent to see if he might have a few days to fit it in, but he passed again; it just wouldn't work for his scheduling. I watched more casting tapes and auditions. Benedict Cumberbatch would get the script next week – another wow! – after one of Riggy's very well-connected contacts had managed to ask him if he'd take a look as a favour. But he was in the throes of childbirth, or rather his wife was, so pinning him down would be hard if not impossible. If he passed on it too, it would go to Sean Bean. I don't know when we had started on this Planet Cuckoo idea that A list actors would want to be in our little as yet unfunded indie, but we seemed oddly confident that this was now the case. At the end of the week, it was clear the multi-talented

Sherlock Holmes actor was not going to be the supermarket manager in our little comedy robbery-moped-driven caper. There's is a fine line between naïveté and plain gullible-daft. We may have crossed that line many chapters ago at this point.

The current London meetings were more concrete than anything I'd ever had. I sat in the BFI cafeteria with the Director of Photography, going over the many files of mood boards, style guides, and storyboard frames that we had produced, discussing camera moves, angles, blocking, etc. The vintage Arriflex lenses that we would use to shoot them all. We both shared an admiration for Conrad Hall and discussed tongue in cheek how we might get a little *Cool Hand Luke* look to *Fizzy Days.* I was further enthused at this latest London meeting as I got to discuss what music tracks we actually had a realistic shot of getting the licences for. The license company had offices off Baker Street, just a few doors away from my old London office. I was still having *Fizzy* conversations and getting assurances from the other producers that there was no need to worry about the money as it would all be in place. We had adjusted the budget to reflect the fact that, in all likelihood, we would have to shoot *Fizzy* for less than originally hoped. By now we had a lot of people involved all keen as mustard to get started. We even set the tentative first day of shooting as May 2nd, 2016. I flew back to the US, now warm and giddy, basking in the glow of pre-production anticipation.

On arriving back in the US, I met Spencer from Kaleidoscope, here to attend the AFM. I introduced him to our production designer on *Fizzy* at Lowes Hotel in Los Angeles and to dot a few i's and cross a few t's while further discussing the forthcoming production of *Fizzy Days* the movie. Again, I found myself at the AFM in sunny and palm-treed Santa Monica, only this time I was a player. I was a film-maker with a project in production, just a hair's breadth away from the shoot date and 'Lights, camera, action!' Spencer, who had given us that distribution and sales deal, the £300K minimum guarantee, affirmed his commitment to me and the project. I couldn't have felt better about *Fizzy*. I took a moment to reflect on where I was years earlier. I had been the kid on the fizzy in my story. I had been here too, at the same event, with my first contract for *Fizzy*. Things had come full circle, not once but multiple times. But now we even had a backup sales deal from another London company in place should we need it. The three of us said our goodbyes, and that it would be great to meet up on location at the shoot or in London during the production. I was looking forward to it!

A hot sunny breezy day at the beach. I sat in the dentist's chair staring out on the street as someone got a traffic ticket on their Tesla one floor below. Hollywood news was piped over the speakers and I waited for my mouth to numb. The news the speakers mentioned this morning was the birth of Benedict Cumberbatch's new baby. ARG had sent us letters of intent from two British actors: Lesley Sharp from Downton Abbey and a young chap, Ben Travollini, whose readings were absolutely superb. But I wasn't too sure what that meant as we were still very much up in the air. Despite no solid offers of further finance, it seemed like it was still all go, go, go! My continuing conversations with music people, production people, DPs, accountants and producers, sound, edit and post people were all still very positive. We really were about to make *Fizzy*!

Wait: Someone with a large pin was jabbing my overinflated balloon. As usual, my rock-solid confidence was misplaced. The noise of everything skidding to a halt and the abrupt imagined record needle jarringly scratching the surface of my dream as it fell from the turntable deafened me. Apart from that meeting with the distributor, Kaleidoscope, at the AFM, things went rapidly and strangely quiet. Very quiet indeed.

Paying work dried up completely. Out of necessity, we sold the house in Manhattan Beach. The need to finance the mortgage payments with the equity in the house couldn't go on forever. It had already made a sizable dent in the equity we'd built up over the years. We moved to Malibu. Malibu is not generally known for its affordability, though the surrounding mountains are a different matter. It does have its sunshine and celebrity cachet. Perhaps if I moved to the place where many of the top directors and film-makers live, I would more easily become one, right? Ha! The place we moved to is called Malibou Lake, not Malibu, but it is nestled in the surrounding mountains. It's spelt slightly differently, but it's very much more affordable to own a property here in the mountains. I sighed with relief as the pressure of making the sizable mortgage payments and fear of default was now lifted and I could concentrate more fully on *Fizzy*!

Most people don't know Malibu even has a lake, just a few miles from the Pacific Coast Highway, or that Malibu is not just beaches and ocean. Its hinterland, including around Malibou Lake, is home to mountain lions, vultures and raccoons. The lake is man-made, dating back to 1923. Back then it was used for hunting, fishing and sailing. Holding twenty-two million gallons of carp filled water, it nestles idyllically among the mountains just off Mulholland Highway. Although it feels like a remote wilderness, on a good day, we're still just fifty minutes away from being able to place our tired backsides on a wooden bench seat at the Hollywood Bowl, maybe catch KC and the Sunshine Band or even Phil Oakley and the Human League forty years on, still asking if you want his baby. It's also where the TV series *M*A*S*H* and *Planet of the Apes* was filmed, and more obscurely, some scenes from Universal Studios 1931 production of the horror classic staring Boris Karloff: *Frankenstein*. Charlie Chaplin shot some scenes here. But the kicker for me is *the* Batman 1966 submarine fight scene and the exploding Shark. All filmed at the (no longer in existence) water tank not a mile from my house on the Paramount Ranch Movie backlot: how cool is that!

This jewel of a place is pretty special, here in LA's backyard, and we were lucky enough now to call it home, for the moment at least. We had settled in and it was time to get back on the *Fizzy* horse. I'd been exchanging shorter and shorter emails with Sara, whilst being busy with our house move, and then came an unanticipated and rather stilted Skype conversation in which she outlined an unexpected change in her own plans.

'I can't work as much on the project as I might want to. I have a new job.'

'You're joking!' I gasp.

This came as a bit of a shock.

'Another film job?' Damn!

'No,' she replied with a somewhat serious face.

'Oh. I thought you had a job, I thought you were our producer on *Fizzy*. So now you have another movie too, are you going have time?'

'I've got another job … in a shop.'

'A production shop, you mean?' I stammered, more than disappointed.

'No, a clothes shop.'

A clothes shop? How many rock-steady producers about to produce a multimillion-dollar movie work simultaneously in clothes shops? Not that I begrudge anyone working in a clothes shop, but it smacked of part-time, kitchen-table, we-are-going-nowhere producing … or if it didn't smack, it at least had the strong smell. I had thought that Sara's income was derived from royalties or some other hitherto unacknowledged private source, and the movies she'd produced; her "slate", which Fizzy would soon be adding to. This didn't bode well.

And, of course, it wasn't well. It was as sick as the proverbial parrot. For a few weeks I heard nothing despite my frantic correspondence; then the reluctant realization we were again going nowhere. The production dates approached, the rehearsal dates came and went. I fielded as many calls as I could, putting off interested parties with excuses. Then on a Monday morning I received a new bombshell from Sara, a bombshell that had hit me many times before.

'I think we need to get a named director someone who is bankable, someone who can help raise the profile of the project and thus get us more finance, someone who is maybe a household name, someone who is … not you.'

'Oh … damn.' I sighed.

'We need you to sign over the project completely, wholly and in perpetuity. That's the way it needs to be, that's the only way we'll get things done, and we won't be moving forward unless you do.'

Hmm …

'You need to sign a contract.'

Hmm …

I mulled over my options, such as they were. It was clear that Sara didn't want to do any more work with me at least. I assumed she had tried her best to raise the money and had failed. The only way ahead that she could see seemed to involve ditching me and starting again. After a couple of days' soul-searching, added to the last dozen plus years of trying to get my movie made, I agreed to let them take the project and see if they could find a "bankable" guy who would help them raise the finance for my little moped comedy film, a director of name and note. After all, a *Fizzy* made is better than no *Fizzy* at all. I would write a letter assigning the option, which I did, and sent. For the rest of the year they would forge ahead without me, as even Riggy, who had worked as tirelessly hard as me on the project for all these years, had now come round to the idea that I should step aside.

A few days later I received an agreement, another contract from Sara, full of legalese, which obviously needed to go to a lawyer. I handed the new contract to an attorney who didn't do entertainment contracts but specialized in divorce, family wills and estates; he said he would take a look if we did a will with him. I did a will (preferable to a divorce). He took a look and promptly wrote back,

'Are you nuts? You are if you sign this!'

It hardly inspired me with confidence, but by way of keeping things honest and open – after all, these were my friends and project partners, right? – I got a second opinion and paid a second lawyer to look at the new contract; with the same conclusion. Keeping things transparent, I forwarded all the lawyers' correspondence to my producing team. Sara promptly replied that I was being completely unreasonable, and tossing her rattle from the playpen, just as promptly resigned from the project with immediate effect. Riggy? Well, he wisely watched from the side-lines as it all fell apart again. We still keep in touch. He and Nut are trying to get a Second World War horror film off the ground at present.

So here I am again. One moment I'm meeting sales companies and distributors, casting directors and potential financiers between London and LA, working with co-producers and accountants all telling me how wonderful the project is and how they are all looking forward to working on it with me and the crew. The headiness of being wined and dined in the fanciest of restaurants in London and LA; choosing the rockingest soundtrack to use for *Fizzy*, complete with Slade music and a Lynsey DePaul track! Then, the next moment, just like that, I'm asked to let go of the reins and sign the whole thing over in perpetuity – lock, stock and barrel – to someone else, someone who probably doesn't even know what a fizzy is.

Someone who will bring in the much-needed finance and who … isn't me.

I was somewhat shocked, a little downcast, but then not really 100 percent surprised. Gone from a man with a vision and a story to tell, with the tools and the trusted, if only moderately-tested, ability to do so, to albatross and pariah of ill omen as deemed by my film-making partners of just a few moments ago, like an unsightly wart needing to be excised and removed.

* * *

I haven't given up. I have had a moment to think; I won't have failed until I actually do give up. I will gain some traction somehow. The script is at present free and clear and just looking for a home! I have sent many emails during the last few months and got a few very positive replies, though still nothing concrete of course. I just need someone who will share my confidence in the project and has a taste for comedy and nostalgia, with the ability to raise finances, to jump on board! Could be any day now. Perseverance pays off in the end, right? So maybe just a few more outreaches, as I like to call them, before bedtime. The night is young, and tomorrow is another day. Of course, I'll need another lawyer, a good one, when it all kicks off again. Anybody know a good and affordable entertainment attorney?

Of course, people today are able to make movies on their phones, but they couldn't back then. So this is an old-school cautionary tale. But remember, mostly: never give in, never surrender! You will never fail if you never stop. Oh, and don't be too impatient! Movies take a long time and a lot of ground work. Oh, yes, and money! Movies also take a lot of teamwork and a lot of financing. A lot of trust and a lot of luck! A lot of everything, really!

So good luck and the best of wishes with your own *Fizzy Days*. Whatever they are.

'Mark,

I really enjoyed the read.

We should talk about it if you have not moved on to another

company already, it's funny. Great dialogue and set scenes. We must talk. The business plan and prospectus look sound.

If your MG is still in play then we could look at how we can ramp up from here and in the UK with the various funding agencies and tax breaks.

How would you feel if the story got reworked for Belfast with a few minor changes?

Do you think we might change the motorbikes for cars?

In short, loved the idea, it's workable and very entertaining. Let's talk next week if you are free?'

* * *

"Like a dog that returns to his vomit is a fool that repeats his folly": *Proverbs 26:11*

'I'm Free!'

July 19th 2022

ABOUT THE AUTHOR

Mark Millicent is a storyboard artist and commercial illustrator whose work has been published in literary Journals both in the UK and the USA. He creates artwork for game companies and advertising agencies on both sides of the Atlantic; whilst working for production studios large and small from Disney to Warner Brothers to RSA and ABC. Mark's illustrations and short films, including Fizzy Days, have been recognised by several awards over the years.

He likes to draw all manner of things and keeps a regular sketchbook – taking time off to fish and walk in the mountains and listen to good music from the 1970's of course.

Learn more about Mark online:

markmillicent.com

www.instagram.com/markmillicent/

markmillicentstoryboards.com

https://adg.org/directory/4783-mark-millicent/

If you have enjoyed this book, please consider leaving a review for Mark to let him know what you thought of his work.